One Wild and
Precious Life

Marie,
Have a great read!

John L. Stump

John L. Stump

Edited by Rosanne Gulisano & Ellie Lockett

FV11

ISBN: 978-1945-190-575

Visit the website: **www.DocStump.com**

www.IntellectPublishing.com
Inquiries to: info@IntellectPublishing.com

"Sometimes it is said this man is the 'Dog' that had nine lives! As you read this story about him, remember his life's motto was 'live and enjoy life to the fullest,' that's why there are very few pictures of Stump without a smile on his face!"
Marshall Cropper, Retired *Offensive End,*
Pittsburgh Steelers

"Stump, I'm not sure if he has more guts or brains but neither are lacking!"
Art Shell, Head Coach – Oakland Raiders (1989-1994)
NFL Hall of Fame - Offensive Tackle

"John Stump, the son of a WWII Navy veteran had a rough start in life. After his ambiguous adoption he saw his real father at his funeral. After the funeral his real mother took off again for fame and fortune never to be seen again. John went on to become a success in spite of the many hardships placed in his path of life. This memoir "makes for very engaging reading."
John Nussear, former Assistant Principal,
North Caroline High School

JOHN L. STUMP

This book title is taken from a poem penned by Mary Oliver and describes John's life for his entire childhood.

This book is dedicated to: Emile, Dalton, Kelsey, Emmy and Emily, our Grandchildren

In gratitude to Nora and John F. Stump

Preface

This book is the outgrowth of many years of stories, questions and travels that have been cultivated over time. Being adopted as an infant, I have to take the word of others for the beginning of my story. It is said I was found on my adoptive parents' porch one cold fall morning. My parents never told me anything regarding the adoption until my biological father's death.

It has taken me fifty years to slow down long enough to get the facts of my early life down on paper and in order. Over that period, numerous people have asked me why I wasn't curious about my family and the reasons why I was put up for adoption. I did wonder for a few minutes, from time to time, but it was history and I was busy making a life and a future as a doctor and a family man. Now the time is imminent, and I have most of the answers to my questions to share with others.

After finishing a professional degree, raising a family and traveling to more than one hundred countries lecturing, I finally found the time to write my story. Many will find adventure, romance and intrigue in this story. Much of the history has been pulled from family albums, newspapers, magazines and other media over the last fifty years. Some people filled in the blank spots of my childhood and my relatives have been very good at helping me coordinate and separate facts from fiction.

This story is about an ambitious young man of the 1960s who demonstrated the power of persistence, tenacity, and determination, and found continuity in the midst of change. I hold no malice or hard feelings toward any who might have harmed me in any way spiritually, emotionally, or physically during my wild and crazy childhood, during my romantic years, or financially during my professional years.

Although the many accidents and injuries I sustained throughout life would have done most in, somehow my injuries just kept me going and coming back to fight another day, like Dharma of Japanese folklore.

Life seemed like a race for survival my entire childhood in one way or another, and now that adulthood is within view, I look over my shoulder and there's no one in sight overtaking me.

John L. Stump, DC, PhD, EdD

Acknowledgments

This book is written to tell the story of one man who struggled through life only to realize life wasn't a competition but was according to God's will.

I enjoy the fact that I am alive and well after enduring so many circumstances that seemed overwhelming. This held true throughout my early years, childhood, and my school years, and I want to thank many people for their help along the path.

When I look back, I did try to thank the folks who helped me at that time—somewhat like paying in cash as you go. However, extra thanks and consideration should be given to Terry Cline, Judy Richards, Rosanne Gulisano and John O'Melveny Woods for the editorial corrections and advice; and most of all to Dianne Stump, my live-in proofreader.

JOHN L. STUMP

What will I do with this one wild and precious life?

JOHN L. STUMP

Chapter 1

"We know that enduring peace cannot be bought at the cost of other people's freedom."
President Franklin Roosevelt

War Cries

This story begins as the end of World War II approaches. The Germans are defeated, Japanese and Italian armies are back under the control of the Allied Forces, and the Allies are now celebrating. President of the United States, Franklin D. Roosevelt, is now trying to decide what to do with all the soldiers coming home.

Among the thousands of soldiers and sailors returning from the war was Curtis Draper. A dapper, twenty-year-old, 5'10", blond-haired, blue-eyed young man from Roderfield, West Virginia. Curt had spent much of the war on a battleship out of Norfolk, Virginia. The *USS Wisconsin* saw a great deal of action and had several near misses, almost getting blown out of the water by depth charges and bombers. But they had The Man Upstairs on their side and limped into port for mending of the ship each time they were hit.

The battleship, built by Philadelphia Naval Shipyard in 1941, was commissioned in 1944 and decommissioned the first time in 1948, finally retired in 1991, in Norfolk, Virginia, and is now a museum ship at Nauticus in Norfolk.

3

The Navy regained possession of Wake Island from Japan. That battle was the last action Curt saw as an ensign in the United States Navy. That year, 1945, after 55 million deaths and fifty-seven nations immersed in the fighting, WWII came to an end on May 8 in Europe. By the time Curt got into his home port in August of that year, the end of the war was a reality, the Pacific was and the American flag was raised over Iwo Jima. The word was that Hitler had committed suicide and the Soviet troops were liberating prisoners of the concentration camps at Auschwitz and others after millions of deaths during the Holocaust.

In August, Curt was back in the States and discharged from the Navy. Before the war Curt was just like millions of other high school graduates who wanted to fight for their country. Curt knew if he went straight back home he was predestined for the West Virginia coal mines like so many in his family.

Curt, with his honorable discharge papers in his duffle bag and all he possessed in the world, took a Greyhound bus from Norfolk, Virginia, to Washington D.C., instead of going back to West Virginia where he had been living before the war. He loved and missed his parents, but felt like seeing what he had been willing to give his life for: the Capitol building, White House, Lincoln Monument, and much of the history of the United States, amassed in this one location. He had never been out of the "hollers" of West Virginia before the war, and had lived only a few hundred miles from the government capitol of Washington until he joined the Navy.

The main bus depot was in downtown Union Station in Washington D.C. People were everywhere, just scurrying around heedlessly it seemed. Curt threw his duffle bag across his shoulder and started to walk. He knew he would have to find a room somewhere for the weekend. He had heard on the ship they were designating places for returning military to stay for a short time, so he began to look for a sign of military activity as he walked.

On the walk from the bus station, Curt stopped one man and asked, "Where is the nearest military flophouse?"

The man looked puzzled at the word and said as he pointed, "Two blocks that way is K Street, you can find about anything on K."

"No, not a whorehouse, I want a cheap rooming house!" Curt said to the man with a smile.

"Yes, they are there also. The two-dollar rooms are on down about three blocks the same way, just stay on K," the man said as he kept walking.

Sure enough, after not more than three blocks of walking, he saw two other sailors. Curt yelled, "Hello, can you guys help me?"

The men, still in uniform, stopped and came across the street to where Curt was walking.

"Can you tell me where I can get a reasonable room?" Curt asked.

The guys pointed across the street to a four-story brick walkup. "There, the Navy will let you stay three days free and then the cost is two dollars a day after that," the taller and larger of the men stated with a Southern accent.

"Hey, where you both from?" Curt inquired.

"We are from the little ole state of Alabama, down near Mobile. You know where that is?" the shorter of the two asked.

Curt was always good at geography in school and was used to reading maps and charts for the quartermaster in the Navy as part of his job as a cryptologic navigator on the ship.

"Yes, I think so. It's near Pensacola, Florida, where my ship was headed once, but got delayed because of a hurricane coming into the Gulf of Mexico and we had to return to Norfolk."

The three young sailors became friends that day, as they got Curt checked in and took him to the local watering hole where they began to drink beer and swap war stories. That was Curt's initiation to Washington D.C.

For the next few days and nights they hit every bar in the four-block area, considered unofficially the Military Zone by the native Washingtonians. It seemed Curt was not the only one who wanted to see what it was they had been fighting for and how it differed from home. The first three days after getting there he did nothing but drink and party with the guys. What started as fun always seemed to end in a fight, usually over some sweet young thing in a bar with hundreds of lonely, virile, handsome young men.

After three days, the two from Mobile, John L. and Mike, along with Curt, a stray West Virginian, struggled to get up that Monday morning; but after showering and a hearty breakfast, they decided to see some of the sights in the city. The starting place they selected was the Washington Monument.

They all climbed the 555 feet of the monument, racing and laughing all the way up like kids. One of the things they liked was that the monument was built in an obelisk on the National Mall to commemorate the first President, the first commander-in-chief of the armed forces.

After spending an hour or more at the monument, they went to the other end of the reflecting pool to see the Lincoln Memorial and read Lincoln's words. They were astounded at their patriotic feeling as they read the words, with tears streaming down their cheeks. They sat down on the enormous marble steps and talked of how bad the war was and how they hoped none of their children or grandchildren would ever have to experience such a war. After talking, they were resolute in their decision to tell their future children the true American history, even though they were all still happy-go-lucky single men.

Next on the list was the Smithsonian Institution. It was a governmental research center Mike had raved about for ten minutes while they sat there at the monument. He was keen on understanding our scientific and historical foundation. Neither he nor John L. was aware just how extensive the Smithsonian happened to be. They had read about the Smithsonian, but no one had ever been to the next stop on the list.

The Smithsonian Institution, established in 1846 *"for the increase and diffusion of scientific knowledge, is a group of museums and research centers administered by the Government of the United States,"* was what was written at the entrance. Mike was so fascinated that after he left he swore he was going to enroll at the University of Alabama as soon as he could after he returned home. John L. was still not sure what he wanted to do, but being around the water and boats was high on the list.

After the visit to the Smithsonian, they were thirsty and hungry and selected a honky-tonk called Dalton's in the Old Stone Inn down in the Georgetown section of D.C. They had gotten wind it was a wild ride, but it was early in the evening, so it couldn't be too bad yet, they thought.

The primary commercial corridors of Georgetown contain high-end shops, bars, restaurants, and the Georgetown Park shopping mall, as well as the Washington Harbor waterfront restaurants at K Street, between 30th and 31st Streets.

The Old Stone Inn was where they ended their day's journey, and all decided to separate to eat and seek out female company on their own. They had found it easier to talk to a girl one-on-one rather than in a group competing for her attention.

This is where Curt met the most gorgeous woman he had ever talked with as an adult. Curt was at the bar of the Inn, watching the news on one of the only TVs in the place, when a beauty sat down on the stool next to him and asked, "Would your wife mind if I sat here beside you? I want to see this new-fangled invention in action … the television," she said.

"Oh, I'm not married," Curt was quick to explain.

"That's good. Then you can buy me a drink and we can spend the next few minutes getting acquainted," she said.

Curt was more than happy to buy this little beauty, named Pansy, a drink. Come to find out, the hourglass figure was on a 5'6" blonde just like Curt. She said she had lived in Washington D.C. for two years, since graduating from high school in nearby Maryland. Her apartment was two blocks from her job as a private secretary at the Canadian Prime Minister's office. She liked the life in Washington compared to her former life in the slow outlying area of Maryland.

They talked from around five p.m. until dinnertime at seven. Then Curt asked, "Pansy, would you like to get a bite to eat?" She agreed, and they went to an Italian place around the corner she really liked. They sat there and talked about how happy they were the war was over and what had transpired on the world scene during the war years as they ate. By the time they had finished dinner, it was nearly nine o'clock. Curt asked, "Would you like to go to a late movie?" She agreed, but warned him she had to work the next day.

They walked several blocks to the Foster Theater, a new Technicolor theater, where the tickets were fifty cents each. "Damn, the tickets were twenty-five cents when we left for the war," Curt exclaimed. "Guess it's this new Technicolor that costs more to operate!" The movie playing was *Thunderhead, the Son of Flicka*. Curt didn't care, as long as it took his mind off the war for a few hours.

He didn't know what was wrong or if it was normal, but for the past year he was only able to sleep for an hour or two at a time. Many of the men on the ship were the same way and would be up walking or smoking at all hours of the night. On the ship,

Curt found it easier to stay up and read or study the maps he was in charge of, rather than try to sleep.

Chapter 2

"I hate war as only a soldier who has lived it can, only as
one who has seen its brutality and its stupidity."
General Dwight D. Eisenhower

Courtship at the Capitol

This was the beginning of a whirlwind courtship. Both Curt and Pansy were smitten with each other, and she invited Curt to live with her in the one-bedroom apartment there in Washington. Things went well until Curt left the city to try to find work. Curt didn't have a car, though he had his eye on a new Buick or Mercury that cost about a thousand dollars. What little money he had saved—about a thousand dollars in his three years in the Navy—was quickly dwindling after running into Pansy.

After he had moved in with Pansy, he went to visit his parents outside of Welch, West Virginia, to tell them the news of his new love and relationship with Pansy in Washington.

The next day he visited his cousin, Bobby Mills, to see if he needed some help. Bobby owned a small mining supply store in southern West Virginia, and often had to make deliveries by truck. Bobby told Curt he could start right away since he had four or five new accounts that had to be serviced. Curt called Pansy to tell her he wasn't coming home for several days, but there was no answer. He called morning, noon, and night. Then when he did get to talk to her, Pansy told him, "I'm not moving

10

to the coal fields of West Virginia for any reason. You'll just have to find a job here in D.C."

After the telephone argument, Curt returned to D.C. to try again to find a job, because he loved her and didn't want to lose his new heartthrob. They were getting along well and having a wonderful time one Saturday night, when Curt decided he would ask her to marry him. He proposed that evening and she said "Yes." They were married the next week in a civil ceremony.

Two more weeks went by and he searched everywhere but could not find a job, even after applying at ten different locations. There was a flood of employable manpower of veterans returning from the war; plus, Curt only had a high school education and no particular skill that could be applied to civilian life.

Curt decided to try employment in West Virginia again. He dragged Pansy to his parents' home one weekend and told her they were going to stay there and work for his cousin in the mining store until something better turned up. Pansy didn't like it, but she loved Curt and agreed to try it for a month or so. She started doing the books for Bobby in the store and things went well for the next several weeks.

By that time, Curt had spent all his savings running around chasing Pansy and taking the bus everywhere to apply for work. This meant he didn't have the money to pay the deposit or rent a house even if they found one. Curt begged Bobby to give him a few months to get on his feet so he could pay the rent or even buy a house if possible.

That started what seemed to be Curt's demise. He was from a family of German and Irish immigrants. The Drapers didn't have much family money, but they had a lot of love and compassion for each other. Curt's family could only offer him the job and a house that someone in the family owned, but they couldn't fix his marriage problems.

11

Pansy would leave on a bus every chance she got and sneak back to Washington. She told her former boss she had a dying aunt in West Virginia and she was helping to take care of her. The doctors didn't expect her to live much longer. "I plan on returning to work within the next couple of months," Pansy stated to her boss.

Chapter 3

*"I don't measure a man's success by how high he climbs
but how high he rebounds when he hits bottom."*
George S. Patton

Heart Strings

Curt decided to leave West Virginia, after struggling and suffering that year without Pansy's support, to try to find work in the D.C. area again. He had built up a few hundred dollars in reserve to live on and had paid his cousin Bobby three months in advance on the house. He called Pansy to tell her of his decision that he couldn't live without her that way. She agreed it was a good idea and best for them as a couple.

When Curt returned to Washington he noticed Pansy seemed to have changed even more. Pansy had dyed her hair jet black and wanted to go out every night clubbing, as she called it. Curt told her he didn't have the money to take her out every night, plus, "I don't think it's good for you in your condition," he told her.

"You'll have to find a job soon because this freestyle life really suits me. I want to continue this lifestyle, either with or without you."

"Pansy, just think for a minute. Don't go off half-cocked and spoil our young marriage and future."

"This is my apartment and I'll do as I please. I'm paying the expenses, so deal with it!" she told him one Friday evening after she came home from work. "Mildred, Steven and I are going to Manhattan for the weekend. There are some musicians and dance halls we want to visit. We have been told the places are wild and fun. Do you want to go?" Pansy said.

Curt responded, "I'm sorry, I just don't have the kind of money it takes to party all weekend in New York City. I'll stay here and keep looking for work and try to save a little expense," a dejected Curt told her.

Curt found that Pansy flitting off from her place in D.C. to New York, Washington, Baltimore, and other cities on the east coast with jazz and blues musicians was not unusual. It was evident after a few more weeks that she was fertile and had been busy because there was a definite baby bump on the normally beautiful, slim and attractive blonde. The question was … was it his or some other stud?

Curt was in love and ready to settle down with Pansy. He was ready to give up the wild life he had during the war years. But Pansy didn't want to stop, and continued running around and fraternizing with the "boys," even in her obviously pregnant state. Finally, she told Curt a week later, "I want a divorce. I don't think you could ever afford me and my taste."

She promised Curt she would deliver the baby before they got a divorce. Curt then began drinking and barhopping every night, coming home drunk. After several months, it was evident Pansy was not in love nor had any intentions of staying with Curt. He packed his bag and left for West Virginia again, never to return to the D.C. area.

Chapter 4

"Men are not prisoners of fate,
but prisoners of their own mind."
Winston Churchill

Sweet Home West Virginia

Curt went back to work in his cousin Bobby's store, driving the truck, and delivering supplies and equipment in the mountains of Kentucky, Virginia, and West Virginia. His life had felt like a Ping-Pong game for the past six months, still in love, thinking about Pansy and what to do. The thought of her delivery coming soon and him not there with her was almost unbearable.

One day he was asked to take a load of wood-beam support timbers down to the deep-coal miners at the U.S. Steel operation in Gary, West Virginia. That is where Curtis Draper and John Fleming Stump got to know each other, nearly one mile under the earth, in a hole thirty-four-inches high. Stump was a section boss and it was Curt's job to supply him with the needed timbers to shore up the mineshaft for the company.

Curt asked Stump, "What is a section boss?"

Stump explained, "A section boss means there are eight men working in the areas where I feel there are the best coal veins to dig coal for the week. We spend the week digging there or until the vein plays out. It's just a term that puts more responsibility on a fella without more pay. It sounds good." Stump started talking to one of his men in the dark, cold hole they were in.

"You mean you guys crawl around in this three-foot-high mine shaft, nearly a mile under the ground, all week, not being able to tell daylight from dark?" Curt asked, shocked and surprised.

"That's right. We're not a very pretty sight when we come out of the shaft in the evening, but we can say we've put in an honest day's work.

"That's why your job is so important to us, to be sure we have the right timbers holding this coal up while we dig it. Some mornings you really don't want to crawl back in there, but you know there's no other way. I started writing a song about coal mining that tells the story in a nutshell," Stump said. "What did you say your name was again?"

"Curt, Curtis Draper from the Mohegan-Roderfield area. I can't believe you all do this day after day. Better you than me. I don't think I could do it. I felt confined on a battleship and I thought the little steel stairwells were narrow, and small. Damn, thirty-four inches and pitch black without your carbide lamps on your head is scary shit when you think about doing it day after day. How long have you been working like this for the U.S. Steel Company?" asked Curt.

" Ten years too long," Stump said, without any hesitation.

Music in the mountains

During the day, Flem Stump was a deep, bituminous (soft coal) miner. After work, he was a musician. He could play anything with strings. Stump loved music. He had a gift of tone from childhood, and was able to hear anything once and then repeat the music on just about any stringed instrument. His favorite instruments were the guitar and mandolin, even though he could play the hand-held fiddle (violin) and the bass fiddle if the band didn't have anyone else.

Stump played in a band called the *Bluegrass Mountain Boys* that was rather famous in the Appalachian Mountains during those days. They played the latest country and western genre by Ernest Tubb, Hank Williams, Merle Travis, Chet Atkins, Hank Snow and others.

Accounts had it that Stump and Merle Travis co-wrote the famous coal miner's ballad of *Sixteen Tons* during that era, then sold it to Tennessee Ernie Ford when things got financially tight in the early '50s. Ten thousand dollars split two ways at that time was a right good sum, and neither Stump nor Travis could turn it down. But the song went on to make Tennessee Ernie Ford, who bought the rights, millions.

We'll never know the complete story, but many of those old Appalachian legends are as good as written in stone when they were carved into coal, like that song done during the heyday of the black gold of the Appalachian Mountains.

That evening the mining section crew met up with their boss Flem Stump; they also invited Curt to join the crew for a beer after work. This was an unwritten tradition—all the men would go to the bar after leaving the mine to celebrate having survived another day in the deep, black hole.

There were six white men and two black men on Stump's crew. Even in those days there was very little separating black from white, upper from lower, and rich from poor, once you'd entered the coal mining world.

"When you guys came in the bar from the mine, I couldn't tell who was black or who was white except if there was blue eyes shining," Curt said to begin the conversation.

"Yeah, there's a bath house, an area to scrub off some of this black gold after work, but we thought we would come straight down here as soon as we could after getting some of the worst stuff off in case you were going to buy us all a beer," Stump said.

As the miners sat and talked about the day over their beers, you could tell there was something bothering Curt, but Stump and the others couldn't determine what it was; there just seemed to be a sadness in his eyes and manner. After a few minutes, the rest of the crew started a dart game and a shuffleboard game.

Stump and Curt sat there talking. Curt asked if Flem was married, "Yes, very happily. Right now we are trying our best to start a family. But it's been three years and still no children on the horizon. The doctor thinks maybe there is a female problem," Stump said.

"How about you? Are you married, Curt?" Stump asked.

"Yes, I got married over a year ago after returning from the Navy. Met this little beauty in a Washington D.C. nightclub and we really hit it off. We started dating the next few months. I felt lucky to have a gorgeous thing like Pansy on my arm and wanted to keep her, so I asked her to marry me. Now, she is a month from delivery but not very happy about it. She is a good-time party girl, not ready to settle down and start a family. I don't know what to do," Curt stated.

Flem said, "Damn, that's a problem I wish we had but I'm sure she'll change her mind when she sees the little bundle of joy the stork delivers on that special day. Sorry, I've got to run. We have band practice this evening and Nora will have dinner ready when I get there. Hope to see you again and best of everything to you and your wife," Stump said as he got up and paid the tab.

Stump left the crew and Curt that evening at the bar while he headed to Welch from the mine at Gary, about twenty miles away around a mountainous two-lane highway. Gary was the coal mining capital of the world at that time. Welch was the area where he and Nora were living since they had gotten married three years earlier.

Baby Blues

The next month was bad for Curt and Pansy. They were arguing, fighting, and fussing late into the night because she would not stay home, and because he was tired from work all day and didn't want to go out honky-tonkin' every night. He pleaded with her to take care of herself and the baby, but his plea fell on deaf ears. She was out about every night that someone would come by to get her. Yes, he thought, he would give her a divorce as soon as she delivered if things didn't change when the baby was here.

Late one night she came in drunk and high, falling all over the furniture. Curt got up and helped her into bed, but she wasn't able to sleep. "I've got abdominal cramps; knew I shoulda' had an abortion like the girls in Washington told me about but I just didn't want to take the time," she told Curt. After an hour of crying, screaming, tossing and turning, Curt got up and called the doctor.

Curtis Draper, Pansy and little Johnny

During those days, Dr. Lincous was the only M.D. for miles around Mohegan, the little settlement where they were living near Welch. He said, "Meet me at the hospital. It's near your due date; that may be the problem." Off they went, Pansy

19

still smelling of smoke and alcohol, unable to walk. Curt carried her to the old black '40 Mercury he had bought used from one of the miners in Mohegan, and put her in the backseat as gently as possible while still hurrying. He jumped in and at a racecar driver's pace tore out of the drive, throwing black coal dust and rock everywhere.

With the windows rolled down, they arrived at the emergency room in about twenty-five minutes on that hot August night—Curt in a white T-shirt with dungarees, and in a sweat from nerves and panic.

The doctor and nurses got Pansy into the ER exam room and determined she was about to deliver. She was hollering, "Somebody do something to get me out of this misery. I don't want this baby, just do the quickest thing to get me out of pain," as they rushed her to the delivery room.

Twenty minutes later the doctor was out of the delivery room to tell Curt, "It's a boy. The delivery went well with no complications." Curt told this to Flem Stump sometime after the delivery.

Johnny became one of the first Baby Boomers of his generation, and with that a new generation was born. Even with this awkward start, Johnny would go on to become a typical Baby Boomer of his era.

This was a rough beginning for the little 5-pound 2-ounce baby boy, who seemed happy, healthy, and as alert as could be expected under the circumstances. A smile, laughter and joy were his distinguishing traits as the nurses played with him day and night. Many came into the delivery room for the next couple of days to see "Johnny, the happy baby."

"It was phenomenal; he only whimpered when he had to go or eat!" stated a delivery room nurse.

For the next few days there were only whimpers and smiles coming from the little, blonde, baby boy in the delivery room.

He was very lively, with no apparent deficiencies, as the doctor checked him, despite his mother's lack of concern for the baby or caring for herself during her pregnancy.

"Pansy did all of the wrong things that were known to be a concern for a baby's health, yet Johnny survived the first trauma of his new life … his birth!" Curt commented as he talked to a friend there at the hospital.

The nurses asked what his name was going to be, and Pansy said, "Whatever they want to call him or Curtis wants it to be. He's going to raise it! I'm outta here just as soon as I can walk. I've been offered a new gig in Los Angeles and nothing's going to stop me, not even a husband and baby."

Then the surprised delivery room nurses went out to bring in Curt. He was elated and relieved everything went rather quickly for him and he was as happy as you could imagine a proud poppa would be. They asked him what he decided for the name.

Curtis hadn't really thought much about a name because they had not been to the doctor but once, to determine if she was really pregnant. It was then at the delivery room he thought of John Fleming Stump, the miner he had just met, and how he and his wife had been trying so desperately to conceive a child.

When they entered the delivery room, Curt said, "Johnny will be his name." He told Pansy to call him Johnny and they would think about a middle name later. The birth certificate simply read: Johnny Draper, born August 29, 1946, Welch, West Virginia, at 4:00 a.m.

What happened next is not clear, and probably never will be, but Pansy did just what she said she was going to do … she left. She packed a small suitcase that Curt had brought and was out the door within two days of giving birth to Johnny. She didn't give him a hug, kiss or a glance—she was outta there!

21

Curtis was beside himself with joy and sadness, but at the same time he didn't know what to do. He couldn't keep the baby and work. He had no relatives in the area to depend on for keeping the baby, except his cousin and boss who had six children of his own. Curtis's parents lived nearly fifty miles away and they were elderly. He hadn't even known how to put on a diaper until two days earlier. How would he feed the baby? He was overwhelmed and called the Gary coal mine to ask for the number of John F. Stump. Curt, along with baby Johnny, went to see John and Nora that evening after work.

The Stumps were surprised to see Curtis and the baby. Curtis explained to John and Nora the unfortunate situation he was in and wanted their input and opinion. The Stumps were astonished that Pansy had up and left without a care at all about her husband and baby. Here they were trying so desperately to begin a family and Pansy was hell-bent on destroying hers.

That evening the situation was not resolved. Neither Curt nor John nor Nora knew the legal ramifications or the procedure to be followed to make it an amicable process for both families. The Stumps suggested he contact his mother and father, sister, brothers and other family members and let them know what had happened, get their feeling on the situation, and see if they could help with the baby, at least for a short time.

Curt agreed he would.

They said good night and they would be in touch in a few days if anything changed. Little did the Stumps know Curt had already asked his family for help and none of them were in a situation to render any assistance.

Curt already knew what he was going to do when he left. It might not have been the best thing but, for the sake of Johnny, it was all he could think of and besides it may be the answer to John and Nora's problem of not being able to conceive at that time.

Chapter 5

"For my father and my mother have forsaken me, but the Lord will take me in."
<u>Psalm 27:10</u>

The Adoption

The Stumps were up early the next day. Flem worked the first shift from five a.m. until three or four p.m., depending on their underground situation. This meant Nora was up at four a.m. to fix the fire in the wood-burning stove to make breakfast, while Flem got dressed and got his mining equipment and supplies together for the day. Flem kept a big stack of kindling for the stove on the back porch so it could be curing and drying for the winter. It was very handy for Nora to just step out the door to grab a handful of wood to start the fire.

That cool fall morning in the mountains it was still dark when Nora rose to start the fire she had made the night before. She put the iron skillet on to warm and let the butter melt and soften while she went about preparing the eggs and bacon Flem liked on Monday mornings. Usually he preferred a bowl of oatmeal with honey and raisins the remainder of the week, but Monday he liked "a good hearty breakfast," he would say. Nora felt fortunate to have several good laying hens, and she had gathered a dozen eggs Sunday afternoon from the hen house.

While fixing breakfast, Nora heard a rustling sound on the front porch, but she was in the middle of fixing the eggs just like

Flem liked them, soft and runny, so she never checked to see the reason for the noise. They had a dog named Popeye and she thought it was probably him on the porch making the noise. Popeye was always around the back door at mealtime. Popeye was a good watchdog, black and white around the eyes—the right was white and the left was black.

Flem came out of the bedroom and sat down at the table. After the blessing they talked of the day's plan and ate their breakfast as usual. Flem got his lunch box and other equipment together and walked to the door. They kissed, as they had every morning before work, but today was going to be different.

As the Stumps opened the door they were greeted with a smiling baby in a large, white-handled, peach basket with a blue ribbon and a note attached with a safety pin:

"Flem and Nora, please forgive me but I am desperate. I love my baby but I must do what is best for him at this time. You two please keep Johnny. We'll work out the adoption terms legally later, as they need to be."
Your friend,
Curtis Draper

Nora and John were astonished and didn't know what to think. They looked at each other, then took the basket with the baby into the house. Nora checked his diaper and all was dry; little Johnny was just smiling and seemed happy as could be.

Flem went to the living room and called an attorney he had done some carpentry and masonry work for a year or so back. It was nearly five a.m. by that time and he was late for work, but this was important and took priority. The men at the job would know what to do.

When he got the telephone connection, he explained the situation to Mr. Swope, the attorney. Mr. Swope was surprised, and advised several things be done while this was looked into.

"Flem, are you willing? is the question. Will you two take care of the baby until all this can be worked out?"

"Yes, sure," Stump said.

"Well, you go on to work and let Nora get used to the baby. Looks like she may get a baby without the labor!" Mr. Swope said with a chuckle.

Rough Start

That was a rough start for little Johnny who was to be put up for legal adoption shortly after his birth. Mr. Swope explained over the phone that evening, "The baby has to be put up for adoption for a thirty-day legal period until all the ramifications can be checked as far as the parents and immediate relatives to see if they indeed do not want the baby left at your home."

Thirty days later, Mr. Swope called and asked how everything was going and if Flem was still as enthralled as he was when he called earlier. He went on to say,

"It took two weeks to find Pansy and a week to get the papers typed up for the court. Now that the papers are finished, and the legal time limit is up, I wanted to call and set up a meeting to sign the papers."

John Stump, Nora Stump and Curtis Draper had a meeting two days later at the attorney's office and signed the adoption papers necessary for the legal adoption.

Mr. Swope said, "John and Nora, you don't know how fortunate you are to know Curtis, the father, and him to be so agreeable with the adoption process. There was no contention or further legal ramifications. I wish you all the best."

Stump said later, "Curt had big tears in his eyes as he signed the papers and hugged Nora and me and said, 'You know I love my baby, but can't take care of him alone. You all want a baby and can't have one. This seems like a match made in heaven, and I wouldn't stand in the way because of pride. I hope you never divulge to him the awful thing his mother and I have done to him at such a young age. Thank God you two were here; I will never interfere or come around and I'm sure Pansy won't either.'" Curt then got up and again hugged both new parents, thanked Mr. Swope and left.

A smile, laughter and joy were Johnny's distinguishing traits at birth and have been his outstanding qualities ever since. When asked about the smile and happy persona in an interview for pre-school nursery, Johnny's new mother said about him , "I don't know why he smiles and laughs so much. I don't think about it a lot. I guess he's just happy!" Nora told the administrator.

Flem added, "It's not something you normally associate with Johnny's personality, but as the old saying goes, it seems his glass is always half-full instead of half-empty."

John Stump laughed after he said this because that was the way he and Nora lived their life after the many trials and tribulations that confronted them and their adopted son.

*****

Born at the right time, I missed the Great Depression, the Dust Bowl, and World War II, according to my adoptive parents. Just to know *Sixteen Tons,* one of my dad's songs, was a hit, and being played, was huge in my opinion. John "Flem" Stump played music on the stage of the *Grand Ole Opry* with the greats of the day in country western music.

I am told I was carried by my new parents to many venues of music like that of Hank Williams, Little Jimmy Dickens, Kitty Wells, Pee Wee King, Hank Snow, Marty Robbins, and others. I guess you can see my genealogy in the country western setting was very entrenched right from the beginning. I grew up listening to Hank Williams and Hank Snow. Wearing my father's cowboy hat he used in his band, I would ride around the house on my broomstick horse. With this great music, you were never prepared for the strong ballad-like songs that were written; no matter how often you heard them it was always like the first time.

My biological dad whom I never knew was a military man, a sailor, one of those who never quite settled in any one spot to put down roots. My life started with a father who had what is now called PTSD (Post Traumatic Stress Disorder) by physicians, from his years in WWII. He died from unknown causes in his 30s when I was only six. My mother Pansy was a real looker in those days but a rather loose woman, as Grandmother Draper described her to the Stumps. She flitted off to New York, Washington, Baltimore and other cities at the drop of a hat before leaving completely.

According to Pansy's girlfriend and a relative, "There was also some rumor about her employer at the Canadian Embassy and Prime Minister William King's office, in Washington D.C., having the 'hots' for Pansy as well. That's how Pansy is able to take off so easily whenever she wants; she just rubs up against them or gives them a little sugar and the old boys go right bonkers!"

Pansy's last contact with me was when a photo of her, me, and Curt, was taken by the Stumps the year following the adoption when she returned from the west coast for a few days. "She seemed to have no regrets about leaving Curt and Johnny," reported Nora, when talking to her mother. Her mom, Rosie

27

Smith Pendergrass, came to live with the Stumps a year after the adoption to help care for Johnny.

Curt and Johnny

Chapter 6

"Whoever receives one such child in my name,
receives me."
Matthew 18:5

Early Memories of Bluewell

Some of the first memories I have as "Johnny Stump" are from when we lived on a small farm in the town of Bluewell, near the town of Bluefield, Virginia. "A Town Too Big for One State," is what the sign reads when you drive in from the north or from the West Virginia side of the state line.

I would hear Dad say all the time, "Koot (Dad's pet name for mom), I just love that sign."

The town started small on the West Virginia side and grew as you crossed the state line and got more into Virginia. Dad, as I always called the only father I ever knew, was working in the area and wanted to be as close as possible to the family while with the Southern Coal Company and U.S. Steel near Bluewell.

The Stumps bought a little farm with chickens, cows, pigs, rabbits, a horse and a pony; they even had a little garden. My first memories are those days when they would sit me on the pony's saddle and let me ride around the barnyard before I could even hold the reins. Mom and my grandmother (Rosie) would go out and gather eggs, milk the cow, and feed the other animals every morning with me by their side.

My grandmother Rosie, my mother's mother, had been married to Tom Smith, a steam engine engineer on the Norfolk & Western Railway out of Norfolk, Virginia. Tom had died, and she remarried a few years later to George Pendergrass. He had passed as well from a sudden heart attack, or so I was lead to believe, until I was older and "could understand adult matters," my grandmother said.

Tom had been killed in an unusual accident four or five years earlier in the railroad yard in Norfolk. Rosie (Lea, as Tom called her) and the family were well taken care of as the result of that accident. That was how Rosie (I called her Granny) came to live with my mom, one of several of her daughters, and her new family. This was also how I got my middle name of Lee, after my grandmother Rosie.

Rosie didn't want to live alone, and Mom needed help with her new addition to the family. Flem was agreeable to Rosie moving in because he often worked late nights when they had to work overtime to get the coal out on time. Dad had to leave for work at four in the morning and sometimes come in from work after midnight when on night shift. Having Rosie at the house was a great help for everyone. The only complication was another bedroom. The house in Welch, West Virginia, had two bedrooms. When I came along they used the second bedroom for a nursery. When Rosie's husband Tom was killed and she

Johnny at 2 years old

30

came to stay with us, we were cramped for space. That's when Dad found the little farm and farmhouse with four bedrooms in Bluewell and they moved from Welch to the Virginia border town.

Bluewell was a quiet, charming mountain community of fewer than five hundred families. There was one gas station, a thrift shop, a small restaurant, a secondhand store, and a hardware store. The town got its name from being halfway between Bluefield, Virginia, and Bramwell, West Virginia. It was not incorporated, nor did it have a post office. All of the community supported the elementary school, having grades one through six. There were large numbers of people who had only gone to school in Bluewell and never completed high school because of having no transportation to Bluefield. The high school was located only a few miles away, but on curved mountainous roads.

The little farm was a happy place and afforded me a great place to start my childhood. About three years later, a new coal company bought the old one out and my dad was transferred to another mine.

I was born in the coal fields but didn't live there long. Dad was always saying, "I'm going to try to get our family out of these coal fields somehow if it's the last thing I do."

He told Nora, "The money isn't worth the danger now that I have a wife and baby to think about."

I learned to walk, talk, and ride a pony on the little five-acre farm in Virginia, but would soon be back in Welch. During those years Welch was a thriving coal community with about 25,000 people. It was the county seat of McDowell County. Mom and Dad really liked Welch, but there was little in the way of work for Dad that paid as well as working in the mine.

31

Dam Right

I remember an incident when I was little more than four years old. Dad, Mom, and Granny took me camping at Bluestone State Park on the 4th of July. The state park was near our farm in Bluewell, but it was getting out of our surroundings and going somewhere different. The park was very beautiful in the summer, with a huge lake made by the dam, with tall oak, sycamore, hickory, and black walnut trees casting shadows and creating cool places to stand and sit. Wildflowers all over the park were as beautiful as a movie set. The state park rangers already prepared the campsites. All we had to do was clean up when we were going to leave. There was no hard and fast written rule about how long you could stay either, because it looked like some people had staked a claim and were there for the summer in their tents and trailers. They could fish and relax and of course hunt small game year-round.

Dad selected a small, quiet place away from the other campsites, so he could fish near a huge, beautiful rhododendron shrub Mom just couldn't keep her eyes off. The purple blossoms were large as your fist, as they hung thick on the widespread shrub nearly as big as a small tree.

Flem worked hard in the mine, and he and Nora decided they needed a few days to sit by the lake, rest, and fish with the family. Nora had prepared a large picnic basket for everyone for the first day there, with fried chicken, mashed potatoes, cornbread, and apple pie, because she knew they would be busy setting up the camp after the two-hour drive through the mountains to get there. That afternoon Dad had hoped to catch a few fish to fry for dinner as well.

The well-laid plans were spoiled by a sudden thunderstorm coming out of nowhere. That afternoon the storm passed around five and the sun came out to brighten up the evening. The camp was soaked and consequently we ended up sleeping in the car that evening, telling stories until everyone fell asleep. Granny told the best scary stories of black cats, witches, ghosts, and people appearing and disappearing. I don't think Mom was pleased at hearing them, judging from the coughs, grunts and "*Mom*" that came out of her that evening, but it was dark and no one told her to stop telling the stories. They seemed so real, and I was frightened at times, but wanted to hear the next thing that happened in her stories.

The next morning the sun was up bright and early and there was not a cloud in the sky. Grandma Rosie was the first one up and there was no sign of the previous night's rain. We crawled out of the car and started setting up camp again. This time Mom asked Dad to take me down to the lake and begin to teach me the skills of how to fish while she and her mother prepared

breakfast. Dad agreed, took an apple and an orange for us to snack on and stuffed them into his pockets. He also picked up a can of worms we had brought with the fishing poles.

Flem was a good fly fisherman in the mountain streams, but he wanted to start teaching me on the still waters the lake provided. He had gotten two bamboo poles about six feet long and tied a fishing line at one end. He clipped the hook so mine wasn't sharp, and let me get used to just tossing the bobber, sinker, and worm

Johnny at 3 years old

on the fake hook into the water and pulling it out. This really excited four-year-old me, and we stood by the bank of the lake fishing together for nearly an hour before Dad finally got a bite and pulled in a large bass.

This was a good opportunity to teach a boy about fishing; this lake, with its smooth water, was perfect for a beginner. We took the fish and put it on a stringer. "A stringer is a line to keep the fish on until we're ready to leave or quit fishing," he told me. We went back to fishing because Dad wanted to catch enough for everyone to have for dinner that evening. I was excited to be a part of the fishing adventure.

Dad took the apple and orange out of his pockets and asked, "Son, which do you want for your snack?"

"The orange," I said. I liked the sweet juice that ran down your throat when each slice was popped into your mouth.

Dad took the sour green apple for himself. Our fishing spots were only about ten feet apart because we had to have enough room to cast our line. Dad went back and began fishing, with his apple in one hand and his fishing pole in the other. I couldn't manage the pole and the orange at the same time, so I yelled that I was going to sit, peel, and eat the orange, and then return to fishing. Dad said that was a good idea. I found a big rock by the lake and sat down to start peeling and eating the orange.

Flem was standing there thinking what a wonderful weekend they were having with preparing the picnic, telling stories in the car at night, and fishing together. All of a sudden, he heard a loud splashing noise and thought I had caught a big fish. When he looked over, there was no Johnny—I was under the water. He had forgotten to tell me not to step on the stones near the water, that the lake was very deep and to be careful of the slippery rocks. When Dad got to the spot, there was no sign of me. My dad jumped in and started feeling around in the deep, dark, water. In just a few seconds that seemed like forever he felt something with his foot; he went under the water and pulled me to the surface.

When Dad got me to the shore, he saw that I had a piece of orange in my mouth and couldn't breathe. He stuck his finger in my mouth and dislodged a huge slice. He then placed me across his knee and slapped me on the back two or three times— out came water and more orange. It looked like I had tried to swallow half the orange at once. Dad got the remainder of the orange out of my mouth and slapped me on the back again. I started coughing and spitting up fluids.

Flem's heart was racing a hundred miles an hour from the incident. I raised up and started crying, trying to explain, "I-I …," between sobs, "I wanted to get back to fishing and crammed the large chunk of orange into my mouth and stood up on the rock to go back to fishing. I choked on the orange, then my feet slipped on the rock and into the lake I landed."

When Dad finally found out how and why I fell in the lake, all he could do was laugh and cry. He was pleased that I was so excited about fishing I couldn't wait to eat the orange before trying to fish again. That made him happy; on the other hand, when he saw how easy it was to almost lose the precious boy that he was just given by God to care for, it made him cry.

He and I sat there beside the big rock laughing and crying for the next few minutes before we realized we were both soaked and needed dry clothes. We went back and tried to tell my mother and grandmother what had happened without scaring them to death. After two tries at me trying to tell the story, Dad had to finish the tale of Johnny's fishing plunge into Bluestone Dam.

This started a life-long knack of getting into predicaments I've needed help to get out of.

Chapter 7

"In the middle of every difficulty lies an opportunity"
Albert Einstein

The Slate Fall

I lived in the coal fields of West Virginia until an unfortunate accident at the coal mine almost ended it all. One day in 1950, Mom received a call from the mine where Dad had been working. A man's voice was on the line, "Mrs. Stump, there has been an accident at the mine. You need to get to the Steven's Clinic hospital in Welch as soon as possible."

This message shocked Mom, and she grabbed me and took off to see why she had been called. There were always accidents at the mine, but most of them just injuries from lifting, straining, falling, or some other avoidable incident. For some reason, judging by the sound of the man's voice, this didn't seem to be that kind of accident. Rosie was away at the grocery store with another of her daughters, and wasn't aware anything had happened.

When Mom arrived at the hospital there were ambulances, fire trucks and rescue wagons, all with their lights blinking like they had just come from a fire. We ran into the hospital and found the entire lobby full of weeping, wailing, crying people. "God," she thought, "What has happened?" Mom finally got to ask a nurse at the counter what had happened and where was her husband, John Stump.

The nurse said, "Let me have that name again."

"John Fleming Stump, born 1909, right here in this hospital," Mom said.

"Got it," the nurse said, as she turned to answer another question from someone standing in line behind her.

"Yes, he's in surgery. All you'll be able to do is take a seat and pray he is better off than the ten we have lost so far from the explosion and slate fall. Seems like there was a gas leak, and someone's carbide lamp sparked off a chain reaction of explosions. That caused one of the walls of the mine to cave in on more than a dozen men between shifts. Thankfully, the men had not descended into the mineshaft for the evening shift or there wouldn't be much chance for rescue of anyone." The nurse continued talking to no one in particular as she hurriedly moved from counter to telephone.

"Thank you. Please let me know when he's out of surgery," Mom said.

Mom took me over to the waiting area and tried the best she could, in between her tearful sobs, to explain the accident to me. I understood an accident had happened, but I didn't quite grasp the significance of surgery and death that I kept hearing people talk about.

Two hours later, the nurse came over to Mom with an encouraging look on her face and said, "Well, John Stump was one of the few lucky enough to escape that death trap they call a mine. He'll be in ward D in about twenty minutes when they bring him out of surgery. They'll take him there where you can see him for a few minutes."

Mom seemed to breathe for the first time in two hours. She shook me awake and told me we would be going to see Daddy in just a few minutes; that he was going to be all right from the accident at the mine.

As we walked through the hospital ward, we saw men in beds on each side of the big open room. They were hooked up to breathing apparatus, and blood and traction devices. There were at least ten men on each side of the room. Dad was the next-to-the-last one on the right side. When we got to the bed, he was still lying with his eyes closed. Mom walked up to the bed and stood there, not knowing what to say. I broke the ice with a quiet yell, "Sure am glad that you are not hurt bad, Daddy."

He put his arms around his head on the pillow, and, opening his eyes, he said, "Thank God I made it."

"What happened?" Mom asked him.

"I'm not real sure yet but I think there was a gas leak and one of the men had not turned off his carbide lamp when he left the mine. It sparked a chain of small explosions that brought the entire outside wall of the mineshaft down, with us under it. Thank goodness my crew was just about out of the area and the evening shift was just going in or we would have been the ones in Heaven now," Dad said.

Mom couldn't do anything except sit there beside the bed with tears streaming, saying how thankful she was he wasn't hurt any worse. We later found out his injuries were bad enough that he would never be able to return to the mine.

His medical report was bad. He had sustained three fractures: right arm, right collar bone and two vertebrae, besides the five ribs that were crushed, a ruptured spleen, contusions, and abrasions of both internal and external organs—and that was just the preliminary report. They advised him not to return to work again in the mine due to the extensive injuries he had sustained.

"You'll be six months getting over these injuries, if infection doesn't set in," the doctor told him. "Don't even think about going back to deep mining again."

With Flem laid up in the hospital, Mom thought she better consider finding a job to help out with expenses. She found a house on McDowell Street about four blocks from the hospital. She went to Tony Lambert, an old friend of the family who owned a grocery store, and asked for a job. She told Tony the story of what happened, and he hired her on the spot.

She was able to get several cousins to help her move that week. Grandmother's son Hillard Smith had an important job at the Coca-Cola Company there in Welch, so they were a big help to Mom. She had made the first big decision without Flem, to sell the farm and buy the house in town, but she figured Flem didn't need any more worries than he already had.

After more than three months in the hospital, he was released to return home, limiting his activity as far as pushing, pulling, lifting, or manual labor—in other words, what he liked and was used to doing all his life he should not do anytime soon.

Chapter 8

"The difference between school and life, in school, you're taught a lesson and then given a test. In life, you're given a test that teaches you a lesson!"
My Teacher, Lois Crabtree 1956

School Bells

I remember being in school at the Welch High School building at the age of six. At that time all grades from 1 to 12 were housed in a huge three-story brick structure with a bell tower you could hear all over downtown Welch.

I lived about a mile across town from the school. After the first grade, Mom let me walk to school with my two neighbors, Sherry who was eight, and Sammy who was nine. Sherry was taller than either of us boys and I was the smallest and youngest. We had a good relationship and talked and joked all the way to school each morning. Only the weather, if it rained or snowed, sometimes made it difficult for our trio to walk to school. On those days, Mrs. Stephens, Sherry's mother, would take us in her car before she went to work.

One day, walking home, two older boys, ages ten and eleven, started asking for money to buy a soft drink. Sherry told them she had no money. Sammy gave them a dime he had in his pocket. They then turned to me and said, "Give us a quarter or we're going to kick your ass, kid." Every day after school for a week this went on; then on Friday they hit me right in the head and knocked me down on the sidewalk. I just lay there, not sure what to do. I had never had this happen before, someone deliberately knocking me down. One of the boys then kicked me in the stomach. The other boy hit Sammy in the face so hard it made his nose bleed. Then they took off running down the street, laughing.

I got up with tears in my eyes and said, "Please don't tell my mother; she won't let me walk to school with you anymore, Sherry."

"Mine either," said Sammy.

"Yes, but what are you going to do if they do it again and each time after that?" Sherry said.

We finally decided it was just an isolated incident and to try to forget about it. That evening when Dad got home from an errand he had been on, we sat down for dinner. I decided to bring the subject up and discuss the circumstances because it had really hurt my feelings that two boys would do that to three innocent people who never bothered them.

"Dad, today one of my friends was beat-up after school by two older boys that wanted some money to buy soft drinks. What should be done about a problem like that? They told my friend Sammy they were going to beat him up every day after school if he didn't pay up at least a dime a day."

"Johnny, that's what we called a schoolyard bully when I was in school. Do you ever see him on school grounds during school?"

"Yes, I think he is in the fifth or sixth grade."

"You are in the second grade now and somehow that doesn't seem right. No, I'm sorry. Your friend is in what grade?" Dad mumbled.

"Sammy's in the third, I think," I answered.

"Let me tell you what my brothers would do. I had five older brothers when we were in school. They would stop that type of thing real fast when we were in elementary school. When we saw the boy again, they would send me up to the bully to explain we didn't want to fight or have trouble at school. If the person wanted to borrow a nickel or dime, we would loan them the money for a week. If they didn't return it or asked for more without paying back the first, their trust would be lost.

"Then my brothers would wait after school and catch the boy. They would tell the boy he had borrowed the money from all of them and to repay the debt. That was bad for the boy, very bad, and they scared him with a few punches to the gut. Usually that was the end of bullying anymore from most," Dad said, as he pondered the grammar school incident in his head.

"Tomorrow, go with your friend Sammy and you tell one of the boys at a time that you don't have the money to pay them and you would appreciate them not fighting with you because you don't have the money. Tell them it's going to be like trying to get blood from a turnip. See if that helps." Dad got up from the table and went in the living room to talk to Granny and Mom as they were sitting watching the news on our new black and white TV.

The 1950s was a decade of the Gregorian calendar that began on January 1, 1950, and ended on December 31, 1959. By its end, the world had largely recovered from World War II, and the Cold War developed from its modest beginning in the late 1940s to a hot competition between the United States and what was then known as the Soviet Union. This was what dominated the news. I rarely listened to the news with the family. I went out to play and think about our family dinner conversations, homework and my friends.

The next day walking to school I told Sammy what Dad had said. "I plan to go to Ronnie at recess and tell him to leave us alone. We have no money and never will, that I know of."

Recess rolled around and I found Sammy and we went to the boy. We found out his name was Ronnie Harris and the other was Jerry Morris and Ronnie was in the fourth grade. He seemed to be the leader. We asked Ronnie to please stop picking on us because we didn't have any money to pay. Ronnie laughed and said, "If you don't have the ten cents by three o'clock today, you are going to get the same thing you did yesterday. The hell kicked out of you," and walked off laughing.

Sammy and I were shocked—we couldn't believe what we were just told. What were we going to do? What my dad had suggested didn't work.

I told Sammy, "We've got to do something first, before he gets a chance to jump us."

"Let's jump him first," Sammy said.

"I'm game if you are. But we can't get Sherry scared and hurt," I told Sammy.

"Right!" we said at the same time.

That day we planned to jump Ronnie Harris after school and before he got together with Jerry or with his other friends that usually joined him at the Tic-Tock Café. This was the hangout for all the high school kids about a block down from the school. The high school kids met there after school to dance, smoke, drink cokes and talk.

There was an empty building with an alley beside the sidewalk where business people put out their trash in the mornings and evenings. That was our proposed scene where the action was going to take place. The alley was dirty from coal dust, with trash and empty trashcans scattered all around. We had selected this area because there were usually no people in either empty store on each side of the alley.

When the final bell rang, I ran full speed down the hill from school to the location of the trashcans and hid. Sammy made sure Ronnie saw him but stayed a safe distance from him coming down the hill. When Sammy got almost to the alley he slowed and started whistling to let me know they were just about there. He slowed down and lingered until Ronnie caught up to him at the opening to the alley.

"Ronnie, please don't bother me. I'm alone today and have no money."

Ronnie laughed; he was about a head taller than Sammy. Sammy kept backing into the alley and begging Ronnie for mercy.

About twenty-five feet into the alley was where the trashcans were sitting and a Bluestone coal truck was parked. Sammy stopped and put up his fist. "Ok, Ronnie, if you insist, we'll just have to have it out."

Ronnie laughed, put up his fist and moved toward Sammy. About that time, I stepped from behind the trashcans with a baseball bat we had brought from the school playground. I snuck up behind Ronnie and whopped him across the back of the head and neck as hard as I could. Blood flew. Ronnie wilted to the ground like a withering vine, right onto the alleyway.

"Wow, that was easy, Johnny. He's out like a light," Sammy said.

"I see that. Should we just leave him or what? I never thought we would get this far!" I told Sammy.

"I've only seen things like this in the movies, Johnny." Sammy said. "What should we do now?"

"Just let him get up when he wakes up," I said.

"Let's you and me catch up with Sherry and go on home."

I put the bat across my shoulder and my other arm around Sammy, and we strolled past the Tic-Tock Café where *Till The End of Time* was playing on the jukebox. We didn't know how much damage we had done to Ronnie, but the bullying stopped—at least for that day.

That evening at dinner my dad asked me about the problem my "friend" had with the bully at school, and how that went after he talked to the boy.

"Well, Dad, I told my friend everything you suggested about asking the bully, who we found was named Ronnie Harris, not to take our lunch money and not to beat Sammy up every day, that he doesn't pay because he has no money like me. I think it worked, because today after school he didn't lay a hand on Sammy."

Dad smiled and said, "I knew you would find a way to help your friend."

"Well, I'm sure he'll want to hear the school bells from now on and not the bells that may have been ringing in his head from our little talk today!" I told Dad.

Chapter 9

I smile because you say you're my sister.
You-laugh because we can't do anything about it.
John Stump

The Adoption Revealed

From that time on while at Welch Elementary School there was no more bullying of my friends and me. Ronnie and his friends steered clear of us, for he told some of his friends we were out to kill him. The word had gotten around school that if you fought Johnny you had to fight Sammy, and vice versa, and neither fought fair. That was okay with us – at least we were not bullied anymore by the older guys.

Walking to school one day the next year, some girls a few years older walked by and said, "Johnny, sorry to hear about your family loss." Neither stopped to explain or bother to let me know who they were. I hadn't had a loss that I knew of in the family.

That evening at dinner Mom looked across the table at me and started crying. Dad didn't say a word at first, he just let her cry. Then he put his utensils down and dabbed his mouth with his napkin as he cleared his throat.

"Johnny you're a big boy now and what we're about to tell you is difficult for us but will be even more difficult for you."

I was concerned now and listened closely. Had I done anything wrong at school in the last couple of days? What could be so difficult for me right now? Everything was good at school—my grades were good, I was playing baseball, and even had been socializing with Penny, the little girl down the street.

Mom said, "Johnny, I don't know how to tell you this other than just to tell you the truth just as it is. You were adopted when you were less than a year old and we became your adoptive parents. Your real father, Curtis Draper, died yesterday and that's what all the commotion is about. Your adoptive father, John Fleming Stump, and I have wanted to tell you but there never has seemed the right time up to now, so we hadn't taken the time to sit you down and explain the whole situation to you. Besides, we gave Curtis our word that we wouldn't tell you unless absolutely necessary."

"Mom, what is adoption and how can I have two fathers?" I asked.

"Sorry if I cry, I'm a little emotional right now," Mom said.

"Johnny, let me tell you the complete story from the beginning; then you'll know the truth and understand what's occurred up this point in your life," Dad said.

This is what happened the day John Flem Stump told me the story behind my adoption and how it had been hidden from me, because my biological parents decided it would be best. Never did they realize what was ahead in life and that I would have to be told at some point. Now, it had been thrust upon me without any warning—"Johnny, your birth father is dead!"

After hearing the story, I just sat there looking at Mom and Dad. After a short time, I remember saying, "Well, I'm sorry Curtis is dead. My mother, Pansy, decided she would rather run off to wherever than take care of me, but the best usually comes out if it's supposed to happen, and I think it did. I'm with the parents I love and who love me. I'm sorry I didn't know Curtis and Pansy."

Then I got up from the table and hugged my mother and in a few minutes came around the table and hugged my father. I looked at both and said, "I'm sorry to have been such a problem, but I sure am glad you didn't have any children when I was born. It sure turned out for the best for me as far as I'm concerned."

About two days later I was told we all had to go to what would be my first viewing and funeral. I went with Flem and Nora Mae Stump, my adoptive parents, but all the time hearing the many people attending whisper about me being Curt's son. I didn't know what to think. Here I was with my "real father" for the first time that I could remember—and he was dead!

I looked at him closely in the coffin. He had blonde hair, a light complexion, and big hands. I couldn't see his eyes, but I knew they were blue like mine. My adoptive father had coal-black hair, was about six feet tall, with a dark complexion. I had always thought I took after my fair-haired mother, Nora Mae, who was much fairer than the Stump side of the family who were part Indian.

That was the only time I saw my biological father and I still do not know if my mother was there or not. People would whisper and point but no one came over except Curt's mother and father and talked to Mom and Dad about the death. They felt Curt drank himself to death grieving over my adoption and Pansy taking off and rarely coming back to see him or let him know where she was. "She seemed to have no remorse," they said, "about the marriage split-up, the adoption, or even now the death of Curtis."

Chapter 10

Love within your soul is what sets you on fire to get out of bed and face the new day; it challenges you and makes you resilient to the everyday happenings of the world. Embrace life with all your heart, Live with Compassion.
Malika E Nura

Southern Thoughts

After my father's accident he was unable to work in the coal mines again. Yet Flem was grateful to be alive, and U.S. Steel had given him a little retirement bonus to live on after surviving the explosion. Flem decided if he wasn't in the coal mine, there was no reason to continue living in Welch.

The only thing Flem could do after getting out of the hospital was sit around, write songs, play music with his friends, and drink the night away. The group of one banjo, two guitars, a harmonica, and Dad's mandolin made for a pretty good sound to lull me to sleep each night. It finally got to where they were playing and singing very late every night after Dad was able to physically sit and handle the instruments with no pain.

One night, around two a.m., the cops came by our house and told Dad it had to stop. This was the third complaint of the noise and music all hours of the night on weeknights, not even weekends. I was listening and watching from the steps up to the bedrooms. The oldest policeman said, "Mr. Stump, not everyone likes country music like you all do. You're going to have to get a recording studio license or stop playing after nine p.m. The

49

next time we come there will be an arrest and a heavy fine to pay."

After that incident, Mom and Dad had a little "come to Jesus" meeting and agreed they had to do something to change. They decided they would make a clean break from the area and their partying music friends.

Mom and Dad put our home on McDowell Street in Welch up for sale and started planning to go to Akin, South Carolina, where Dad heard jobs were plentiful, and these were jobs he was qualified to do without being in the mines.

Flem Stump was a miner by chosen trade because of the top dollar he could earn, but he also was a mason and musician. He contacted his Masonic Lodge in Welch. John F. Stump was the son of John Ben Stump. His father had introduced him to the Masonic Lodge a few years after his 21st birthday. Flem didn't know much about the Masons except the fellowship and secrecy, but he knew his father always contacted the Lodge when there was a crisis in the family or business … and this was a crisis in his life. He was told by the Lodge Master to use the fact that he was a Mason in good standing wherever and whenever he applied for a job, like a reference.

Dad was from a large family, five brothers and three sisters. His mother, Texas Cooper Stump, said to Mom, "Nora Mae, several men in the family are also Masons and should be able to help Flem get work there in South Carolina. It's a big move but it may be the only way out of this coal country you have been born into." That was the first time I heard the words South Carolina.

My grandmother, Texas Stump, then explained to me that Sam, Bob, Charlie, and Buddy, were my uncles. And then there were my aunts, Sally, Myrtle, and the oldest sister, Edder. I'm not sure if I ever met everyone, or whose children belonged to whom, but there was a lot of visiting at that time and a lot of goodbye tears with the Stump family.

It was the same with my mother's family, the Smiths. I remember we spent a lot of time visiting Hillard and Lula Smith, Mom's father and mother. They had three children whom I met on different occasions: Big Doug, Nellie and Rink, or Bill, as they sometimes called him. I really liked Douglas and Nellie. They were not much older, just teenagers, and we talked and played together when I was at their house. Grandma Rosie was their mother and she was my favorite of all the relatives.

At some point Mom and Dad had visited most of the family and said their goodbyes, and I haven't seen some of them since. I have often wondered about my friends and those relatives, but at that age, when you moved a thousand miles away, you couldn't think about "back home" very much.

The Move South

In 1952, brick and block masons were being hired by the dozens at the construction site at the new DuPont Plant in New Ellington, South Carolina. The Bomb Plant, as it was termed by everyone, was being built by U.S. Steel Corporation with DuPont Corporation. Dad had good references from the Gary Coal Company as a section boss and all the Masons had written references as well. The mine was owned by U.S. Steel, and he had good credentials for the brick and block masonry work he had done building Stone Churches, as well as a brick-block service station for Mr. Clifton in Welch who gave him a reference.

Dad had worked under a Frank Lloyd Wright trained architectural firm in West Virginia. This firm had directed a job for C&O Railway and John D. Rockefeller, building railway trestles of concrete in place of the old wooden trestles throughout West Virginia. The Justice family attorney who helped with my adoption had a prominent family name. But Rockefeller was the most prominent political name in West Virginia.

Names carried a lot of weight, and Dad was hoping these connections would help his effort to break free of the coal country ties he and his family were born into. I was told that the Stump family had been supplying timbers to the mines of West Virginia miners for at least a hundred years from around Stumptown, West Virginia.

John F. Stump was hired within two weeks of filing his application, as a masonry construction assistant to the engineer. Stump was told by his doctors not to do much physically, but still qualified for the construction job.

I remember the move from Welch to South Carolina. I was still young, but old enough to remember most everything that was going on at the time.

Our car was a big, black, 1952 Buick Roadmaster. Mom had it packed to the brim with about everything you could think of for the trip. It probably contained our entire family fortune, truth be known. It was fun for me—I was stuck in the back seat surrounded by pillows, blankets and clothes. I spent most of the morning we left West Virginia in the early dark, curled up in a cocoon I made for myself.

One of the first things I remember was being in the mountains of North Carolina after lunch. I was sitting in the back seat with Granny. We had stopped and picked up Granny after leaving our house that morning. Dad was driving, and Mom rode shotgun. While going around a curve, there was a big bang, Dad had trouble steering, and the Roadmaster slowed and came to a stop on the shoulder of a very steep mountain. Dad got out and looked to see what had happened. It was a blow-out he called it, in the front right tire. He went back to get the spare tire to change for the damaged one.

We had to unpack a stack of items like bed linens, dishes, and clothes, and finally got down to where the tire should be and there was none. It seems Mom had forgotten to put the tire back in because she was so determined to get everything else she wanted packed in the trunk. She just left it sitting beside the house in the dark when we left.

Dad was not pleased. It cost us several hours because Dad had to walk about two miles to find a station that had tires for sale and would fix the blowout for a spare. We finally got off the mountain that evening, but had to spend the night in a motel before crossing the state line into South Carolina—something they hadn't planned.

Dad located a house where our family could begin a new life in New Ellington, South Carolina, based on the recommendation of a fellow worker at the new company. We knew no one and no one knew us and that was how it would be until I started school in the fall. The area was totally different, with no mountains. It was hot and dry, not like the cool mountains of West Virginia.

My brother Douglas
becomes a musician

Chapter 11

Never be afraid to start over. It's a chance to rebuild what you want. You're fortunate if you're given a second chance.
Malika E Nura

The Southern Way

I found our new home in South Carolina a little difficult to get settled into. The house was about half the size of the place we had in Welch. It was a one-story and the old home was two-story, and we were in the country instead of town like in Welch. But I figured my mom and dad knew what they needed. Back at their home on McDowell Street they were always having company on weekends, sometimes late into the night, and at times they were still there when I woke up the next day.

Dad had been a miner during the day and a musician at night; he could play anything—guitar, mandolin, banjo and fiddle. It was a gift, everyone would say. My dad had not gone to school or learned how to read music from anyone that I knew of and I heard many say he had a musical genius. Dad had taught Mom the guitar so she could go with him to the gigs he played.

When they were first married, he had been in a band that played every Friday and Saturday night. There were five men in the band before they added Mom (Nora), who was also known as "Koot." She became the lead singer and played a Gibson flattop guitar. After I came on the scene, if they wanted to practice and party all night, it had to be there in Welch at Flem's (also called Slim Stump by several band members) and Koot's place.

This group of musicians was known all over the Appalachians as the *Blue Grass Mountain Boys*. After my arrival Dad curtailed his music activity by at least fifty percent.

I heard Mom tell Granny that she was going to stop going on gigs with the group. She and her mother (Rosie) would stay at home and sing and play together with Bessie, a big woman who came over to help Mom before Grandma Rosie arrived to live with us. Nora was on the guitar, Rosie the mouth-harp or harmonica, and Bessie played a mean violin or fiddle, as they all called it in West Virginia.

While the *Bluegrass Mountain Boys* were playing in Nashville, Dad's favorite gig, he was asked by another musician by the name of Merle Travis to co-write a song with him. Since Dad had been a real coal miner for over ten years and knew the trade, he agreed, and he and Merle Travis sat down one night in Nashville with their instruments. Stump, with his background in the coal mine, and Merle with his musical ability, put together the song *Sixteen Tons*.

Sometime later, both musicians were strapped for money after their time together in Nashville and decided to sell the rights to the song to another musician by the name of Tennessee Ernie Ford. "The rest of the story is for the music history books; that's as close to fame and fortune as I ever got," Dad would tell others through the years.

Mom told another story about Dad to Granny while we were traveling. She said it was before Johnny was walking. "Flem, they called Slim, had been invited to play with a group of musicians in Nashville that were thinking about putting a

recording album together. Flem was introduced to everyone there. One of them, called 'Hank,' had just had a number-one hit the year before called *Lovesick Blues* that Flem really liked. The men got to talking and drinking that night and Hank Williams asked Flem to come play on his broadcast at KWKH radio in Shreveport, Louisiana. Dad agreed, but when he returned home and realized how much time and expense he was looking at for no guaranteed income, he ended up calling Hank Williams back to cancel his playing gig. Hank went on to star at the *Grand Ole Opry* and become a short-lived sensation, dying at the age of twenty-nine from a heart defect.

Dad and Doug Practice

"After that music jam encounter in Nashville with Hank Williams and a host of up and coming musicians, Flem went on to make several albums with other musicians and even two with me in a duo production. When we decided to leave the McDowell Street house and move south, we wanted to make a clean beginning, and as a result, we even sold our instruments or gave them to friends and family," Mom said with a tear in her eye.

"There was a time when we thought music could get us out of the coal fields but that never happened for one reason or the other. Now we have another chance and we're going to take it," Mom said, as she drove and Dad slept.

School Days

I liked the new school in New Ellington but had to make my way up the pecking order for the first several months. I found it much easier here than in Welch where all the grades, one to twelve, were in the same school complex. Here it was just grades three to six, and I was in the middle instead of at the bottom of the order.

The first few days of school were fine, with Mom dropping me off and picking me up. On the fourth day of class at the new school, I was waiting for the bell to ring to go in the building where I had been dropped off a few minutes early with my books and bag lunch in my hands. Without warning, my books were knocked from my hands along with the bag lunch. Several boys would race by and slap the books out of your hand. It happened so fast that you were preoccupied with trying to catch your books and whatever was in your hand, so you didn't get much of a look at the offenders. This happened not only to me, but several standing waiting for the bus or for the bell to ring to go inside.

This seems to be the happening thing to do here at this school, I thought at the time. I was surprised, to say the least, and turned around to find two boys standing there laughing after about the third time I had been a victim.

"What's the matter, Johnny, drop your lunch?"

About that time the bell rang and everyone scurried right on by, getting to the designated rooms. I had to scramble to pick up everything and get to my room before the tardy bell rang; of course the class laughed as I walked in with my books all dirty and covers torn. What made me really mad was that my peanut butter and banana sandwich was smashed when someone stepped on it in the rush at the bell. Mom had always made peanut butter and jelly, but after moving to South Carolina it was banana; this was a good change.

As a punishment for near tardiness, I had to sit in the back instead of at my normal desk. While sitting there in the back, I soon spotted the two who had knocked my books out of my grasp, sitting on the far side next to the window. One was about my size and the other a little taller. I was rarely the biggest kid in school, but I was always one of the fastest.

During lunch sometimes I sat and talked with another new student by the name of Vernon Robertson who lived near me. Vernon was in a grade ahead and had been held back because of moving to South Carolina from a place called Winston-Salem, North Carolina, in between semesters.

"My sandwich is dirty and smashed but I'm going to eat it anyway 'cause I'm hungry," I told Vernon. I didn't mention the book incident anymore and neither did Vernon.

The next morning, I sat my books down on the ground and got behind a post at the school. As soon as the two boys rounded the corner, I hit the taller boy right in the nose, which started to bleed, and hit the other boy in the jaw because I missed his mouth as he started to say something. I didn't even look back as I walked into the classroom. That was the last time anyone knocked my books from my hands. From then on, I was part of the class and they would come and ask if I wanted to play with the other kids at recess or play ball after school. I readily agreed.

Vernon and I became good friends. Vernon was a diligent student. He was a Boy Scout and his father let him camp out on the family farm between my house and Vernon's place, about half a mile apart. Dad would let me camp out with Vernon since it was so close, and Vernon had been over to our house on his bicycle several times.

Vernon had a sister by the name of Faye. She was a year older than Vernon, around twelve. She would sit by the campfire with us boys into the night and we would talk. Faye was almost like one of the guys at times. We were all at the same junior high school and felt a kinship in that regard.

One moonlit Saturday night, after eating hot dogs and making something like S'mores, with graham crackers, peanut butter and marshmallows, we sang and told ghost stories till nearly midnight. Faye said she had to pee and was going behind the bushes where we all had done the same thing dozens of times in the past. In about five minutes, she called to Vernon and he went to see what the problem was.

In another few minutes they called me. When I walked around the bushes, I found them both undressed and stark naked. I had never encountered such a thing before, especially a brother and sister. I wasn't sure how or if I was supposed to participate.

Faye and Vernon both assured me it was an "educational" experience to let me know what older girls liked. I followed Faye's lead—I was there to learn. She said: "Us girls liked this sort of play because it was "safe"—no risk of pregnancy."

Vernon and I got the beginnings of our first-hand sex education that night from an unexpected source—his big sister.

Afterwards, Faye got on her bike and rode home, while Vernon and I stayed at the camp. We talked of girls, sex and things my friend Vernon seemed to know much more about than I did.

***

It usually took very little time for us to get to the other's house by bicycle. The only problem was all the roads were sandy and it made riding very tricky, especially at night. Where it had been very mountainous in West Virginia, here there were rocks everywhere and the ground was hard like pavement.

One day as Vernon and I were riding back toward Vernon's place we got into a race, as boys tend to do. Vernon was a little ahead when he hit a sand pile and it caused me to hit his back tire with my front tire. We ended up crashing and Vernon fell on his handlebar, which had no cover, and it rammed into his ribs and chest. He was lying there bleeding and screaming for me to help him. When I came over to see what the problem was, I

School days

could see the handlebar was stuck into his chest. I said, "Stay there, try not to move around, it will make it worse! I'll go get some help." I tried to get my bike out of the entanglement to ride but realized the front wheel was all bent and wouldn't turn. I threw it down and took off running. I got to Vernon's house and told Mrs. Roberts what had happened. She jumped in their new blue Oldsmobile and drove it like a wild woman as I directed her.

When Mrs. Roberts and I got to where the bike accident had happened, Vernon was still writhing around moaning and screaming. His mother pulled him off the handlebar that had him impaled and blood shot up from Vernon's chest. She carried him and put him in the car. She told me to stay at her house and tell her husband when he came from work what had happened, she was going to the hospital with Vernon.

That minor accident, causing a lung clot, nearly took my best friend's life that day. Mr. and Mrs. Roberts moved back to

North Carolina shortly after the accident. I was never sure if the accident was the reason or there was some other reason for their sudden departure, but we never got to fulfill all the things Vernon had envisioned us doing together.

That playful accident and their abrupt departure caused me *not* to become further "socially educated" by Vernon and Faye. This bike accident also caused me much grief and heartache at almost losing my best friend.

Dad and Mom Celebrate Anniversary

Humiliation

I still remember watching the Friday Night Fights with my father back in the 1950s. It was a ritual for my father. I remember the old beer commercials and the company that my father had at the house when we watched the fights; usually my uncle Gilbert and uncle Jimmy were always there. They were not my uncles, but I had to call them that.

I was young, but I clearly remember. I didn't know who was fighting but I just loved being there with my dad. I would ask my father, "Who are you voting for?" He would laugh and say, "You don't vote for the fighters, son." I didn't quite get it yet. Sometimes I would see what appeared to be an opening and yell out to my father, "How come he didn't throw a punch?" His answer was almost always, "It's a lot harder to see those things when you're in the ring."

I would run around the house throwing punches at imaginary opponents. I wanted to be a boxer. My father had some old leather boxing gloves and a speed bag in the garage. I would punch away at the bag without any real knowledge of what I was doing. I just wanted to feel like a boxer.

When I was older I came to understand that the 1950s was one of the greatest eras in boxing, and some of the best fighters of that time would appear on Friday nights. Guys like Sugar Ray Robinson and Carmen Basilio, Chuck Davey, Chico Vejar, Kid Gavilan, Gene Fullmer, Johnny Saxton, Tony DeMarco, Charlie Powell, and so many more that I would never be able to mention them all. It was a "Golden Age" for boxing.

I was lucky enough to be born at a time when I can still remember it. A little fuzzy perhaps because I was young, but still I remember those nights in our small front room in South Carolina, watching the fights, my father and uncles standing and yelling at the television, their hands swinging away, beer cans in their hands, hoping to be heard by their favorite fighter. Those were special days.

Then one Saturday we were coming home from Myrtle Beach and somehow the conversation got on fighting. My grandmother said, "I know I had to learn how to fight. I was next to the youngest. My oldest brothers taught us all how to fight."

"Same with me, Rosie. With five boys in the family you better learn how to fight. Sam was next to the oldest and he was a natural boxer. He was tall, fast and tough. He taught us all the basic three boxer's moves, then it was up to you to use them.

"I was never the toughest of my brothers but they never wanted to start anything with me either; they knew they would get a bloody nose, if nothing else."

Going back home we were going through New Ellington and I just happened to see a Golden Gloves arena sign. I asked Dad what that was and if anyone could go see it. He said he would check on it. A few days later he asked me to go with him into town; we pulled right up to the Golden Gloves gym. "Come on in. I want you to meet some people," Dad said.

After going in, I saw three big boxing rings with people in all three. "Mr. Stump, you did come back with your son," a slender foreign guy said in broken English, with a smile

"Yes, this is Johnny. He is a student over at New Ellington Junior High and wants to learn the skill of boxing. He watches Gillette Friday Night at the Fights with me and some other men and has become interested. I thought you guys could teach him the ropes, you might say."

"Yes, for sure." And the man looked at a sign on the wall reading, "Welcome students from twelve to eighteen." I looked at my dad; he never said a word.

Another man they all called "Lightning" took us over to the ring in the very back and asked another man to get me fitted for some gloves. "You can stay, Mr. Stump, if you want; we do one-hour sessions. It's five dollars an hour, cash and carry terms. You understand we have a high dropout rate because people don't like to pay for their kids getting punched and beaten on."

"I'll stay for a while," Dad said.

Two guys took me over to the area where there were gloves and a punching bag. The men put these big gloves on me and stood me in front of a mirror and made me understand what a boxer's stance was for five minutes. I was always to have that pose anytime I was in the ring.

Next, I was taken to a large leather bag filled with something heavy—it probably weighed more than I did. The man told me to get in the boxer's stance and hit the bag like this, and he demonstrated the punches: one high with the right hand and one low with the left hand, twenty-five times. Then switch, with the left hand being the high strike and right being the low strike, for twenty-five more. After that was completed, he asked me if I had ever jumped rope and he brought out a short jump rope. He jumped it a few times to show me and told me it was to learn foot speed.

That was my introduction to Golden Gloves Boxing. I stayed with the routine they assigned of two days a week of practice and three days of running. After a few months, they thought I was ready for the ring.

Saturdays at nine a.m. started the Gong Show for me. There were three fights before me—two older fighters then a junior division like me (12-18). The older fighters had three two-minute rounds and the younger junior division had two one-minute rounds.

I thought this was terrible—we should have three two-minute rounds just like the upper division. Soon I heard "Stump" and another name. We were called to the center of the ring, told not to hit below the belt, to follow the rules and to listen for the bell that would be the end of the round.

We went back to our corners and I heard Lightning say, "My money is on the little white-headed boy." Then I heard the bell, and the fighter was in the center of the ring before me. He was a few inches taller than me because he was twelve or thirteen by the rules. I was really only eleven, but my father couldn't wait to get me started.

As we started punching, the gloves seemed to weigh more and more. I wanted to lower my shoulders to rest my upper arms. I suppose my opponent felt the same arm fatigue I did because I saw him lower his right arm. That was all I needed to give him a hard shot to the jaw and that caused him to fall backward. The next round we exchanged a few punches until again he lowered the same arm in the same way and I did the same thing, with him not getting up so quickly that time.

For the next two Saturdays I was again victorious. My father was very proud and was telling all he could about his boxing son doing so well. Then he brought my mom and my granny to see me on the fourth Saturday, the finals.

Again, I watched two matches prior to hearing my name called. Everyone cheered and jeered when we entered the ring. The guy I was matched against was tall, a head taller than me, and probably thirteen; but the most outstanding thing was he only had one arm. He was just like me—he had won all of his preliminary matches. We were fighting for the junior division title for the year.

We both came to the center of the ring and the referee gave us the talk. I said, "Excuse me, but he only has one arm." The referee said, "Yes, just remember you said that." We went to our corners and came out at the bell. I stepped in and punched one time to his face and stepped back.

From then on I was backing up trying to dodge the flurry of fist coming from that one arm. I thought the round would never end. Lightning came over and told my corner man, "Stump can't be afraid to hit him, even with one arm." The next round, at first I threw a few punches but then it started again. The burst of lightning-fast punches caught me and I went sliding across the ring on my back.

After the match was over and they raised the one good hand (the left) of the one-armed boy named Kent, I was forever humiliated. I had my family there to watch me win and become the junior division title-holder for that year, but instead they watched me get pummeled by a one-armed fighter.

I never went back to the Golden Gloves gym after that fight. I was just too ashamed. But I heard the boy Kent went on to win the State Title that year!

I was given all the coaching talks about, "It's not how many times you get knocked down that's key, it's how many times you get back up." Good adage but I didn't learn that until later in life.

Cotton Top

Later that year my dad was still upset at me for not going back to practice after getting my ass whipped by the one-handed fighter. It took a long time to live down that embarrassment. Part of the way my dad had of teaching me was by work.

That summer, I didn't want to do anything after my thrashing in the boxing ring. I wouldn't go watch the Friday night fights with my dad and uncles anymore; my pride just felt crushed. After a few weeks of this moping around, my dad told Mom at the breakfast table one morning. "Take Johnny over to Mr. Bishop's Gin Mill and see if he can give him a summer job."

Granny said, "I saw some people out there in the cotton field yesterday. They must have just started pickin' because I come out and sit on the porch while I have a chew in the afternoon and I have not seen anyone in the fields until yesterday."

"Flem, it's just a few weeks until August 29th and that is important."

66

"I know, I know, but I think a few weeks is enough time to bring Johnny around and out of this funk he has been in since that fight where he got whipped by the one-arm kid."

"You should tell him what you found out," Granny said.

"No, not until he comes around to acting normal. Many people lose at things in life; that fight is a small battle to lose, and he's acting like it's the end of the world."

The next day Nora took Johnny over to Bishop's Cotton Gin located across a hundred-acre cotton field. They went at eight a.m. in case Mr. Bishop wanted him to start work that day. Sure enough, Mr. Bishop knew Dad because Dad had done a little masonry work for him and Mr. Bishop loved what he did.

"Yes, if the question is anything to do with work."

"Our son, Johnny, has several weeks before school starts. He's bored and wants to make a little spending money. Can he have a job picking cotton or on the line here at the gin?"

"He sure can. We'll let him start today picking. The pickers have to have several days' head start before the gin gets started. If you want to you can come back over and get him around noon. They get a lunch hour from twelve to one and then work until after five, if they want," Mr. Bishop emphasized.

Mom said, "He has work clothes on; let him go to work this morning."

Mr. Bishop took me in the back and began explaining the cotton-picking process to me. Mr. Bishop never asked my age or anything along the personal line since my mother had brought me over.

I was given a burlap fifty-pound bag and told to just pull the cotton out of the cull and put it in the bag; when the bag became filled, to just ask the field foreman for another. I was to pull the bag along with me by tying it on my belt loop.

"Just follow Jason on out to the field; he's our field foreman, and he'll get you started.

I followed Jason out to the field. He looked at me sorta funny and said, "I guess you've never picked cotton before, have you?" I said, "No, I haven't but just give me a chance."

"Oh, you'll get your chance, that's for sure."

He showed me what a row was considered, then how to pull the cotton out of the cull of about five or six cotton pods. Then he said, "You are on your own. You're finished when you reach the end of the row or fill the bag. Here's a few blue ribbons to tie on your bag when you finish. Everyone has his or her own color," and he pointed to the other pickers in the field. Most were black but there was one other old white man two rows over.

I started picking and by ten a.m. I couldn't believe how hot and tired I was, and I only had the very bottom of the bag full. I was at least picking toward our house and thought I could use a rest for a few minutes at lunch.

Well, in two hours Jason came to tell me it was lunchtime and to be back at one p.m. I tied my ribbon on my half-a-bag of cotton, left it, and took off for the house. I ran just about all the way across the field, following my row, and then walked to the house.

"Well, I know one thing; we have to get you a hat or a bonnet like Granny wears. You are as red as the lobsters we used to catch," Mom said with a laugh, when I walked into the kitchen.

I hadn't noticed but when I looked at my arms they were very red as well. "I'm hungry. I didn't know pickin' cotton was so hard but there are several old black women that can pick about as fast as you walk down the row. They have two bags full and I only have a half a bag full.

"How do they pay you? by the bag?" Mom asked.

"Well, I'm not real sure but I saw a truck in the field with a hook on the back of the truck. It seemed to me they were weighing the bags when they were picked up. I'm not sure, it just looked that way, I was in such a hurry to get home to eat."

"We'll ask Granny when she comes in; she knows a lot of things like that."

"Okay."

Granny came in a few minutes, but Johnny was so busy eating his peanut butter and jelly sandwich he forgot to ask her. Instead, she asked him, "Johnny, how many bags have you picked this morning so far? I could see your head across the field. It looked like a moving cotton ball." And she laughed. "I'm going to make you a hat that will help protect and block you from some of that hot sun," she said.

She left the room and went in to where Dad sits and reads his paper in the evening. She brought back a great big piece of paper and placed it on the table in front of me.

"Let me show you this folding so if you ever need a hat in an emergency you'll be able to make it yourself. I learned it from a Japanese lady named Kazuko who worked in the rice fields over there somewhere. She became my friend in West Virginia, where we picked apples together."

All the time she was talking and folding on the paper. I had to ask her, "Show me that fold again," several times before I got the fold correct.

But when it was finished it was very neat and reminded me of a big paper triangle. By the time she finished the hat and I learned how to wear it, my time was up and I had to run out with the hat on.

When I got back to my pickin' spot; I was the only one back there. The others that had started with me were much ahead of my position, even the little old man. I started pickin' again; after a few minutes a big shadow came over me. I looked up and a huge black man said, "Hi there, little cotton top, are you lost out here?"

"No sir, I'm working for Mr. Bishop. My mom got me the job this morning. Look, I've picked nearly a bag of cotton." I

69

lifted the bag and it was heavy to me but he laughed.

"Let me show you a little trick." He pulled out a hand full of small stones that my dad called pea gravel in building work, but he called them anchors and laughed when he said it.

"They anchor the cotton down so your sack weighs more when the boss man weighs it. You get paid on the weight not the size of the bag." He put two little stones in the bag and gave me two more to put in about an hour later. "Then when the truck comes around to pick up the bag, you'll get more money at the end of the day."

At six in the evening my bag was full. I proudly raised my hand and waved for the truck to come over. The driver looked at me and grinned and said, "This is your day's bounty, young man."

"Yes sir, my first bag I've ever picked, but after I get the hang of it I'll do better!"

"Well, that bag is worth a dollar. I'll let you do the math since you are still in school and hopefully do more with your life in the future."

I went back home that evening tired and hungry. I talked about the job all through dinner and I told Dad and Mom, "Well, you can mark off two professions for me not to become … Prize Fighter and Cotton Picker."

We all laughed.

Chapter 12

A new baby is like the beginning of all things wonder, hope, a
dream of possibilities.
Eda J. LeShan

A Big Surprise

After we moved to South Carolina and I got started in school, Dad's work was steady and Mom seemed to be very content.

School picked up for the better with no more pranks, and my teacher, Mrs. Crabtree, helped catch me up on what I may have missed earlier that year with the move to New Ellington. Baseball got my attention and I stayed after school and played almost every day with the school team. There were no uniforms. All we needed was shorts, T-shirt and sneakers.

One day when I got home from school my mother told me, "I have good news to tell you. We'll talk more about it when your father comes home for dinner." I went into my room to finish my homework. In about an hour I heard my father come into the house. He did his usual routine of cleaning up before dinner, and then we all sat down to eat.

Mom could hardly wait to talk, but she politely asked how Dad's day had been. He said, "They were on time with the construction and maybe a little ahead of where they thought the job might be at this time last month. There was a minor accident, but not on our crew." Mom said, "That's a good reflection on you … a feather in your cap. But I hate to hear of an accident, it brings back bad memories."

Then she said, "Well, I got some good news today from Dr. Milland when I went for my check up."

"What's that?" Dad asked.

"We are going to have another baby; Johnny's going to have a little brother or sister!" And she smiled from ear to ear.

Dad said, "Are you sure? Dr. Lincous said he thought you couldn't get pregnant."

"Well, Dr. Milland says otherwise. I'm two months along."

"That's great, but it complicates things a little," Dad said.

"Why, what do you mean?"

All this time I was sitting there not saying a word but listening intently. I also had understood from earlier conversations that Mom couldn't have a baby and that's one of the reasons why they adopted me.

"When you are further along in a few months and need some help," Dad continued, "we have no one down here to help us with the baby. Your mother is back in West Virginia or Kentucky with some other family member."

"Yes, you're right, I didn't think of that," Mom sighed.

I didn't think much about it, but later I thought about the circumstances. Mom was happy and more relaxed, and the environment was good for my parents to have another child; yet I had always thought, but was never told, that Mom couldn't get pregnant.

Mom and Dad were glad to see me active with the other kids because they were now busy with planning for my new sibling who was to be born soon. He was to be named after Mom's nephew, Doug, who was Uncle Hilliard's son, if a boy, and Sally, my father's sister, if a girl.

We finished dinner with talk about my schoolwork and general conversation about the day's activities. But there was a question still hanging that was not discussed at the table that night. Who could help Mom?

Four months later I got the answer. I was re-introduced to my grandmother, Rosie Smith Runyon Pendergrass, whom I had not seen for a few years and didn't remember very well. She was dark-skinned, thin, and tall like my mom. Now, I could understand where all the talk about being Indian came from. My dad looked Indian and so did his brothers and sisters, but they didn't brag about having Indian heritage.

Since I was a little older and could notice the difference in people's skin color and ethnicity, I could see then that her mother was of Indian descent. However, Mom was light skinned, with light brown hair and no Indian look to her at all. She said, "That's because I took after my father's people, not my mother's."

In Welch we had lived among blacks, Italians, Poles, Russians, and other Europeans. Dad worked with all the different ethnic people and didn't show any antagonism toward any. My exposure to musicians at a young age brought all those different kinds of people together as well. But now that I thought about it, there were no blacks, Italians or Indians in school with us now. What had happened, by moving to a different state? Was there a different attitude here? I would learn about that later as I got older and further along in school.

Chapter 13

"Half the time when brothers wrestle, it's just an excuse to hug each other."
James Patterson

A New Brother Arrives

Later that year in April, I was taken to the local hospital and introduced to my new brother, Douglas Howard Stump. Douglas was named for Granny's nephew, Doug, a huge man, over 6'6," with dark brown curly hair. Howard was for Granny's oldest son, William Howard Smith, an Army Master Sergeant and a hero in WWII.

I wasn't quite sure what to think about a new brother. I had been told I was adopted because Mom couldn't have children and now she had a baby. How did that work?

I soon got used to everyone swooning over little Douglas, though I felt somewhat pushed to the background. That was where Granny came in. She became like a big sister to me, taking me on hikes, going on campouts with our Boy Scout troop, and field trips with the school. It was like I was learning from a real Native American every day. Soon, I could identify plants, animals, and types of wood, as well as to trap and track animals and humans. She even taught me how to make and shoot my own bow and arrows.

Granny told me one day after she had been there about nine months, "I really came down here to stay with you and your family to help with the baby, but Koot and Flem have been so absorbed with little Doug it has left you and me time to get to know each other much better, and I like that."

"I really like it too. I've learned so much from you. You are a better teacher than any I've had in school," I told her. "Granny, will you stay with us or do you have to go home now that Doug is here and all right?"

"I'm here for as long as your mom and dad want and need me. As far as I can tell that's going to be several years!"

"Don't you have a husband?"

She laughed. "Johnny, I've had several husbands, but life has seen to it that they are no longer here and that my time is in demand somewhere else."

"How does that work? All the other kids say their parents have just been married once."

"Normally that's true, but if your husband dies or leaves, you have the right to marry again. I have had two husbands die and one leave and return and then leave again. My third husband only stayed a week after we first got married and he took off for greener pastures. He returned several months later and wanted to come back. I allowed it, he stayed several months then disappeared again, that time for good because I told him if he showed his face again I would shoot him!" she said with a laugh.

At that, we went out to shoot the bow and arrows where Granny had set up both moving and stationary targets.

Back to West Virginia

For reasons I don't recall, several months later we were in the big, black, Roadmaster Buick headed to West Virginia, but without my dad. I remember sitting in the front seat with Mom. Doug was in the back seat with Granny.

As we went around a bad curve on a mountain road in North Carolina, I heard a loud *pop* and Mom started to wrestle with the steering wheel. I looked outside, and we were just inches from going over the side of the mountain. "There's no place to pull over," Mom kept saying. It reminded me of our trip down the first time. The wheel kept wobbling, but Mom wouldn't stop. There was an awful smell of burnt rubber, but she continued.

After another curve and up ahead about a hundred yards was a sign for gas and drinks. We went on until she reached the Mobil gas station with a flying red horse on the sign. We all got out and looked at the tire. It was shredded, and the rim was chewed up.

She went in and made some type of deal with the station owner because he came out with a helper and began to change the tire. Mom bought a 3-cent postage stamp and mailed Dad a little note on a postcard, while the rest of us ate a little snack of bread and something called *Nucoa,* or margarine, supposed to taste like butter. Granny had brought some New Orleans-made *Brer Rabbit Molasses* for the bread. We were back on the road in a few hours.

"I want to try to be off the Skyline Drive before dark if we can," Mom told Granny.

"Nora, can we do it? is the question," Granny said.

"If not, we'll have to spend the night because it's too dangerous to drive on these roads in the dark."

The old black Roadmaster just hummed along, riding as smoothly as a flying carpet like the book I was reading. Little Doug was sleeping soundly since shortly after leaving the gas station; I was nodding off as well. Granny turned on the radio and tuned in some Tex Ritter. Mom and Rosie began to sing.

"Koot, you know all the words to these songs; that's really good. I wish I could remember lyrics like you. I have rhythm, but my singing is not the best," Granny said.

"Yes, Flem and I used to play these songs on the radio and at different gigs all over the South when we were in Welch."

I soon fell asleep listening to the two sing.

In a few hours the sun began to sink behind the mountains as they drove along the parkway. The bright green foliage would soon be hidden in the dark shadows of the mountains and the women knew it was time to be looking for a place for the night there on the Blue Ridge Parkway.

Granny saw a sign advertising a phone and cooking facilities in each cabin for $25. That seemed a little high to her, but if it was safe and they could heat up a little food it would be fine. They turned off Skyline Drive's main highway north and followed a sign saying *Sleepy Hollow Cabins* with a directional arrow. They followed the two-lane gravel road about a mile until it turned from gravel to rock and black dirt and the trees seemed to be closing in on them.

Mom turned to Rosie and said, "Damn, I hope we didn't make the wrong choice coming off the road way up here in these mountains. You know what they say about those Hillbillies from these parts."

"No, Koot, I don't know what they say about folks in these parts–tell me."

"Well, Mom, if you've seen a donkey before, they say if you can get past the smell they're really hung. Supposedly the Hillbillies don't care what they partner with, human or animal." They laughed so hard it woke Doug. I had been listening and reading but now everyone was awake.

As Granny laughed she pointed toward a barn-shaped structure on the right side of the road about one hundred yards ahead. As we got closer we could see cars and trucks parked around the building with a sign that read, *Office - Sleepy Hollow*. There was a gravel parking area around the front of the building. The windows were large and the double doors looked commercial. As Mom and Granny got us kids out of the car,

Granny stuffed something into the belt of the dungarees and big blue and white chambray man's work shirt she was wearing.

Now fully awake and raring to go, I asked, "Are we here yet?"

"We're going to see if we can get a room," Mom said, as they opened the door to the spacious store front office. It was set up with the office to the left and an eating area to the right. A sign pointed to the restrooms where Granny was taking us while Mom checked on a room.

"No, lady, we don't have a single room left, but I think we have a $35 cabin left that sleeps six." I heard as we closed the door to the toilets.

When we returned, Mom was asking again in a pleading tone, "That much for a cabin? We can't afford that much, we have a long way to go and not much cash left after a tire blowout and wheel incident earlier today."

The bearded man said, "I'll make you a deal. For $25, we have one place left all the way in the back, up the hill a little. It doesn't have a TV but it's a real cute spot, a little hard to get to, but you'll wish you were staying here longer!"

"We can handle that," Mom said. She paid him the cash. "Our cabin number 7 is all the way in the back and up the hill a little. Let's take everything to the cabin, get settled, and then we will come down to get something to eat for dinner."

"That sounds fine," Granny stated, as we left the office area.

The one-room cabin was very Spartan indeed. No extras except an old black telephone and a radio sitting on a night stand beside the two double beds. There was even a hand-pump for water at the back door.

We only had a few things to unpack before going down to the office to eat. Granny told Mom she was going to get her plug of Apple tobacco and go out back for a chew before dinner.

Granny never smoked but usually had a chew of tobacco in her jaw.

We heard Granny make a noise as she was sitting on the old wooden bench. Out of the corner of her eye there was movement to the right of her and the door. She told us later, "I didn't move a muscle, just watched. After a few minutes, a big snake slithered up the bench about three feet from my feet. The snake was shaking its six rattlers. I counted them as I watched it move up the wall. In a split second, the rattling stopped. I jumped up and pulled the .38-caliber from my belt and blew the head right off the rattlesnake."

Mom rushed out to find Granny with the snake, trying to measure it while it was still slithering around on the little log porch.

"Nice one, about six feet," Granny said.

"Mom, did you bring that gun?" my mother scolded.

"Now, Koot, you know I don't go anywhere away from home without Tom." Tom was the name Granny had given her gun after her deceased first husband, Tom Smith, the father of her four children. "Tom told me this gun would help take care of me and to keep it close, and it sure has helped in many a situation."

Mom came back inside and told me, "Go out and look at the big snake your granny shot, so you'll know what a rattler looks like. Be sure you stay away from it, because they say it can even strike while dead until the sun goes down!"

Nora knew she was in good hands with her mother. Rosie could rope, ride and shoot better than most any of the men. Her husband, Tom, had been an engineer on the Norfolk-Western Railroad and was one of the first men to run a steam engine from the east coast to California on the west coast. Tom was an adventuresome man, but Rosie was even more so. The Cherokee Indians had raised her and her three sisters from a young age.

Chapter 14

"It is located just a few minutes from the hustle and bustle of the highway and its summertime visitors is an incredible natural phenomenon known as the fields of fireflies. Over the past hundred or more years this breathtaking show put on by nature resembles a psychedelic combination of stars falling and fireworks exploding, but you have to be present to enjoy it."
John F. Stump 1955

Fireflies in the Smokies

As we went out the cabin door that evening for dinner, Granny looked up at the twilight sky with her eyes closed and said, "This is going to be a special evening. Look at how the setting sun is reflecting off the orange, white and pink clouds and they are casting strange shadows in the mountains. This will be an evening to remember!"

I looked but wasn't sure what I was looking at, what made the evening special; it looked just like any other evening to me.

I told Granny, "You must have a special eye that can see something before it happens."

"Sometimes, Johnny, when you get to be old and experienced, it seems like you are seeing into the future, but it's just because you've been down that road before," she said.

We went in the cafe and sat down at an old wooden table made from big old oak and maple logs. There were about ten other families and people in the establishment eating and we figured they were staying at the cabins like us.

The cheeseburgers tasted good, the side was a freshly made potato salad and green beans. We all sipped Pepsi-Cola since they didn't have the chocolate milk I would have preferred. Mom and Granny made plans for the next day's travel. They said the plan was to get up at seven a.m. and get packed up, not have breakfast at the cabin but get something on the road when we stopped for gas.

Doug started crying because he had been awakened when a loud noise outside of the restaurant startled him. I even jumped myself. Come to find out some big truck had brought a load of empty barrels to the place to be picked up by another truck and taken to another location.

Granny said, "These barrels are often sold to a moonshiner, or someone who makes illegal whiskey, here in these mountains. They are very sought after because it gives the whiskey an earthy rich taste from the old oak they are made from. We've got our share of moonshiners and bootleggers in Virginia and West Virginia so we can't be pointing fingers and whispering about others here."

Johnny and Granny

Mom said, "Of course, baby Doug will get his breakfast on time every time, won't he Mom?" She looked at Granny and winked.

"Yes. Douggie can't wait like the rest of us," Granny said.

We went out the door after finishing our meal and headed toward our cabin. I noticed it was as black as pitch, not a light anywhere. You could hardly see your hand in front of your face.

Mom said, "You all wait right here." She turned around and went back in and asked the man at the office counter what the story was with the lights, and that we couldn't see to get back to the cabin.

"In just a few minutes you'll see a marvelous sight you won't see again after you leave these parts, unless you live in this area."

"What is it?" Nora asked.

"Lightning bugs, but special ones."

I ran back in the restaurant door just hollering at Mom, "Look at the lightning bugs, Mom, look, look! Mom come on you're missing them!" I was excited, to say the least.

I grabbed Mom's hand and pulled her out the door and pointed, "See the fireflies, they started lighting a few minutes after you went in ... it was like God switched them on all together."

Mom looked up into the dark sky and just as she did there was a flash of light like a miniature lightning bolt lighting up the pathway to the entire cabin area all the way back to our cabin. I was just amazed. Doug, of course, slept through the entire firefly show without so much as a stir.

The cabin was all the way in the back of the complex, nearly fifty yards away. It only had one light above the door that showed the number 7 and we had forgotten to leave it on because it was daylight when we left.

The lightning bugs were in harmony, glowing together, on and off, every few seconds. They were like nothing I had ever seen before against the eerie black sky here on this strangely quiet night in the great Smoky Mountains. I had seen some lightning bugs before, but these were certainly different, blinking in synchronicity.

Mom said, "That's really strange. Our lightning bugs are more individual, just blinking at their own rate. These are hundreds or thousands that blink at the same time, like a flash."

"This was what I was trying to say about this being a special evening. These synchronous patterns are the fireflies giving off signs and mating signals by the flash of their body. We had a great Chief of the Cherokee tribe that could tell you when, where, and why the bugs would appear here in the Smokies at this very spot and time. This is a very rare evening for sure.

Many of my original Indian ancestors talked about these lands being sacred. This is just one of the reasons—the synchronous fireflies, or *Photinus carolinus,* are one of the fourteen species of fireflies in Great Smoky Mountains National Park. They are considered sacred," Granny told us. It was amazing to me how little formal education Granny had (Mom said third or fourth grade), but how much she knew about everything—like the fireflies!

"Johnny, can you remember how special this night is now after your grandmother telling you about the fireflies? See if you can keep this moment as a treasure in your memories," Mom said.

I told her I would, and I did. Every few years going north or driving south through those same mountains, I would tell Dianne or the kids the story about the fireflies until they got tired of hearing it. It was never enough for me because I was just at the age where it fascinated my curiosity about the how, what, when and why of the biological process. I think that was part of the reason why I went on to study the biological sciences at the University of Maryland.

The next morning was crisp and chilly, as the sun's rays were trying to appear over the mountains. We pulled out of the

Sleepy Hollow cabin office, where Mom left the key, at exactly 7:30 a.m., the clock read.

We were not back on the road north a minute before we saw a sign saying, *"You Are Now Entering the Great Smoky Mountains National Forest."* Mom and Granny talked about the forest and all that it provides for people and how nice it was the Federal Government recognized its importance and made it a national living monument so long ago. Their conversation was interesting, but I needed more pictures to really understand better.

My grandmother always had a story to tell. "Johnny, let me tell you a little of the history of this area. Before the arrival of European settlers, the region was part of the homeland of the Cherokees, our tribe. Frontier people like my father, George Runyon, began settling the land in the 18th and early 19th century.

"In 1830, President Andrew Jackson signed the Indian Removal Act, beginning the process that eventually resulted in the forced removal of all Indian tribes east of the Mississippi River to what is now Oklahoma. Many of the Cherokees left, but some, led by a renegade warrior called Tsali, hid out in this area known now as the Great Smoky Mountains National Park.

"My father was one of the white frontiersmen who respected and worked with the Cherokee Indians. When President Jackson began a disbandment of the Cherokee tribe, George, my father, married a beautiful girl, the Chief's daughter, who later became my mother. Some of their descendants now live in the Qualla Boundary south of the park called the Eastern Band of Cherokee Indians.

"As white settlers arrived, logging grew as a major industry in the mountains, and a rail line called the Little River Railroad, was constructed to haul timber out of the remote regions of the area. Cut-and-run-style clear-cutting was destroying the natural beauty of the area, so visitors and locals, along with my father, banded together to raise money for preservation of the land.

"The U.S. National Park Service wanted a park in the eastern United States, but did not have much money to establish one. Though Congress had authorized the park in 1926, there was no nucleus of federally owned land around which to build a park. John D. Rockefeller, Jr., contributed $5 million, the U.S. government added another $2 million, and private citizens from Tennessee and North Carolina pitched in to assemble the land for the park, piece by piece.

"Slowly, mountain homesteaders, miners, and loggers were evicted from the land. Farms and timbering operations were eventually abolished to further establish the protected areas of the park. During the Great Depression, the Civilian Conservation Corps (CCC), the Works Progress Administration (WPA), and other federal organizations hired hundreds of men, including my father, his sons, and their families, to work. They made trails, fire towers, and other infrastructure improvements to the park and Smoky Mountain roads. My father left a lot of blood, sweat, and tears in helping to build a park right here in the Smoky Mountains."

By the time Granny finished telling the tale of the Cherokees helping to establish the Great Smoky Mountains National Park, we were almost to the turnoff at the West Virginia line. I had paid close attention for most of the conversation and history talk by my grandmother, but I'll have to admit my eyes got pretty heavy during the part where she was trying to explain the people involved from a hundred years ago. It was a shame no one ever wrote down that part of the early history of the Great Smoky Mountains National Park.

Chapter 15

Better is not something you wish,
it's something you become!
Author unknown

Runnin' Wild

Mom drove to Welch, I saw the Welch city limit sign, and then on to a smaller town called Roderfield. We pulled up to a white house up on a hillside about three or four feet higher than the road. The house was large, with big white columns in the front all the way to the second story, with green shutters on the front windows. There were five bedrooms and three bathrooms. It was the largest house I had ever seen, I thought, as Mom showed us the house. It was located just beside a grocery and deli called Nick & Geno's, across the road from a railway stop. Both passenger trains and coal drags stopped in Roderfield, as a suburb of Welch.

I later found the house was not ours, we had rented it and it belonged to the owner of the store, Mr. Geno Valente, where Mom was to work as a cashier.

This was a part of the family history I didn't know at the time ... why we were there and how Mom got to know Mr. Geno, and how they became so friendly. He was always coming over to the house and talking with Mom and Granny in a whispered tone.

The Valente family was large and lived in an even larger home several blocks from the railway station. Mr. Valente's brother had just moved out of the big white house we were now occupying. I still wasn't sure of the reason we were now back in West Virginia, but Mr. Geno seemed to know. The house had been vacant several months before we returned to West Virginia. There was a lot of scuttlebutt heard on the three-mile school bus ride to Welch Elementary School that crossed a mountain from Roderfield.

Nick and Geno were having trouble, and they had a big fight that split up the whole family, was what Mom repeated to Granny, was all that I knew for sure.

Talk was, a woman that worked as a cashier there was seeing Nick on the side. Nick's wife caught him with the woman and blamed Geno for having that kind of woman working at the store. Geno got mad and fired the woman and kicked his brother out of his rental house.

Geno knew Dad and Mom from riding the train that stopped there in Roderfield coming from the Gary coal mine where Dad first worked. In addition, Geno and his wife Angelina were enthusiastic country and western fans and they knew Dad had records out and had been instrumental in the song *Sixteen Tons* that Geno loved. When Dad called him to see what had happened to him and his brother, it was just at the right time and the house was empty. This was how Mom moved into such a nice house right from the start.

Mom said Dad had finished his contract job at the DuPont Company in South Carolina and had not been assigned another location for DuPont or U.S. Steel. Mom never liked South Carolina much and when this West Virginia opportunity came up, she told Dad she wanted to go back to the Welch area.

Mom went ahead and left with Granny, little Doug, and me in the beginning of the month of September and was to get the house set up for living. Dad was going to come when he finished at the end of the month. That way they were able to get me in school sooner and Dad could avoid driving in bad weather in the mountains during the holidays.

Granny stayed with us. She had a big blue and green flowered bedroom all to herself and took care of little Doug during the day while Mom worked at the store next door. Dad was still in South Carolina where he had sold the little house we lived in and sent the money to Mom to take care of things with the family.

Dad moved into a small trailer he was calling home for the remaining weeks. He was the contract overseer, and the time on the job turned out to be months because of a problem getting the job finished.

***

I became heavily involved in school activities. I was now in the sixth grade and had become bigger and more filled out. My speed was still pretty good from all the sports I had played in South Carolina. The weather was so mild there we could play outside nearly year-round.

One day, Coach Walters saw me run in physical education class and said he was very impressed. He asked if I would come out for the football team, even though I was only in the sixth grade. Normally, a student would have to be at least in the seventh grade to be on the Junior Varsity or Varsity team to play football. "I am willing to make exceptions to the rule once in a while," Coach Walters said.

Love of the game

I had only been in school less than a week and all the boys had been practicing from the end of August to fight for their positions on the team before I had even gotten there. That day all the boys playing football were asked to report to the locker room after school. Coach Walters made a special announcement regarding the practice over the intercom that morning.

I showed up just like the other boys. I was a little smaller than most of the boys and not nearly as heavy. *"This is nothing to worry about,"* I thought, as I stood in line with the others to get shorts, a T-shirt and special track shoes they were giving out. The gear was handed out by grade, age and size. Well, you can imagine where I was on the list … next to last.

Yes, as nearly the last person to get the running equipment, "the pickin's were slim," as Granny would say. When the coach came in, he saw me and said, "I'm glad to see you, Johnny. You know you are the only sixth grader we've allowed to try out for the varsity team in over five years."

"Why is that, Coach?" I asked.

"Well, truthfully, you may be as fast as some of our varsity running backs and split ends. I want to run you in the time trials for a few days to see. Don't worry about the equipment or your placement at this point. Just run your best," Coach said.

As I continued to look through the equipment, I only found one helmet that would fit because my head was so small, and it was an old leather helmet that looked a hundred years old. I put it on and asked the equipment manager if it was the right fit.

Sonny was the equipment manager and was really liked by everyone. He was in the eleventh grade and was like a young coach to me.

Sonny looked at me and laughed, "Damn, I hope you can run, 'cause everyone is going to be chasing your ass to get a look at that helmet and face. There's not even a face guard on this helmet, it's so old. Here's you a set of shoulder pads, practice jersey, pants and thigh pads, but we are out of hip pads for the time being until somebody quits, which won't be long once coach starts running the hell out of the first and second string. Your cleats are over in the shoe repair area. What size shoe do you wear?" Sonny asked.

"Nine," I answered.

Even though Sonny was in the eleventh grade, he was about my size, and he was not very muscular at all. He had a charming smile with perfect teeth, a real heavy head of black hair, and a faint black beard. I didn't know Sonny's last name, but we became instant friends as we were getting the equipment together.

That day, all coach had everyone do was just run around the track, sprint for ten seconds, then a slow run for twenty seconds, then sprint, then slow again, sprint. The varsity players knew this drill very well and led every drill with high intensity.

In practice the next day, the players were to meet on the regular football field that was up a slight hill from the practice field about 100 yards away from the field house. As I got dressed, I needed Sonny's help because I had never played contact or worn the equipment before. Sonny was very quick and had me ready to go with the others. Being the youngest as a sixth grader, the older boys pushed me to the back of the pack as they moved up the hill. I figured I would be the punching bag for the next year, but I knew I had to pay my dues.

There were about sixty players on the field in the few minutes it took to get up the hill. Coach blew a whistle, and everyone dropped down to a one-knee position. Coach started talking to the players about sportsmanship and a champion's attitude. I listened intently the entire ten minutes, then I heard my name called by the assistant coach, Mr. Viloni. I didn't know what to do other than say, "YES, SIR!" Coach Walters asked me to stand.

I stood up. Everyone laughed. Coach waited a few minutes to let the laughing die down before he started to talk again.

Coach Walters said, "Most of you won't be laughing by the end of this practice. I promise you." And he hollered for Sonny to come to the front, as he often had.

"Coach Viloni, line them up for time trials. We need to loosen everyone up first with a few sprints. Sonny, you stay here and I'll go down to the fifty-yard line and stand. You and Coach Viloni start them, and I'll turn them around."

When Coach got to the fifty, he lifted his hand. Sonny said, "Everyone down in a four-point stance. Now bear crawl down to coach on the whistle." A bear crawl was a basic exercise used by players where the players stay on all fours while they are executing the desired maneuver, in this case running on all fours.

I had done this exercise but never in competition before and started slowly. The further I went the easier it became, and soon I was among the leaders and finished fourth.

Coach bellowed, "Up, jump and grab all the way back to Sonny and Coach."

I was third that time.

Coach Viloni then said, "Everyone down and duck-walk down to Coach."

That time I was again third—two halfbacks and the quarterback beat me by about ten yards. After the duck-walk, Coach Walters had all the linemen and all the backs get together in separate groups.

"Linemen down, sprint all the way to Sonny as hard as you can go," he blew the whistle.

Ancil Sparks clearly won the linemen's run. Ancil was a huge guy, over 6'6'' and around 250 pounds. He was a senior and planned to go to the University of West Virginia in the fall.

"Good hustle," Coach yelled.

"Stump, you didn't run with that group, so I guess you're a back?" Coach said.

I didn't know what to say. I had only played sandlot football and always played where they needed someone because I was usually the smallest and youngest on the field.

"Well, let's see where you fit in; backs down and sprint all the way to Sonny," he instructed.

That time Sandy Bright won. He was the fastest and almost the tallest guy on the team, almost as tall as Ancil. I figured, *damn, he's fast too!*

Then Coach hollered for them to run back, this time in pairs closest to their speed and to run hard, like it's a race. They did, and Sandy won again with the same two guys second and third. The linemen ran about the same, with Ancil again winning by 20 yards.

Now everyone was on Coach's end of the field, and he called everyone together and said, "This is the reason Stump was asked to come out even though he is only in the sixth grade. Sandy, get up on the line, Roger you also. Now Stump, you get three steps behind them," Coach said. Coach Viloni stepped off three steps for me.

"When I blow this whistle, run as hard as you can towards Sonny. The one that finishes first doesn't have to run back, the other two do." They all smiled except me; I was worried. Why was he giving them a head start when I was much younger and smaller?

Coach said, "Ready, set," and the whistle blew. In ten steps I had caught them and started to pass when Roger said, "If you pass us I'm going to kick your ass." I slowed and fell into third place, one step behind the other two.

Coach hollered, "I'm not so sure about that finish. All three of you run back and the last one can do a hundred pushups after practice." The team snickered, and murmurs could be heard as to whom everyone was betting on ... and it wasn't me!

We all three lined up together this time when Coach Viloni started us. Coach Walters wanted a different finish.

"On your mark, ready, set … go!" Coach said.

The two older boys were ahead of me by a step or two and each time I would move up on them they would step in front of me. At about the 30-yard line, I decided to chance it and I ran up beside Roger, who immediately tried to elbow me in the face. I was so short the elbow went over my head and I gave a little dodge, but that caused Roger to go off stride, stumble and fall to the ground with a big thud.

I never looked back. Sandy and I were even, stride for stride, and that's the way we finished.

Coach Walter yelled. "Much better and that's a little sixth grader, you guys! It looks like he's going to play some ball here at Welch."

I tried to never win by much, but I made sure I never lost by much either. From that day on, all the older school boys and even some of the girls were friendly and helpful. I even got my football name that year, "Stumpy," given to me by Roger, Ancil, and Sandy.

Chapter 16

Be the energy you want to attract.
Author unknown

Girl Power

I was in the grocery store next door one Saturday talking to Mom when a nice-looking girl about my age came in and said, "Hello, Mrs. Stump." She continued to walk right on past me without a look and to the office in the back of the store. She opened the door, walked in, and started talking to Mom's boss.

I asked, "Mom, who was that cute girl who just spoke to you?"

"Oh, that was Mr. Valente's daughter. She is about your age but goes to another school, a private Catholic school, I think."

When the girl came out of the office fifteen minutes later, I asked my mother to introduce us. As she came by the counter, Mom said, "Ellen, I want you to meet my son, Johnny."

I quickly stood and said, "Pleased to meet you. I'm sorry I didn't catch your name."

"Oh, it's Ellen," she said politely.

"What grade are you in, Ellen?" I asked.

"The sixth, but I go to St. Mary's in Welch. It's a Catholic school on McDowell extended."

"We used to live on McDowell Street in town, next to the railroad trusses," I told her.

"Yes, I know where that is, we go right by there on our way to St. Mary's every day, under the railroad truss that forms a bridge."

"Yes, that's where we lived."

She asked, "Where do you live now?" as she continued to walk toward the door.

"We live in the house right next door. What are you going to do now?" I asked.

"I'm going to stay here until my dad leaves at four o'clock today. It's only ten now, so I thought I would go play in the basement where dad keeps storage and files. I'll usually go down there and listen to the radio and read. Want to come see?"

I turned, yelled to Mom I was going with Ellen to play and would see her home later in the day. Mom continued waiting on a customer and didn't ask where we were going, if she heard me at all. We only lived about twenty-five to thirty yards from the store and I was in and out several times each day.

The store was a large wood and brick structure with a huge basement and a second floor. I had never been anywhere except the main retail area. Ellen was now leading me around the back and down five concrete and stone steps to a big steel door, which screeched when Ellen struggled to open it. I gave her a hand getting the big red door open.

We walked in and she turned on the light next to the door. When our eyes adjusted to the light in the dark basement, I could see the records and files stored from the ceiling to the floor. There were cobwebs over many of the wooden and cardboard boxes. As we walked down a long hallway, on the right were stacks of big cans of different foods—green beans, tomatoes, corn, and it seemed like every other vegetable for winter or summer. These were not grocery store cans, they were big industrial size cans, the largest I had ever seen and the most at any one time. The shelves were made from big, thick timber like the ones used in the coal mine where dad had worked. I didn't realize the Valente family owned two other eating establishments until Ellen mentioned it when I asked her about all the big cans of food.

"The next light switch is on the right down at the end of this row of cans. Found it … God … look at the size of that spider. It's nearly three inches big around and has long, black legs," she stated.

I had always liked insects ever since my trip from South Carolina to West Virginia where I saw the swarms of lightning bugs. I looked up every bug and spider found in the encyclopedia to find the specifics about the creatures. This one I had never seen alive.

"Don't bother it, I'm scared of spiders, they creep me out," Ellen said.

I didn't pay much attention to her and just got closer and closer to the spider to get a good look. It moved slowly back to the center of its large web. Before it moved out of my range I poked at it. It reared up on its back legs and when it did a large, red, hourglass-shaped spot showed on its abdomen.

"Wow, my dad has told me about these spiders and how dangerous they are. They are supposed to be able to kill a horse or a person in one bite. It can jump nearly two feet to get its prey," I explained to her.

"Well, you are just inches away from it being on your nose. Come on, let's keep moving," said Ellen.

"Okay, but remind me and I'll come back and catch him for a show-and-tell in science class at school."

"I can see already you're nuts. That spider has probably been under here for as long as we are old, and my dad said if you leave most creatures alone they will leave you alone, so come on."

Then she laughed and got hold of my hand and pulled me along the hall. I got a fluttering in my stomach when she took my hand. She was cute in her pink and blue frilly dress down to her knees. Her dark brown hair was curly like that girl on TV called Shirley Temple.

We followed the long dark hallway into another room, this time with old furniture stacked high almost to the ceiling. There were several old stoves, iceboxes, refrigerators, and store display cabinets, as well as chairs and tables like you see in restaurants.

"What is this room? Why does it have a partition between the other section, Ellen?"

"This is the storage area under my uncle's part of the store. He has a Deli, like a small Italian eating establishment, for the railway. He and my father share the building all the way from the basement to the second floor and scary old attic. I've found some really neat hiding places in this building over the years, especially here on my uncle's side. We're not supposed to go on each other's side of the property without permission, but I hate to ask every time I want to go exploring down here."

"Damn, you could get lost down here with no light on," I told her. I reached my hand down on my jeans to feel for the knife in my pocket Granny had given me for my last birthday. Granny had said then, "You never know when a little pocketknife will come in handy."

"The Deli is just above us now and usually has a crowd of customers. There is another floor usually rented out to people that come in on the trains and need to stay somewhere for one or two days, never more than three, or my uncle gets mad. The same is true with the second floor above the store, but it's for longer stays like a week or a month.

The Deli is very popular since they sell the popular drinks—sodas, beer, wine and coffee. The only thing my uncle and my

98

father don't sell is liquor and whiskey. Whiskey has to be brought in from a separate building and it is a mile away from the train station and too far to walk for most people, so they just drink the beer or soft drinks," Ellen told me. "One more turn, another light switch, then we'll go to the left just ahead. There's a door that has a lock on it, but I know where the key is hidden. The key is over the door on the ledge. We'll have to pull a chair or box over to the door to reach it."

"No problem, here's an old orange crate that should be tall enough to stand on." I crawled up on the crate ran my hand along the ledge. "Found the key, Ellen," I said.

I was interested to see what was behind the locked door. When Ellen pushed the door open, it was as dark as pitch until she switched on a light. Beside a big, blue couch there was a small lamp on a table that Ellen found in the dark and turned on. It lit the room pretty well for a small lamp.

We sat down on the couch and began talking about each other's schools and what was wrong with them for about fifteen minutes. It was then that Ellen asked if I wanted to play a game she had learned from her older sister.

"Sure," I said.

She reached over to the little table with the lamp and pulled open a drawer where there was a deck of cards. I was familiar with cards but really had not played any card games because mom and Granny felt they were the cause of some type of evil. I didn't say anything except, "You'll have to teach me. I'm not well versed on card games 'cause we don't have them at home."

Ellen smiled, "Neither do we, but this game is special and usually played with only a few people. The last time I played it was with my sister and her boyfriend." She took the deck, shuffled the cards and dealt each of us a hand of five cards. She told me I had to pick up the cards and not let her see them. Ellen then explained basic poker to me. We played a few hands of the new poker game until I seemed to understand what I was doing. Then Ellen said, "Let's make the game more interesting. If you lose a hand then you have to remove a piece of your clothing and if I lose I'll do the same."

This sounded strange to me but I thought, *"What difference does it make, it's just a game?"* I asked, "Do shoes and socks count as clothing?"

As we began to play we each had lost two hands and had removed our shoes. Then the next two hands I lost and removed my socks. Then she lost a hand but had no socks on and said she would remove her sweater. I had never seen a girl's underclothes up close and became excited because it brought back memories of Faye and Vernon in South Carolina.

I lost the next three hands and had to take off both my undershirt, my top shirt and my belt. I couldn't decide what was next if I lost. If I lost it was down to my jeans and underwear. Sure enough, I lost the next hand. Off come the jeans and now I was almost naked, only my white cotton jockey underwear left.

Ellen said, "Well, do you give up and I win?"

"No, let's play it out; I don't think I'll lose again."

Suffice it to say, I could have used my friend Vernon's advice at this point. The game continued to its inevitable conclusion until we were both stripped bare, enjoyed a good look at each other, smiled, and got our clothes back on.

Chapter 17

"You were born an original - don't die a copy!"
Author Unknown

Cowboys and Indians

I wanted to establish my first highly charged young romantic relationship with Ellen that year, but her parents sent her to her uncle's place in upstate New York for the summer.

While Ellen was away for the summer, I was having a good time with my cousin, Smitty Horton, and his friends who were a little older. Smitty was the son of Henry and Lucille Horton. Henry was the son of my Aunt Sara Horton, my grandmother's sister who lived on Long Island, New York.

Smitty was a year older and had a sister named Betty. They also went to the McDowell School system in Welch. We lived about three miles apart, but that was no problem on our bicycles; except that Smitty lived on the side of a big mountain called Premiere Cut that I had to climb each time to go see Smitty or his family. Smitty's father, Henry, would laugh and say, "Yes, this way I can tell who really likes me … they won't complain about the walk or the drive up the mountain from Welch."

I had gotten to where I could almost ride my bike all the way up the mountain by doing zigzag patterns all the way, except for the very steepest part. That section was very steep, with rough terrain, big rocks and loose coal on the road.

One day, Smitty, two local boys I didn't really know, and I were playing cowboys and Indians in the mountains near our home. We were probably almost a mile back in the deepest part of the forest on the mountain. We were in a spot I had only played in one other time, among the huge oak, maple, and hickory trees, biting briers, poison oak, wild flowers and unending rock cliffs. It was beautiful, yet intimidating to look at.

We always flipped a coin to see if we were cowboys or Indians and who was on sides.

"Johnny, you're a cowboy with Nelson and I'm an Indian with Bud," Smitty said, as we all decided on our sides in the game.

We all had real BB guns and Nelson and I had real bow and arrows, but we were lending them to the other boys for the game this time. I was a pretty good marksman since my grandmother had taught me to shoot a .22-rifle and use a bow when I was quite young. It was rare that I let anyone use my bow since Granny made it from ash wood gathered in the forest several years earlier.

I was always amazed at how much Smitty knew about natural things in the forest, but his grandmother was my grandmother's sister and it stood to reason she probably learned about the same things at about the same time as Granny did when they were young girls. I could remember Granny saying there were no school buses, and she had to walk several mountainous miles through the mountains to school with her sisters and brothers.

In the cowboy and Indian game, the rule everyone agreed was to aim below the waist with either the arrows or the BB guns. The cowboys got a ten-minute head start in the woods, and the Indians had one hour to track them down and capture them. I always liked being an Indian because of my experience with tracking, hunting and shooting. The only problem was there was no snow or soft ground up here to go by. This time I had agreed to be a cowboy and even wore a Hopalong Cassidy black hat given to me by cousin Smitty's sister, Betty, as a birthday gift.

We took off on the designated signal and ran as fast as we could into the forest. I was smaller, slimmer and faster. Nelson was older, taller and heavier, almost fat, and couldn't run as fast. I took us up the mountain where it would be very difficult to climb and shoot. I got to a rock formation and quickly scaled the cliff about thirty feet high. Nelson found it difficult, but finally made it up the cliff. On the other side of the cliff was a shallow cave. I suggested that Nelson hide in the cave while I climbed even further up the cliffs to get a better view. In the ten minutes lead-time, we had probably put nearly a mile between Smitty's Indian partner and us.

I found a huge oak tree growing through a rock and it had a crevasse large enough for me to squeeze into. I could see down the trail where I figured they would come to look for us at some point. I was within shouting distance from Nelson and thought it was a good ambush spot. I then pulled a limb of the oak over top of me, but had to pull off my cowboy hat to cover myself with the limb, then waited.

I thought about the time I went deer hunting with dad and Uncle Hillard, and they taught me about camouflage when hunting or being hunted. We had to stay squatted down in a similar spot for hours before the deer finally wandered into our ambush. I knew about the importance of surprise attack and camouflage.

In about fifteen minutes, I heard Smitty and Bud coming through the woods. I was not going to show myself and hoped Nelson wouldn't either. Let them spend the game time looking for us. In fifteen more minutes they were under the cliff and within firing range of either rifles or bows. Bud didn't want to climb the steep cliff because he figured Nelson couldn't, so why should they spend the time climbing the rock formation. Smitty felt just the opposite. "I know Johnny!" he said.

"Johnny will be right at the top of the hardest thing to get to, like that cave near the top, so let's go see," Smitty yelled to Bud.

Nelson and I heard the command from Smitty. Nelson came from his hiding place in the cave and started firing at Bud who was in the front. They both hid behind the trees scattered at the bottom of the cliffs. Smitty took a position under a large sycamore tree with its distinctive bark, while Bud knelt down behind a big rotting mossy oak stump with wild holly bushes around it.

I had not made a sound or fired a shot. They didn't know my location; their concentration was on Nelson.

"I'm going around and up the cliff," Smitty told Bud. "You stay here and keep firing at Nelson. I'll try to flush Johnny out."

The one advantage cowboys had over the Indians was the ammo. Smitty only had four good arrows left, and Bud had used two of his six shots at Nelson already.

The cowboys were to have ten BBs in their guns, but who really knew?? The Indians were allowed only six arrows.

I rose up to see Smitty scamper up the rock cliff like a mountain goat about a hundred feet from me. I knew I would be found if I stayed where I was. I moved even further up the mountain, staying behind the trees, but forgot my hat in the rush up the hill.

"Okay, I've shot my last arrow!" Bud yelled to Nelson. Nelson began laughing and started to descend the cliff when Bud came up under him.

"Oh, sorry Nelson, I found another arrow on the ground that I'll use to shoot you unless you surrender." With that, Nelson was captured.

Smitty was still chasing me and the game was ten minutes from a finish. I had not fired a shot and Smitty had only used two arrows to flush out one of my hiding spots behind a clump of small maple trees. I was moving from one tree to another with Smitty now right on my heels. Only about twenty-five feet separated us. I was aware how easy it was for him to pick me off at that range. I either had to draw him out for a good shot or I had to put more distance between us.

"Give up, Johnny, you're just as good as caught," Smitty yelled.

"No way," I voiced back from behind a small clump of saplings. I didn't think Smitty could use the bow and arrow well enough to hit me, so I moved toward a larger old oak tree. When I did, my shoulder stuck out from behind the saplings before I could run. *Whoosh*, was the only sound I heard that day as the arrow buried itself into my right shoulder.

"Damn, Smitty, you aren't supposed to shoot for the head!" I shouted as blood shot from my right shoulder. I lay there with an arrow sticking out of my shoulder, bleeding like a stuck pig, as Granny would say.

"Well, that was all I could see of you and I figured if we were going to win I had to get you in the next few minutes. I really thought it would stick in the tree and add some dramatic effect to the capture," Smitty added.

"I'm glad we were just using target arrows and not playing with hunting arrows or you really would have stuck me good. This is painful enough. You think you guys can help get me down from this cliff with this arrow sticking out of me and get me to a doctor?"

The three helped me down the mountain that day while I bled all over everything and all over them as each took his turn letting me lean on him coming back down the mountain. They finally stopped a few minutes down the cliff. Smitty told Bud,

"We have to break this arrow off so we can wrap his shoulder." As I was standing leaning on Bud and Nelson, the biggest and hopefully the strongest, took the arrow in both hands and snapped it in half. The pain shot through my shoulder and down my arm, I felt faint and weak. They wrapped Bud's T-shirt around my shoulder to stop some of the bleeding.

After an hour or so we finally got back down to the road, but I was so light-headed I couldn't seem to think or stand up at all. The boys decided to flag a car down and ask for help. Smitty stopped a car, told them a version of what happened. When the driver saw the arrow sticking out of my shoulder he got the boys to put me in the backseat of his car. He drove me straight to Stevens Clinic, the large emergency care facility. Somewhere in that entire scenario of events I lost consciousness.

I awoke several hours later in a hospital bed with my right shoulder wrapped in white tape and strapped to my body so it couldn't move. I first saw my mother sitting in the room; then I knew everything was all right. I laid my head back on the pillow, closed my eyes and went back to sleep. I guessed my friends had gotten me to the doctor. I later learned I had to have eight stiches in my right shoulder to close the wound from Smitty's accurate arrow. I also learned it almost cost me my life playing a cowboy in the mountains that summer.

Chapter 18

"Your attitude determines your direction"
Lao Tsu

A Jump into Life-Saving

Toward the end of August that summer I was all healed from the shoulder wound and had been invited to Lincous Park with a group of kids from school for a summer party before school started. The location of the party was to be the site of the new municipal swimming pool for the Welch residents. I had just learned to swim a year earlier while living in South Carolina, but was still not comfortable in the water. I knew I needed more practice.

There was a cute girl in my same grade I wanted to get to know by the name of Gail Hall. I was hoping to run into her because her girlfriends had told Smitty she and her cousin, Brenda Rice, would be there Saturday at the swimming party.

That morning was beautiful; the sun was bright, there were no clouds in the sky, a mild breeze from the mountains was blowing across the municipal grounds beside the Tug River. The only problem was the Tug ran black because of all the coal that was filtered into it from all over southern West Virginia. Granny had told me when she was a girl the Tug was clear as a crystal.

We had to cross the swinging footbridge to get to the park. I told Mom Smitty and I were going to the pool to meet with our friends for the party. Mom wanted to take me to the party, but

Dad was gone somewhere in town that morning and had not returned when I wanted to leave. I certainly didn't want to be late for the party if Gail was going to be there. I decided to ride my bike. I asked Mom and she thought it would be all right. I jumped on my old Schwinn bike and rode the five miles to the park without any problem.

It cost a quarter to use the pool all day. The park opened at ten, I paid my money after getting there at about 10:15. I was a little early because I wanted to practice my swimming before the others got there at eleven that morning. I had only been swimming a few times since learning, but felt good in the water and wasn't afraid.

Only three people were there when I got to the new Olympic size pool, the first of its type in southern West Virginia. The construction had only been completed that spring, just in time for summer. I had been laid up with the shoulder injury since early July and couldn't get in the water.

I put my clothes into a basket in the men's locker room, then jumped into the cool clear water and swam up and down the pool about ten times and did a few more laps before getting out. It was only a short time before I saw my friends' parents drive up and drop them off at the swinging bridge then leave.

By eleven a.m. the pool was getting crowded with small kids and a few adults. Our party of eight moved to the deep end of the pool to get a little more private space, where there was a large concrete picnic table to sit and talk or eat. The pool was fifteen feet on the deep end and three feet at the other, with a huge white and blue rope down the middle at the five-foot depth marker. Only good swimmers were to go past the rope to the deep end where I had moved with friends. Around 11:30 I felt a tap on my shoulder.

"Hi, Johnny."

I turned. "Hi, Gail." I smiled from an inward happiness and said. "Glad you were able to make it. Did Brenda come with you?"

"Yes, she's over at the gate talking to Billy Tolbert. She's hoping he asks her to the teen center dance this week."

"Well, bring your things over and sit here with us." I took her arm and guided her to our big concrete table where two of the other guys were sitting with two girls. Gail was taller than I, a pretty blonde with a long ponytail and big blue eyes. We all went to the same school but were in different grades and classes. I was well known for being one of the youngest on the varsity football team, so I got to hang with the older kids.

When Brenda came over, she had invited Billy. Our group was getting larger so we covered two large concrete tables with our towels and cover-ups. The tables were under big green umbrellas to protect against the hot August sun. I had to sit under the umbrella because I was of such light complexion and I had learned by living in South Carolina I couldn't take much sun exposure. Gail was a pale-skinned blonde and also got a place under the shade of the umbrella with me. Most everyone was in the seventh grade and up. I was only in the sixth but it didn't bother me.

Gail seemed like nearly a head taller when we were walking but when we were sitting we were just right. We had laid big towels out on the concrete to lie on to talk.

I was totally absorbed by the tall, blue-eyed blonde and had been in a daze, not knowing what she was saying but just looking at how beautiful she was and how lucky I was to be there with her. There was a commotion just beside the pool on our end that demanded attention.

"It's Ronnie and Connie. They're fighting but it looks more like they are killing each other," someone said.

109

"Ronnie is going under again, someone needs to get him!" a lady shouted. No one moved, as everyone was in shock with their eyes glued to the scene and mouths open.

I ran without hesitation and jumped in at the site of the commotion and swam toward a splashing redheaded boy. Later I was told Ronnie and Connie were two redheaded twins who were always fighting, either someone else or each other. It looked like they had been arguing and got into a pushing match and Ronnie fell in and pulled Connie with him. Neither were very good swimmers.

I wasn't sure how this was done professionally, but I had seen a TV episode with Tarzan saving someone in a river jungle scene and I thought I remembered how it was done.

When diving in, I realized I had never attempted this before, but someone's life was on the line. It didn't matter if it was done perfectly, just get the job done, was what I was thinking as I went under the water. I swam up behind Ronnie who was thrashing around in the water. I tried to get hold of him, but he hit me in the face. A little blood ran down my nose and lip onto my chin, but the hit was an accident I was sure.

"Ronnie, relax, relax. I've got you," and in three or four strokes I pulled Ronnie to the side where several people grabbed and pulled Ronnie out of the water. Mr. Wiseman, the pool supervisor and lifeguard was there in a minute asking, "What happened?" Everyone started telling the story from a different perspective.

I was helped out of the pool by an older tenth grader who was on the football team. He said, "Stump, you saved the day. That boy would have drowned if you hadn't jumped in between them. How did you know what to do?"

"I didn't; it was luck. I didn't know exactly what to do but I knew something had to be done. When I jumped in, I automatically went to the bottom and came up under him and behind them both. The only trouble was, from under the water they both looked the same. I just swam between them, so they couldn't fight. After I had Ronnie around the neck he went limp in the water. So, I just swam to the side with him. Connie was still beating the water trying to get out of the way and to poolside. I wasn't sure if someone might have helped him, but I see that he made it to the side."

"Well done. I'm a Boy Scout and that was a storybook save. I can't wait to tell our Scout leader. We're taught lifesaving in Scouting and you just came along and put it to use in the most practical way. Can I invite you to our Boy Scout meeting next week to tell about the incident?" he asked.

"That would be fine. My father told me he was a Boy Scout. He'd be pleased if I attended a meeting," I told him.

I was a hit with Gail and Brenda and all of our friends when I got back to the poolside table. Ronnie and Connie seem to calm down after the incident at the pool with no more fighting that day. You rarely heard or saw them arguing and fighting again after that day. I became good friends with both of them through the years.

I went on to take Gail to the movies and a dance or two but at some point I had eyes for her redheaded cousin, Brenda, who was older, after I got to know them better in school. Brenda was what they called a tease, always coming up hugging and kissing guys in a playful manner.

Just Whistling Dixie

Gail and Brenda both lived down by the Pentecostal church where they went every Sunday. One Sunday morning, I told Mom I was going with Gail and Brenda to the Pentecostal church. I didn't want my parents to take me to church and I didn't want to ride my bike. "Well son, it looks like you're going to walk," Dad said.

After I decided to walk up the railroad track toward the church, I wondered if I made the right choice. The walk was lonely as I kicked a Prince Albert tobacco can down the track and it seemed like it went on forever in the shadows of the blowing weeping willow trees and poke berries that grew along the track and the river. I had never ventured into this area, but I knew I could save fifteen minutes walking time to church by coming this way. I was trying to learn how to whistle using my fingers to make the sound much louder like some of the older boys.

All of a sudden, a big man with a scruffy, dark beard and dirty, plaid torn shirt, with old overalls, was standing right in front of me. His rumpled clothes harkened back to better times for him. Was this a hobo all the adults talked about? I had seen some of these men at a distance but had never talked to one. Dad said they were usually harmless, down-on-their-luck men going from one place to another, and found hitching on the trains the cheapest and fastest way to get where they were going. Times were hard for most folks, that's why Dad and others had to travel a long way to get work.

"Where you going, little boy?" he asked.

"I'm going to the Pentecostal church up here about a half mile to see my girlfriend." I wasn't sure if she was my girlfriend, but I said it anyway.

"Do you go there every Sunday?"

"No, this is really my first time because my parents go to another church. I'm really going to meet these girls."

The big man smiled an almost toothless smile and started walking along with me. I kept moving because I didn't have much time to waste.

"Do you think they would mind if I attended the church service today?"

"If they're like my parents' congregation they'd welcome you to join the service."

"Do they have food and coffee after the service?"

"Well, I'm not sure if they do, but the Baptist church my parents go to always has a big spread of fried chicken, green beans, potato salad, pie and cake for everyone after church; it's like a picnic."

"That sounds mighty good. Mind if I walk along with you to the church?"

"Not at all. Can you whistle real loud like this?" and I put my fingers in my mouth and blew out a big breath of the loudest sound I had ever made—even I was surprised.

"No, I can't like that. I do it like this," and he blew a loud sound simply by jutting his jaw and puckering his lips in a different manner.

"Wow, that was louder than mine. Teach me how to do that whistle, mister."

As we walked down the endless steel rails and cross ties toward the church, the hobo explained how the sound was pushed out of his mouth.

In five minutes, after he demonstrated by whistling "Dixie," I was whistling very loud without ever putting my fingers to my mouth.

"Boy, just wait until Monday. All of the guys are going to want to know how to do this type of whistle. Do you mind telling me your name so I can tell them where I learned it?"

"Just call me Jimbo. That way you can remember Jimbo the hobo taught you," and he placed a big hand on my blonde head affectionately.

We went on to the Pentecostal church. I introduced Jimbo to Gail and Brenda and the preacher, who invited him to wash up in the back room before service and to join us in worship.

The service was long, very long—the gray-haired preacher just went on and on with his message of trusting your neighbor, and all I could think about during the service was what would Gail think about me asking Brenda to a dance and would Brenda go. I might lose them both with my over-zealous attraction for this redhead.

We all ate the good food, drank tea, coffee, pop, and all the fixin's made by the women of the congregation. I never saw Jimbo after that morning but I thanked him again for teaching me the new whistling method before we parted.

Later, I asked Dad about the travels of hobos and told him how Jimbo taught me to do a special whistle while walking down the railroad to the church. Dad told me, "Hobos are much like Gypsies and do not usually put down roots in a place for very long. But I would never close a door to them because we never know when they might be coming back on a return trip.

"I remember back in the 20s when I was young, my mother would feed hobos. One time this poor old hobo ate beans and cornbread with us and a few months later, a big bag of poke salad and other greens showed up on the front porch just when the greens were desperately needed by our big family. There's always a streak of good in most people if you just give them a chance to show it."

Mom was not so supportive in my taking up with a stranger and taking him to church with me. "What if he was a deranged killer and did something awful to you or those two young girls you were meeting? No, Johnny, you are much too friendly with strangers," Mom said rather sternly.

But just the same, I'll never forget the hobo and the whistle he taught me that Sunday morning walking along the railroad tracks.

Chapter 19

"Your attitude determines your direction."
Author unknown

The Tragic Flood on Tug River

I came home from being out on my bike all day in the rain, riding through mud puddles and holes, with two of my new friends who lived in the neighborhood. We had not lived in this neighborhood or house very long—about six months. Dad was doing well and Mom wanted a house closer to town and near the black waters of Tug River that ran through Welch. Mom said she loved the sound of the flowing water.

It was cloudy and had been raining for the past three days. For us kids it was fun to play and ride in the rain. The boy I played with most, George Ayers, was my age and cussed all the time. No one in our family cussed and used profanity; Mom wouldn't allow it in the house. To me it was like learning a foreign language; I wasn't sure when to say what, as I repeated one of his classics: "bullshit." I had been out that day learning, "piss, shit and son-of-a-bitch." George said it even around his mother and everyone. His mom thought it was cute, and would bring the guys over to talk and listen to our new foreign language.

That day George had taken Billy, another neighbor, and me through all the big mud puddles he could find. George was the leader in this game he put together called "Follow the Leader," where we had to do anything the leader did. That morning was the third day of a steady downpour. We were filthy from head to toe when we went to George's house for hot chocolate. His mother would not let us come in the house with our wet and dirty clothes. "Take those clothes off outside and come in and sit and dry with your hot chocolate I've made for you." We did as she demanded and stripped down and she threw all the clothes in a washer. She gave us each a large towel to wrap up in while we talked and sang songs.

**

There was a car in the driveway I didn't recognize when I got home. When I walked in the house my father grabbed me in a big bear hug and we wrestled around in a playful manner for a few minutes. I hadn't seen Dad for over two months.

"Man, you have really grown since I saw you last; what's it been, over two months?"

"Yeah, I was beginning to wonder where you were. You said the job was almost complete this summer and you would be home … and here you are finally." I smiled to let him know I was pleased. I was very happy to see my dad. I was beginning to think there was something wrong between my parents, but Dad just needed to get the job completed before he could leave and come back home; it was just too far away to drive until he finished.

We soon had to move because the Valente brothers ended their family quarrel, and Ellen's uncle wanted his house back. Mom and Granny had to move, and that's how and why we acquired the house by the river. I still don't know how Mom managed to do it all without Dad. Mom's family did a lot to help us during that time.

I went to the Welch Boy Scout meeting in the beginning of September and was urged by Dad to join the Scouts. He had to report to a new job sometime after Labor Day and wanted to see me in the Scouts. I went on to become a successful Life Scout and earned 25 merit badges while I was in the troop.

I learned that year in our West Virginia state history class that in the first half of the 20th century, during the opening of railroads and coal mines throughout the region, Welch became a prosperous city. It was the hub of retail business for McDowell County, which approached 100,000 in population during that time, and was the location of three hospitals. After the productive boom of World War II, oil began to supplant coal in many areas of domestic fuel supply. Mechanization of coal mining reduced the number of laborers needed in coal production.

McDowell County's population peaked in 1950, and began a decline over the next few years. McDowell County still ranked number one in the United States in total coal production. The City of Welch proudly proclaimed itself "The Heart of the Nation's Coal Bin" by the Chamber of Commerce.

When I told Dad this about our state history, he just shook his head and said. "I'm sorry, it sounds better in print than it does in real life. That's why I had to be gone for over two months to finish the construction job in South Carolina. I had a job that could be done without going back into the mine and didn't want to lose it.

"Many of our friends have to think about moving or finding other jobs like I've done. I'm just lucky I picked up the skill of masonry from working on weekends when I was younger, not thinking I would ever have to depend on it. I really thought the mining business would go on forever. It's called black gold, but I guess everything changes and for sure the mine has changed with the loss of much of the work for the miners."

The following year, with an early spring thaw, Welch sustained a terrible flood. The Tug River ran through the town. Our nice little house, just on the river's edge, was completely washed away. In February of 1957, heavy rains caused disastrous floods in southwest Virginia, eastern Kentucky and southern West Virginia. A dozen people died in the region, and hundreds lost their homes.

President Dwight Eisenhower declared twenty-eight Appalachian counties disaster areas, and the National Guard was called in to help with relief efforts. Eisenhower called the 1957 flood the worst in almost 100 years for our area. Our newspapers from Welch and Bluefield were full of news about the flood that devastated our family.

My family, including Granny, who had moved with us from Roderfield to Welch, was now without a home. Mom and Dad's relatives, especially Shirley Gibson's family, another of Granny's children living in North Welch, sure helped. They knew of a house for rent we could move into that weekend. The house was about ten miles north of Welch and in another "holler" from the Gibson family.

Shirley, Mutt, and a whole house full of six children ranging in age from about four to twenty, lived on the mining road. The Gibsons lived about another mile up a black dirt unpaved "holler" from the little settlement called Brown's Creek, where our new rental house was located. The two oldest sons, Hoot and Don, were out of school and drove big coal trucks that brought coal from the mine's coal tipple to the location for the train to pick up out of the holler. The rest of the children were in school and all walked a mile out of the holler each morning to catch the school bus.

I caught the bus down on the highway. I had tried to ride my bike up the holler to visit with them, but the road was so rough and steep, it was impossible to drive anything there except a truck, Jeep, or some kind of vehicle that could take that kind of abuse. I couldn't believe the conditions; it was worse than Smitty's place to get to, even if walking. You had to walk around the large stones, rocks and boulders that sometimes rolled out of the mountain during a rainstorm.

I had to quit the Boy Scouts in Welch before earning my next rank because Dad came home and told us we had lost everything in the flood and there was no insurance, things would be rough for a while. Little did I know how bad that would be. Dad did save the car and the tools he had in the car, and some kitchen supplies we all grabbed on the way out of the house during the sudden surge of water.

After the flood, my parents couldn't afford any extra expense. Doug was still a toddler, Mom had quit her job at the Roderfield store and had to go to work at a grocery store in North Welch for the next year to make ends meet.

It wasn't so bad; it could have been worse. There wasn't much money to buy extra clothes or extra toys, but we found other things to do like ride our bicycles, play hide-n-go-seek, tag, or rover. Many of the kids in the neighborhood where we lived liked outside games.

Doug and I were told what to do for chores and Granny was there to guide us. With everyone pitching in to help it didn't take long; it was just heavy and difficult at times. Granny gave us directions in getting the chores completed. Chopping wood, carrying coal, cleaning the ashes, and preparing the stoves were the main jobs Doug and I had to do each day. We were fortunate, Granny said, "because we lived here near the forest. Some people had to buy wood, we only had to go into the woods and drag out the dead stuff and a few big logs for the fireplace and long-burning heat in the stoves.

"Your Dad found a good old wood cook stove for the kitchen and a good wood and coal heat stove for the living room. The fireplace doesn't have to be used for heat now. The only problem is, that means wood has to be chopped and stored under the house in the basement each week."

We went through a great deal of wood in a week now there were two stoves to feed. "Since both your dad and mom must work, that leaves you and me and Doug to get the wood in and prepare the stoves. You know Doug is too young to do much, so that leaves you and me," Granny told me the following week after Dad found the stoves.

Chopping wood for two stoves was an arduous task for a 12-year-old, but I could handle the job, I felt. Dad showed me how to swing the big two-bladed axe, and how to use the short-handled hatchet for the smaller kindling to start the fires. It took me several weeks, but I finally mastered the job after getting blisters on about every finger of my hands and breaking an axe handle in the process. It was harder carrying the heavy coal buckets up the hill twice each day, morning and evening.

Granny was always there to help me and give me hints on how to do things faster, better and easier. She would carry the smaller kindling up to the house to the back door, so it was simpler and quicker to bring into the house in the morning when it might be raining or cold and damp from the night before. Dad taught me about lighting and starting a fire in the stoves because Mom and Granny might not be available, so I needed to know everything about keeping a fire going, something I have never forgotten in all these years.

Tilley's Juke Joint

Down the mountain about half a mile, where everyone caught the bus and were let off their rides because it offered a parking lot large enough to pull off the road. It was a little place called Tilley's. The Tilley family that owned the store were extremely large individuals, giants everyone called them. Joe at 6'10" and 400 pounds was the father. Mantilla at 6'1" and 300 pounds was the mother. Then Gladys, at 18 and 350 pounds, and Marilyn, the youngest girl, at 15 was 250 pounds. Then the boy Joey, 16, was 6' and 260 pounds and played football for Welch High School. All the kids that got off the bus there loved to gather at Tilley's by the jukebox and dance every afternoon after school.

Marilyn and I would dance until almost dark many afternoons. When I told her I had to go home and chop wood for the evening, she would hug me tightly and tell me she would see me tomorrow. I knew Gladys was older but I wasn't sure how much more than Marilyn. I thought she was around 15 because she didn't talk about driving yet.

For the next few days I wasn't allowed go to Tilley's for being late and not getting the wood in on time. As a matter of fact, I was not sure if I could go after that. I didn't want to hurt Marilyn's feelings, but I wasn't sure I could handle dancing with her and the work I was expected to do. She was twice my size and older as well. Would the girls at school laugh at me for hanging with the Tilley family? Then I thought, what the hell, I'm just going to have fun dancing and let people think what they want. I just won't stay as long; that way I can get my chores done on time. When I got home the evening I was late, I was reprimanded. I told my parents about the situation and they agreed to let me stay an hour after getting to the bus stop.

"I really like the Tilley family and it seems all they really want to do is have fun and see that everyone has a good time.

Everyone talks about them being so big as if they have a disease. Why are they so big—are they giants?" I asked Dad and Mom at dinner.

"No, Johnny, not really. They have what's called Thyroidism; their thyroid works overtime and pumps a hormone into them that keeps them big. Joe used to be a coal miner, but he got so big he couldn't go into the mine anymore. That's when he and his family decided to open the little store and luncheonette. It became so popular, they expanded their hours to evening and included the jukebox, dancing, sandwiches and soft drinks for the kids. Now you see how popular it is, he has to run people away at night to close at nine p.m."

"So, you think it's okay if I dance with the girls and have fun?"

"Sure, go ahead and let them teach you all the dancing you want. That's something I couldn't do because I was always the one making the music with the band," Dad said.

Mom said, "I'm not much of a dancer either, even now. I was young when I married your father. I learned how to play the guitar and sing to be with him, so I really never learned how to dance much. But it sure looks like fun." Granny just shook her disapproving head.

Doug asked if I would take him to The Juke Joint, as Dad called it, to watch us dance. I started to answer yes, but Mom cut me off and said, "Let's wait a little longer for you, until you can ride your bike down there like Johnny."

Granny sat at the table that evening without saying much, only that they didn't do much dancing when she was a girl ... there was too much work to be done. "Our family didn't have anything musical except a banjo and a big wooden radio as tall and nearly as big as the table. My father sat beside it and listened to some program from Richmond, Wheeling, or Charleston every evening when he came home from work. We kids were all

122

made to go outside and play until time for dinner in the evening. Me and my brothers and sisters played checkers, marbles, tag, and games like hide-and-go-seek until bedtime. Not much else to do, but we didn't mind. We had a good time with all six of us together in our one-bedroom cabin in the mountains."

Chapter 20

**"Reese's Peanut Butter Cups are small
and maybe too good!"**
John F. Stump, 1957

Too Much of a Good Thing

One evening after dinner I went upstairs to my room, also known as the attic loft. I had asked if I could sleep up there when we first moved in because there were only three bedrooms for my parents, grandmother and brother.

There was a tin roof and I could hear the gentle rain sounds at night, plus it was big, and I could spread out, put all my books, papers, baseballs, and footballs from school on the shelf Dad made me. He made me a big wooden desk with secret drawers I kept for years. He made all these things from the extra lumber he brought home from his new job building the service station.

I marveled at my father's ability to build things. If you asked him he would say, "Oh, I haven't made one but if someone else did it, maybe I can do it also." Sure enough, he would build something just like the one I would show him.

He told me, "It's like my mind takes a picture of the object, big or small, and it stays with me until the job is complete, regardless if it's wood, brick, or stone. It works the same way with playing music; I hear a song or play the music and it stays 100 percent in my mind." I often wished I had the ability he talked about, but couldn't seem to make the image stay in my mind day after day like he could.

That week went by fast, and when Friday rolled around Dad asked me if I would like to go to work with him on Saturday. I enjoyed watching him build things and wanted to learn that skill someday, so I jumped at the chance to go with him.

Dad and his crew of another mason and two helpers just about had the gas station finished. Dad was putting the final touches on the place—wood trim, some stone work around the gas pumps, as well as a large stone flower box between the highway and the station. My job was carrying stone and fetching tools so I would learn what stone craft was all about.

The owner of the station was a friendly, balding man about my father's age named Bill Clifton. As I was coming by the office just after our morning break at ten a.m., he asked, "Are you hungry or thirsty? Your dad rarely has anything but a Coke and a pack of Nabs before lunch. It's just eleven and you both won't eat lunch until noon today. You've been working carrying heavy stones and block, sweating all that time; you need a break."

Well, I couldn't disagree. I was tired and hungry, but told Mr. Clifton, "Thank you, but I'll have to ask my dad if I can have something. I'm making a dollar an hour and will have ten dollars if I work all day! I'm saving my money for some clothes that I want."

When I went back for another load of stone, I told Mr. Clifton, "My father told me I could have what I wanted. Just put it on the tab, whatever that is." Bill laughed and said, "How about a Coke and a candy bar?"

"No. How about a Pepsi and a Reese cup? These Reese cups are small so they will be fine before lunch."

Bill smiled and handed the items to me, saying, "Find a seat for a minute or two and eat your snack."

125

I really liked peanut butter and Pepsi and felt it was a real good combination for a snack. I rarely bought anything like that because I was always saving for something I wanted or needed. At the end of the day, after five, Dad went in and asked if Bill had seen me.

Bill laughed and said, "Yes, quite a few times. He came in here about every hour after lunch asking for another Pepsi and a Reese cup."

"What? Let me see that ticket." Dad looked at the ticket and burst out laughing.

I had eaten four Reese cups and drank four Pepsi Colas. The cost came to about half of my pay for the day. But the funniest thing was when Dad went to his old green Dodge work truck to put away his tools. I was lying in the front seat rubbing my stomach. I told Dad I thought the peanut butter and jelly sandwich we ate for lunch was bad.

"It's funny, I ate the same thing you did and I'm not sick." Dad started laughing and could hardly stop when I told him the incident in my own words.

"Do you really think you can eat four Reese cups and drink four Pepsis in a few hours and not feel sick? I would be sick too. Oh, I paid your tab and it was almost five bucks for this little workday of yours. At this rate you would have to pay them to work here." And he started laughing again.

By the time we got home, I was vomiting up chocolate. My stomach was bloated out like a toad. I went upstairs to go to bed. When Dad told Mom what was wrong they both had a big laugh together. From that day to this, I don't eat chocolate or drink Pepsi!

****

Granny and Mom were just back from a trip to Lambert's Grocery. I watched Granny pull sugar, flour, coffee, and a big

126

can of Crisco out of one of the paper pokes and set it on the table. The last thing out was a can of Clabber Girl baking powder. The next poke was larger and contained cabbage, celery, and a big ham that was wrapped, but had sugar or something on it to make it white looking.

"What is that white stuff, Granny?" I asked.

"This is a sugar-cured ham from the Smithfield Brothers farms in Bluefield or Princeton, I can't remember which, but they sure are good."

"I can see we're in for a good meal this Sunday for some reason."

"I'm going to make ham, biscuits and gravy, and greens for a little celebration I'm planning. But you all have some work to do in the garden before we discuss it, maybe at dinner," Granny said.

That afternoon coming down from the hillside garden behind our house, I was talking with Granny and Doug. He was being taught how to work the garden right along with us, even thought he was only half my age.

"It's our job to carry the rocks larger than a golf ball away from the garden site and stack them on the fence line about 300 feet away," I told Doug.

He would carry the small ones and I got the bigger ones. Granny would pull all the weeds trying to grow between the rows of plants my parents had planted. They had rows of peppers, broccoli, cabbage, kale, beans, peas, tomatoes, potatoes, corn, and squash. I remembered there were ten rows because it would take Granny and me an hour to hoe each row and carry the rocks away. It really puzzled me to do this job in the garden, because it seemed like when Doug and I carried the rocks away and stacked them and returned a few days later, they were right back. Little did we realize until later that erosion caused further rock exposure!

How did that happen? I wondered when I returned the next time on that row. We were on the last row we were going to do that day before going in to get the wood. Then all our chores would be done before Granny prepared for supper.

Granny looked hot and sweaty. I said, "Granny, do you want to sit down for a little break and rest? You look hot." I didn't know how old Granny was but she had long gray hair.

"Johnny, don't you know what we Southerners say about girls sweating?"

"No, Granny, what do they say?"

"Ladies don't sweat, horses sweat, men perspire, and women glisten and glow."

I laughed—I had never heard that before, but I didn't say anything … she was definitely sweating!

I really didn't know how old you had to be to have long gray hair and wrinkles on your face. In my mind, that made Granny too old to sweat like me and other male laborers I had seen work with my dad, carrying mortar, block, and brick, and I urged her to sit and rest while Doug and I finished the garden.

"Now, your dad and mom will be home from work soon. Flem picks her up from work at the grocery store in the evening since they only have one vehicle. The flood taking the other one makes it difficult to juggle the time schedule. A lot of people took a big hit when that flood occurred; it affected all of this area. If our family didn't help out, I don't know what would have happened."

Granny continued, "Your father has five brothers and two sisters here in West Virginia, I believe. Almost all of them helped out during the flood. There's Dad, Sam, Bob, Charlie, Buddy, Edder, Ester and John, his dad. I think your dad is the youngest. They're the ones I can think of right now. I'm sure there's a few that I missed in there somewhere. But they all were affected when all that water came down the mountains."

As we started down the mountainside after sunset, Granny said, "What would you think about moving from here if your dad got another job? He's just about finished Mr. Clifton's filling station and snack shop."

"Where would he go? Does he always have to go by himself?" I wondered out loud.

"No, that's why this time Flem wants the whole family to be together and move to Florida. There's a big job down there building a space launch center and your father would be doing a lot of the construction of the buildings and launch pads. They think it would be three or four years' worth of work for him."

That evening when we all sat down for dinner, I asked about the possibility of moving to Florida for the new job.

"Dad, Granny tells me and Doug you've applied for a new job in Florida."

"Yes, Johnny, if this new job comes through it would mean all of us moving to Florida. Would you like that or do you care too much about leaving your friends here in Welch again?"

"Dad, I want us all to be together; I really don't care where we live."

With that statement, Dad said, "Well, it's settled then. I got word today I have been hired to help build the largest space launch facility in the United States right on the east coast of Florida. The job is scheduled to start in a few months, so we'll be moving very soon. I am one of the contractors in charge of building the concrete foundations needed for the buildings and the launching pads for the space ships."

"Space ships! That sounds exciting!" I was thrilled.

With that decision made, we all went to bed thinking about a new adventure in Florida, the land of constant solar energy … the Sunshine State!

As we were getting things together for our trip to Florida, we went to Welch one morning to get new tires and the oil changed at the car dealership where Dad bought the new vehicle. He traded the old Chevrolet he had almost lost during the flood and bought a new Buick Roadmaster earlier that year because Mom liked the way it handled and felt heavy on the road, like an expensive Cadillac.

On the road to Welch we passed a line of painted wagons with pictures of dancing girls, prancing horses, and big muscled men riding the horses bareback. I could see the muscles in the horses' legs strain as they climbed the mountain road pulling the wagons toward Welch. I asked Dad and Mom who they were. "Those are our Gypsy Circus friends that pass through each year," they responded. Everyone was a friend to my mom and dad.

"What do they do?"

"Remember the hobo? Gypsies are much like hobos," Mom said.

"The Gypsies come each year and set up a circus tent show on their way to Florida. I think they are with Ringling Brothers and Barnum Bailey and usually come from Chicago or New York and follow the good weather down south. They end up in Sarasota, Florida, like where we are going later this month. I'll check when we're in town to see if we can catch a show while they're here," Dad said.

Then Mom said, "They are much like a migrating flock of birds, returning to the same area each year. They'll stop somewhere before they get into town, set up their wagons and tents into a little village for a week or so, and invite the town folks to see their shows. The only problem is, I never want us to go because of the drinking, girlie shows and gambling that goes on in the back tents. If Dad and I take you and Doug, it will be during the day and just to see the animals and the rides. In the evening the men get tempted by evil that goes on there."

"Okay, Mom, I understand; just seeing the animals will be fine."

Later that day when the car was being serviced and "getting new shoes," as Dad would say, we ate in a place on Main Street called DeFliece's, an Italian bar and grill, a place Dad knew well. Doug and I had pot roast, potatoes, and carrots, and got a piece of pie if we finished our meal. Both Doug and I scarfed up the lunch and had pie. Mom and Dad shared a milk shake after their spaghetti and meatball special. Mom said, "That was the best spaghetti I ever had." Of course, I learned she said that after every meal she didn't cook. She and Dad sat there and smoked a Camel cigarette, something they rarely did except when they were playing music and drinking beer.

On the way out, we all stopped in front of a big poster to read about the circus coming to town. There was a beautiful woman with big gold earrings on the poster with dark olive skin, big dreamy almond eyes, and coal black hair that hung past her shoulders. The sign read, "Come and see what Carlotta can tell is in your future."

Mom pulled on Dad and said, "Let's go; you've lusted enough over that poster. That kind of woman can get you into trouble when they come to town."

Dad laughed, "I beg your pardon. I was about to explain to the boys what Gypsies are and where they come from. I wanted this to be a history lesson for them."

"You know Johnny and Doug aren't old enough to hear that kind of history lesson. All they need to know is that the Gypsies are nomads and have loose morals, and sometimes get into trouble when they come to town. The local women hide and the men lose their money. Is that what you were going to tell the boys?"

We went home without seeing the circus that day!

The next day was Sunday and Mom told Dad she wanted to go to church to see everyone before they left for Florida. The church we went to for morning service was not the same one I visited that evening. The morning was, as usual, at the Baptist church, with singing by the choir that Mom participated in. This time after the singing she whispered to several of the women that she was sorry she would be moving and wouldn't see them again. They all cried together for a few minutes.

Then it was time to pass the offering and I watched the dollar bills drop into the big silver plate. Most gave a dollar, but several dropped in a five-dollar bill like my dad. I guess because he was happy to have the money to give. The preacher delivered a message about "keeping your brother safe from evil." I guess that's what Mom had done the night before for Dad, and it must have been why he put in a few extra dollars that Sunday morning!

That evening we went to a church where Doug and I rarely went. It was called a Holiness Church and was way back in the holler near Mohegan. Doug and I sat in the back of the little church, while Mom and Dad sat on the third bench from the preacher. I counted thirty-five people in front of Doug, me and Granny, Mom and Dad being up a little from us. Doug and I were the only kids there. If I had ever been to this church I really didn't remember, and I'm sure Doug hadn't. Evidently, they all knew Mom, Dad and Granny because they called her Rosie.

The service started like most I had been to, with singing and different people testifying to be forgiven of their sins, or to mention the sickness or death of a family member or friend. After about a half an hour of this, a tall, dark slender man with a black suit got up. He had a black vest under his coat and a little white collar at the top of his shirt. He reminded me of the men we had seen on the posters and painting of Doc Holiday and Wyatt Earp. He had a Bible in his left hand and started to talk low and slow, pointing with his right finger to the sky while he shook the Bible with the other hand.

Most of the sermon I really didn't understand but it seemed like every person around us did because they would suddenly yell out, "Amen, Praise the Lord." Then another would say, "Hallelujah, Jesus, hallelujah." Then another would stand and start talking in some foreign language I didn't understand. Doug was not very impressed because after about an hour of the service his eyes got heavy and he began to fall asleep and I had to elbow him several times to keep him awake.

By that time, the preacher had taken off his black coat and rolled up his sleeves, walked to the back of the church and started asking people, "Do you believe, brother? Do you believe, sister?" and hit them on the back and they would go up front and kneel and begin praying at the altar. Finally, he got to Mom and Dad—they were already crying like most of the people—and when the preacher asked them, they went to the front to pray, but Granny stayed back with us.

The preacher had gotten all the way to the back of the church and everyone he touched had gone to the front to pray, except a few. The preacher brought a large black cage-box down the aisle with him when he returned to the pulpit. He lifted the box and repeated several times in a very strong and loud manner that woke Doug up for sure, "DO YOU BELIEVE, DO YOU BELIEVE, OH, YOU SINNERS, DO YOU BELIEVE?!"

Then he reached into the box and pulled out a big snake that coiled around his brown muscular arm. Then he pulled another and another. He started handing them to different members of the congregation as they stood and shouted, "Yes, I believe, I believe, Jesus knows, I believe,"

I counted about fifteen snakes that were taken out of the cage. I even saw Dad get up and grab a big black and brown snake and start speaking the foreign language as he was going around holding the snake all twisted around his neck and arm. I tapped Mom on the shoulder and asked what he was saying, and she said, "Not now, Johnny, can't you see your father's talking to the Lord?"

"But what language is that? I didn't know Dad could speak a foreign language. Do you think he would teach me?" Mom just looked at me and said, "Hopefully, yes, someday."

This went on another half-hour. Doug asked me, "What is happening?" I told him I wasn't sure, I didn't think I had ever been to a church service like this before. We would just have to wait and see. Later, one of the deacons of the church started collecting the snakes one by one. He would come to a person who had stopped shouting and just grab the snake and put it in the cage without a word.

Dad gave his snake up when the deacon came to him. Dad came back and sat down with us without saying a word, just like he had been in a trance and didn't know where he was or what he had done. It was a strange experience because no one mentioned anything that happened that night to anyone. It was like it was erased from our minds by Mom and Dad, but Doug and I remembered it for sure.

Chapter 21

"What will I do with my one wild and precious life?"
Mary Oliver

The Sunshine State

Late that summer Dad moved our family—Mom, Doug and me—to Florida, where a job and a new venture awaited.

The new mason job he was sure he could handle; but the space technology he was unsure about. But he was going just the same, because it was a relatively long-term job. Besides, he would be doing the building construction, not anything to do with the secret technology to be developed there. Yet there was some reason why he had to have a security clearance that had taken nearly a month to accomplish, but now it was done. He had his security ID photo badge and was to report to his supervisor in two weeks.

On the way down to the Cape, as it was called, we all studied and quizzed each other about some of the facts that were sent with the photo ID. Dad was to work at Cape Canaveral, a name from the Spanish *Cabo Cañaveral*, a cape in Brevard County, Florida, near the center of the state's Atlantic coast. It is part of a region known as the Space Coast, and is the site of the Cape Canaveral Air Force Station.

Other features of the Cape include the Cape Canaveral lighthouse and Port Canaveral, one of the busiest cruise ports in the world. The City of Cape Canaveral lies just south of Port

Canaveral District. Mosquito Lagoon, the Indian River, and Merritt Island National Wildlife Refuge and Canaveral National Seashore are also features of this area, as I later learned.

Of course, my dad could not tolerate all the development happening on Merritt Island and the Cape area, even if he was part of it, so he found a place to take us like no other, in Palm Bay, Florida; it was called Jungle Park.

It was a full twenty miles south of the Cape, on the shores of Indian River. There were monkeys in the southern live oaks, palm trees blowing in the sea breeze, big hibiscus flowers, and beautiful multicolored parrots everywhere you looked. It was like paradise looking out over the blue-green Indian River, a stone's throw from our front door. *How did dad find this place*, I thought?

Across the street was A1A where a long wooden fishing pier and restaurant owned by Frances Langford, a famous movie star of the 1930-40s, was the most outstanding feature on our stretch of road. Mom and Dad went to Club Frances, located beside the restaurant, every Saturday night for the first month we were in Florida. Doug and I were not allowed in the adults-only nightclub. Doug and I could go out on the pier to fish, and stay until late in the night, since it was legal to fish all night if you pleased.

"Johnny, I think you like this fishing down here on the pier," Doug said.

"Yes, it's great, and can you believe how warm it is here? You hardly have to wear anything to be comfortable."

"That's true, so far but when fall and winter gets here I'm not sure what the weather will bring. It's our first time in Florida and as such we'll just have to wait and see."

"Well, it's a week until my birthday, August 29, and I think school starts here on the Monday after Labor Day. I want us to fish everyday, unless dad has something for us to do at home.

He hasn't told me anything since we finished the unpacking except to help with the boxes, as Mom needs. I can't do anything until Mom knows where she wants things."

"You know mom—that could take weeks the way she moves things around in the house," Doug said as he laughed.

That year I was going to be a full-fledged teenager. I had tried to act like one a year or two earlier, but now I was coming into the home stretch. About a month had passed since we had seen Granny. Mom said, "Granny arrives today on the Greyhound for Johnny's birthday." She wanted to be at my "teen party," but, as it turned out, there was really no party except for the family dinner, because we knew no one to invite. It was fine with me just to have Granny back with us again.

After Granny heard all the fishing stories from Doug, she bought me and Doug brand new spinner fishing rods and reels, top of the line. She said they were for my birthday and for Doug's as well in case she wasn't there when Doug's birthday came in April. She didn't say where she might be going and no one else asked.

We were so proud of the rods and reels that we hung them on two brackets over our bedroom door like hunters do their guns. We cleaned and oiled them every night before putting them away. We would talk about fishing until late in the night, because Doug and I shared a room until Mom decided where Granny's room was going to be.

About two weeks had passed and school was to begin soon. I was walking by our next-door-neighbor's yard admiring all the beautiful flowers and shrubs they had grown. The lady who lived there was watering the flowers with her back to me. I yelled to her, "I really like your flowers; they are beautiful. My mom comments on them almost every evening at dinner because our table sits facing your yard."

"Hello, young man. Your mother has a very good eye for

plants."

"Yes, my mother and my grandmother both really like plants; I suppose that's where I get it from. Back in West Virginia, I never saw some of these types of plants." I pointed toward a large broad-leaf plant.

"That's a banana plant. You certainly have eaten those enough to remember that plant."

"Oh, that's where bananas come from?"

"Yes, there're different varieties but that tall bright-green variety provides bananas to thousands of people." The woman had a Latin accent. "That's because they are tropical plants, which means they'll only grow in warm temperatures. I am from Puerto Rico and my husband is from the Caribbean Island Guadeloupe, and tropical plants are all that we know. But your mother can ask me anytime about plants. I like talking gardening. My husband works on a banana boat out of Miami. He is the boat captain who brings the bananas from the islands here. Cuba is where these plants came from about three years ago."

"I'll bet that's fun," I told her. She just laughed.

"I'm Johnny, and this is my little brother Doug. If you need help, we will be glad to help you doing anything needed. I'm trying to get enough money to buy me a bike before too long. See you later; we're going on home now. Bye."

We went on to the house and never thought anything of the conversation, except that I had forgotten to ask her name. But I figured I could do that another time when she was in the yard.

Chapter 22

You never fail until you stop trying.
Author unknown

Football – Southern Style

Southwest Junior High School in Melbourne, Florida, was where I was enrolled for school. It was a new brick one-story building with a main corridor for staff and teachers, and three fifteen-room corridors for classes.

I only cared about and anticipated one thing—football. After the third day they did not announce that boys interested in football should report to the locker rooms, like they did in schools in West Virginia. I felt that something was wrong and I was going to ask my Physical Education teacher that day. Coach Carver was on the name plaque on the door. I knocked and waited.

"Yes, sir, young man, what brings you here?" The tall, dark-haired man said in a gruff voice.

"My name is Johnny Stump and I transferred from school in Welch, West Virginia, this summer. I want to play football, but I haven't heard any announcement for those interested in playing. Did I miss the announcement or something?" I asked the coach.

"Well, yes, in a way. You were not here when practice started earlier this month before school even started. Come on with me; I'll take you out to meet the football coach and see if we can't get you fixed up with some gear for practice."

As we walked, the coach asked me several questions about my athletic interest. I was honest and told him I liked almost all sports but only played organized football and baseball in elementary school.

"You look pretty fit and well developed. What grade are you in?" Coach asked, as we walked out to the field.

"I'm in the seventh grade and weigh about 155, I think."

"Coach Walker, we need to talk." The other PE coach, called Coach Scotto, yelled to someone when we got about halfway to the group of what I thought were PE students. As the two coaches walked toward each other, I followed the PE coach. When they got near each other, the PE coach introduced me to Coach Walker, the head football coach.

"Hi, Johnny. Coach tells me you are interested in going out for football; is that correct?"

"Yes, sir, I sure would like to."

"Have you played football before?"

"Yes, sir, last year I was on the varsity team at Welch High School in West Virginia."

"Johnny, you're telling me you played varsity as a sixth grader?"

"Yes, sir. They said I was only the second boy in over ten years that played varsity in the sixth grade at Welch High School," I told the coaches.

"Well, let's see if we can't get you started down here in Florida. You know it takes more fuel to play ball down here because of the heat and humidity." He looked at the PE coach in disbelief.

He blew his whistle and motioned for everyone to come over. When the twenty-five or thirty boys got to the coach, I noticed they were all in shoulder pads, helmets, and shorts. I didn't say a word but listened to the coach.

"I want you guys to meet a boy straight from the coal fields of West-By-God-Virginia. He tells me he played varsity football last year. What position was that Stump?"

"Backfield. Coach Walters called me a scat back if that's anything special," I told him.

"I'll believe what you say if you demonstrate to me you can run with my fastest four guys to those goal posts up there. Let me have the fastest seventh and eighth graders up here with us." And Coach pointed to the goal post about seventy yards away.

"Coach, I don't have any football shoes on and they are at a disadvantage in shoulder pads," I said to the coach.

"I don't care—can you run and can they catch you is the question? If they catch you they will tackle you like they would any opposing halfback," Coach said, with a sly grin.

"Okay, Coach." I kicked off my street shoes and said, "Okay, throw me a ball and pick the men."

Coach's eyes brightened and he smiled. "Now ... it's game on."

"Give him a ball, Marty," Coach said to the manager. "Stump, you get three steps then I'll blow the whistle."

"Jake, Irvin, Stewart and Billy, go get him." We all took off toward the goal line. After about twenty yards, I looked back and they were ten yards behind me. I slowed and let them get within a step or two; I then sprinted away again, this time making a sudden cut to the right. As they followed, hot on my heels, I started playing games as I ran toward the goal. I decided to do a circle to the left almost to the sideline and then back in the opposite direction for ten yards, then back up the field almost to the goal post. When I was within about ten yards of the goal post and they were still five yards behind, I turned and sprinted back to the coach with all I had, leaving them twenty yards behind coming back.

"Damn, I believe we have a real runner here," Coach Walker

said to Coach Scotto.

I heard someone say, "Look at his feet." When I looked down at my feet they were bloody and full of little ball like spikes.

"Damn, Stump, didn't you feel those sand burrs?" Coach Scotto said.

"I felt something but I wasn't about to stop. What are those things? We never had those in West Virginia. We ran barefoot all summer and all we had were sharp, hard rocks sticking up out of the ground in different places."

"Well, go in the locker room and let Marty pull those sand burrs out of your feet and put something on them, so you can dress out tomorrow. I'm pleased to welcome you to Southwest Junior High football."

"Okay, Coach, see you tomorrow. But I still have no shoes to run in. They furnished the spikes in West Virginia. My father just got a new job and we just moved here and have very little extra money," I told him.

"Here, Marty, take this money," Coach handed Marty a ten-dollar bill. "Take Stump to buy a pair of sneakers until his spikes can be fitted."

"Sure thing," Marty said.

That was my first day at football for Southwest. I went on that year to play first team halfback and second team quarterback. I could throw the ball accurately for 25-30 yards and I scored fourteen touchdowns the first year and sixteen touchdowns the second year. Melbourne High School called me up to play on their varsity squad when I left the eighth grade.

I really liked Southwest Junior High. I found it was a little difficult in the beginning trying to fit in, because I didn't know which group to hang with. All I knew was I wanted to be an athlete, but even that was hard. The older guys were hard on me because I came from the North and was going to play first string

… before I even practiced two weeks.

Later that week, several of the guys I was hanging with in my class mentioned that some of the older guys were gunning for me. I had become Coach's pet because I was faster than the older boys. I wasn't happy about the way they felt, but wasn't going to worry about it either.

One morning as I got off the bus, several of the older guys yelled for me to come over where they were, they had something to show me. The school was new and there was no hiding anything. You could see everything because of the openness of the architecture of the one-story brick and concrete building. Most of the landscaping was not even finished. I walked over to where a small group was gathered.

"Hey, Stump, we hear you're real fast. Want to see how fast you are compared to Julio here." The boy talking pointed to a tall kid standing with him.

"I'm not claiming to be the fastest person around but last week on the football field I was asked to demonstrate my running … is that what this is all about?" I said.

"We hear you were bragging how fast you are and how slow we are down here in Florida."

"I never said such a thing. I wouldn't do that. I want to help the football team not hurt anyone's reputation," I tried to explain.

"Hell, we ain't playing with the football team or any other team. We are the bosses around here and were told you didn't want to play by the rules."

"I'm sorry, I didn't see the rules. No one gave me a copy when we moved here. Where I come from, each person stood for what they believed, and I believe I can help the football team. That's all that I was trying to show."

"Let's see what you've got, hillbilly," someone said from the back of the group that had gotten larger. Someone pushed the taller boy out of the crowd and toward me. He stepped in front of me. He was a few inches taller, but we were about the same stature. He just stared at me and I returned the favor. I wasn't about to be bullied for being fast and playing football.

"I'm about as fast as they come around here. I'll bet I can whip you in a short- or long-distance race. The loser has to kiss the ugliest girl in school today," the tall boy said, as he stared at me.

"Where do you want to run for the short distance?" I said, because time was getting close for the bell to ring.

"Race to the next building and back," someone said, "it's about fifty yards." "Yes, yes," several agreed. I looked, and the distance looked about forty or fifty yards and would only take a few minutes. "Let's do it," I said.

The mouthy boy that was the first to yell at me lined us up side by side. He said, "You'll take off on three. One … Two … Three," he called.

We took off. The boy was fast; he was two or three steps ahead before I could get traction from the shoes I had on. He stayed in front a step or two until on the way back, as I was about to pass him, he stuck his foot out and tripped me causing me to fall and lose the race.

"What's the problem, Stump? Can't stand up?" I finally pulled myself together from the fall and went back and got my books and was about to go to the toilet and wipe off the blood from the scrapes of hitting the ground.

"Don't bother washing off the blood; there will be a lot more before I'm finished with you," the runner told me.

I just put my books back down on the ground and looked the boy square in the eyes. The strike happened before he knew it. I hit him as hard as I could in the face, hoping to bloody his nose. Right on target, my second punch was for his jaw, which staggered him, and my third punch was to his other jaw that landed him on his back—he didn't get up.

Again, I went back to my books, picked them up and started toward the building as the bell rang. *What a wonderful way to begin the day*, I thought, as I trudged toward the entrance. My hair and clothes were a mess from the race, my hand was bleeding, either from me hitting the boy or him bleeding on me but, either way, I needed to clean up.

I went in homeroom, set my books down, went up to the teacher and told him I had fallen and scraped my hand and would like to go to the lavatory to clean up. The teacher excused me for five minutes.

That afternoon there was a talk at practice. The incident had gotten all over the school that I had gotten into a fight with a townie called Riccardo, who was someone not on the athletic teams and usually associated with the townies of Melbourne. I didn't know there were different sections of the town that were ethnic in origin. Back in West Virginia everyone lived together, but I guessed down here you had to choose an allegiance. Well I wasn't going to. I liked dealing with people on an individual basis.

The next morning as I was getting off the bus, a gang had gathered to see if there was going to be more trouble between the factions that had started yesterday.

"Stump, you want more?" The mouthy guy said. I didn't say a word and just kept going toward the school.

"Hey, you chicken-hillbilly, I'm talking to you."

I stopped and turned around and looked at the guy. "If you want a piece of me, all you guys line up today after 3:30 at the gym and we'll fight one by one."

"I'll be there, hillbilly," the kid said.

"See you then." I wasn't for sure what I was going to do, but decided to face them all at once rather than deal with someone wanting to fight or jump me when I least expected it. I wanted to try to get along with everyone, especially the ones who played football or some other sport. I was new here and didn't know anyone unless they were in my class.

That day, one of my classmates said, "Hi, my name is Ricky Lloyd, and I'm from Michigan. We moved here last year, and I know exactly what you are dealing with right now. I want to help you just to make everything fair for all. I'm the offensive end on the football team. I didn't know if you recognized me without my uniform on."

"Oh, now that you say that, I can put two and two together and see you on the field now. You made that great catch in practice when Roger threw the ball all the way down to the goal yesterday. Yes, that was a good catch for sure. Did you play before coming here to Florida?"

"Yes, I played in Detroit until my dad got laid off at the car company up there and joined a company here in Melbourne. Up there we started playing tackle in the sixth grade."

"Yes, we did too," I echoed.

Johnny at Melbourne Beach

That afternoon I went to coach Scotto at the gym and told him the whole story and my plan to fight with each one. He didn't agree with my plan and he felt he could not condone the violent behavior it would bring out. He had another plan.

When the 3:30 bell rang, and all the students started to pour into the gym for the after-school recreation activities, Coach wouldn't let anyone go into the locker rooms until most were in the gym.

"I want to make an announcement. There has been some disagreement about athletic ability, and someone challenged Johnny to a fight this afternoon. I can't let you fight bare-knuckled, but I can put you in boxing gloves and let you all fight all you want."

"Where is the first challenger?" Coach asked, as he laced up a pair of boxing gloves on me.

"Right here, Coach. I'm the one that made the challenge this morning to him in front of the school as he was getting off the bus."

"Why are you challenging him? What's the reason? He's not a fighter, just a football player," Coach asked.

"I saw him hit Riccardo yesterday and knock him down for no reason. Riccardo is my cousin and I'm picking up where he left off."

"Is that true, Johnny?" Coach looked at me.

"No, not exactly. I did knock him down but with good reason. I want to say something, Coach. I'm new here and have nothing against any of you, but if fighting is what you want, I will accept the challenge. However, we have to agree, if we win or lose, we will let the decision be final. No carrying a grudge and have trouble from then on about everything. I'm here to go to school and play sports."

"It's agreed," said Hernando, who was an eighth grader.

Coach called us to the middle of the floor. Mr. King came in and Coach called him over to help be a referee for the match. "They will fight three two-minute rounds. Mr. King will give the points of each round. Do you each understand?"

"Yes," we both said out loud.

As soon as Coach blew his whistle, I hit Hernando right in the face with my left hand. It didn't let the blood fly like it would have with just our bare fists. Hernando didn't back up but one

147

step, and then he came at me with a big haymaker swing with his right hand. The punch just missed my nose by inches and I struck him in the mouth and a little trickle of blood started coming from his upper lip. I ducked another swing for my head and it hit my right shoulder.

I thought I better work on his split lip. I let go with a left to the left side of the face and then a right hook that struck him in the mouth, again splitting the lip even more. Now the blood was dripping down his chin and he was upset. He had been wounded. He started punching wildly with both hands and that's when I knew he was finished.

My old boxing coach in South Carolina had taught me if you just deliver three successive punches to the face you will beat most opponents. If they stand in there, you have a fight on your hands. Well, Hernando lost his composure and was now swinging wildly. When I got a good look at him, one of us had wiped the gloves with blood across his eyes and this caused him to squint and blink several times. It was then that I stepped in and punched hard as I could to the nose and face. It landed hard and I felt the resistance of his face against my right glove and then the left. Hernando was going down, he was on his knees when Mr. King and Coach stopped the fight.

"It looks to me like we need to stop this match here," as Hernando was helped to his feet by Coach and Mr. King.

"We need to call this a draw since we hadn't even finished the first round," Coach said.

"Mr. King, let's take them into the locker room and clean them up so we can now go out and play some ball."

"Sounds good to me," Mr. King said.

That fight was the end of trouble for me at school; as a matter of fact Hernando and I became good friends. I even talked Hernando, and he talked Riccardo, into joining the football team.

Chapter 23

What you allow is what will continue.
Author unknown

A Southern Moon

That year was my first exposure to Florida. I was still astonished at the beauty, the sight of the flowers and fauna, the feel of the sea breeze breathing in the salt air in the evening. My bedroom window faced the Indian River, and I could feel the breeze and smell the salty air at night. I still wondered how Dad knew this place existed? He had never been here, but it was a perfect spot if romance and tropical island breezes were on your mind, and they seemed to be on my mind more each day.

I was now a full-fledged teenager and Mom and Dad gave me permission to attend a local community dance one Saturday night there in the town of Palm Bay, sponsored by the Lions Civic Club.

Palm Bay was a small community a few miles south of Melbourne. There was a town center with a Civic Center, a few businesses including an auto body shop, grocery store, hardware, beauty shop, barbershop, police and fire station, a tavern and a restaurant.

At the Jungle Park shuffleboard court (I found shuffleboard was very popular in Florida, especially with the retired people), I heard several teenagers my age talking about the dance that Saturday night. I was never shy and I asked if anyone could attend. Several of the younger girls immediately said, "Yes, if you are a teenager you're eligible. Please do! We'll see you there … we're going."

The dance was from seven p.m. until eleven p.m., and was for the teenagers of Palm Bay only. I was excited, really hadn't attended a community dance before, and didn't know what to expect.

That evening around 6:45 I told my mom I was ready to go. My mother looked at me and asked the usual questions, "Did you shower, brush your teeth? Are those clean jeans? Was a white shirt your choice of clothes? And comb that hair," she said, before I could go out the door.

After football season was over, I was going to let my hair grow, but couldn't decide whom to model myself after—maybe Elvis? I put my trusty black flexible nylon comb in the back pocket of my jeans, flipped up the collar of the white dress shirt, with the top two buttons unbuttoned, and I was ready to go. This became the young male fashion for several years during my teenage days.

Although big for my age, I knew I was still only thirteen. Dad told me to be home around midnight since the dance was over at eleven p.m., "That gives you an hour to socialize and the fifteen-minute walk home." I agreed, but reminded Mom and Dad it was more than a fifteen-minute walk from the teen club from home there on the river at night.

It was evening, and the majestic golden sun was setting, casting a reddish-orange hue to the entire western sky during my walk. I was amazed at the beauty of even the undeveloped land; the bananas, palms, and poinsettias grew wild down here in Florida.

As I walked along the unpaved, sandy, gravel road, not a car passed. It was hard to believe only a year ago I was concerned my father would leave us to look for work down here without us. Now we were living here in this gorgeous location, Florida, a place I had only heard grown-ups associate with movies and vacations.

In a few minutes I was off the short back road and walking straight to the teen club where the dance was to be held. By the time I reached the building, there were already around twenty teens there. I saw no one I recognized and walked toward the double green front doors. I wondered where some of these guys came from. They sure didn't look like my teenaged friends, but I couldn't forget teen meant all the way to nineteen.

Inside the door I paid two dollars, got stamped with red ink across the backside of my hand and had to show my Southwest School ID. I was proud of the ID photo because I thought I looked like Elvis. My hair looked darker in the picture. I went in, and very shortly found several of my school buddies. Billy, Jackie, Rose Marie, and Sammy were all standing together talking when I walked up.

"Hi, everyone. What a great place to have a party," I said.

"Hello, Johnny," they all said at almost the same time. There were no couples in the group; we were just all school friends at that stage. Only Sammy was in the same grade as me, the others were a grade ahead. I couldn't believe I was here with other teens at a community teen center, attending a real dance.

I remembered I could dance from my friendships in West Virginia. My mind jumped back to the days with the Tilley family at the little Juke Joint. Those days were fortunate for me because I could now dance a lot better than most of the guys my age.

We had only been standing there talking for ten or fifteen minutes when a tall, dark-haired, very striking girl came over and introduced herself as Frances Eastwood. She was taller than any of my friends and looked to be at least sixteen. She had on tight jeans and a blue striped top with a black leather jacket. She was built well, and because her breasts seemed to be at my eye level, they were hard to take my eyes off.

"You guys, keep your eyes off my chest, I just want to dance." I smiled and said, "Let's do it, sister." I grabbed her hand and pulled her to the middle of the dance floor. When we were in the middle of the dance floor we started rocking to *La Bamba*. In just a minute, I had the rhythm of the music and was rockin' and rollin' with Frances all over the dance floor.

After about four songs I saw a football buddy and broke off the dance. I left the floor before a slow dance came up. Frances just looked at me, and then drifted back to her friends. I stayed and talked to my teammates. There was a tug on my sleeve; turning around, I saw Rose Marie, a beautiful Latina girl in the eighth grade who had been talking with Sammy and the others when I first got to the teen center.

She said, "Come on, Johnny, slow dance with me. The others don't want to dance, and I really like this song," she said.

"Sure thing," I said, as she pulled me to the middle of the floor.

She felt so good in my arms dancing. She was hardly there, so light and yet so present. Rose Marie's hair was jet-black, her eyes big, almond-shaped and brown. She was several inches shorter and more attractive than Frances, the girl I had been dancing with earlier. Rose Marie just seemed to melt into my dance embrace. She put her head on my shoulder and we just glided around the floor like being on the ice rinks in West Virginia. After three or four more songs, Rose Marie pulled me off to the side and asked me to walk her outside, she wanted to get some fresh air and show me something.

"Sure, I can go for that, it's getting hot in here anyway. What is it that you want me to see? Don't tell me you have a Corvette or something."

"No, I don't even have a car, but don't worry, you'll like it just as much." We walked out the door and down the front path toward the ocean that we could hear after getting away from the music.

"The palm trees block the scenery back at the dance," she said, as we turned the corner. Then I saw what she was talking about. It was the biggest, most beautiful moonrise I had ever seen. The pale yellow-orange moon was almost full, but captured the evening regardless of the stage.

"I would like to sit for a few minutes and just look at this beautiful moon. I know just where we can go; a few yards this way there's a park bench near a beautiful palm tree with a flowering hibiscus under it. Come let me show you."

I just could not believe I was experiencing this. I was going to wake up soon I was sure. We sat on the bench looking at the moon for a few minutes, when she started to say something. I reached over and put my finger to her lips and said, "Words will only ruin the moment, and a kiss will seal the deal." A phrase I learned from Vernon in South Carolina. We leaned together and kissed for what seemed like several minutes before we ever pulled apart.

For the next hour we just sat there and looked at the moon, listened to the faint wave sounds on the shore of the Indian River, kissed, kissed, and caressed.

"It is getting late, we better get back," Rose Marie said. "My mom is picking me up at 11:30 and I have to find my little sister in the dance."

As we strolled back hand-in-hand, I still couldn't believe what the night had brought; it just kept getting better. I still thought I may be dreaming and would soon wake up. When we got to the teen center and were about to enter the front door, a big, dark-haired, ruggedly nice-looking older guy in a black leather jacket and white T-shirt stepped in front of me. "Hey man, can I talk with you a minute?"

I told Rose Marie to go and find her sister and I would find her later. I turned to the guy, wondering what he wanted.

"You know the girl Frances you were dancing with earlier is my sister?"

"No, I didn't know. I just met Frances tonight. She's a great dancer and I really like dancing with her. Is there a problem?"

"The only problem is she really thinks you are cute and would like to see you again but wasn't sure how to tell you. She's only sixteen but looks twenty."

"I see," I said. "That's not a problem except I'm only thirteen and a lot shorter than she is. I didn't think she would want to be seen with a runt like me."

"Not a problem, Daddy-O," he said and began to walk away.

"Hey, what's your name?"

"Louis or Louie; I am the leader," he yelled back.

"Leader of what?" I yelled, as I left to go try to find Rose Marie before starting the walk home. After the wonderful night on the beach under the beautiful moon with Rose Marie, I wanted to be sure she felt the same way.

Chapter 24

Being Happy Never Goes Out of Style.
Lilly Pulitzer

Naughty Sisters

I called Rose Marie that week and asked her to go to the movies. She could not go unless she took her little sister with her, she told me.

"Not a problem," I said, as we planned our next rendezvous.

We met at the movie on Saturday afternoon, in downtown Melbourne where I had hitchhiked that morning to be sure I was there for our afternoon movie date. I couldn't believe my eyes. The little sister, Vivian, was the cutest little thing and looked just like her sister, but there was something even more appealing. That day in the movies I found Vivian's hand on my leg several times during the movie when I was trying to cuddle with Rose Marie.

This is going to be interesting, I thought. *Do I choose or play both?* I had never been in this predicament before. Vivian and I were in the same class at school but I never noticed her because we only had one class together.

It was not as I suspected. One afternoon at a matinee movie two weeks later, Rose Marie went to the concession stand to get everyone popcorn. I was left to secure the seats. Just as soon as Rose Marie left, Vivian moved into her seat and laid a very passionate kiss on me. I was taken by surprise and started to push her away. Then she said, "Wouldn't you like to experience two naughty sisters at the same time?"

I wasn't sure what to do. I knew Rose Marie would return soon and I didn't want her to think I was after her little sister while she was gone. It seemed like only a minute until I felt Vivian's hand back on my leg. *Seems like she has done this before*, I thought. I was even more puzzled as to what to do.

"Wait, wait for me. I don't want to miss any of the fun," Rose Marie said, as she slid into the seat on the other side of me.

We three were sitting in the last row, in the right back corner of the dark movie. Lights were very dim, almost yellow in the old theater. You could see cobwebs around the lights. There were about twenty or twenty-five people in the afternoon matinee about ten rows to the front and no one was paying attention to us. *This was going to be a great afternoon,* I thought!

That afternoon at the movies I became great friends with Vivian, as well as, Rose Marie. Later, I found she and her sister were well-known in school for their friendly ways with the boys. However, it was also known that they only played and didn't go any further. I remained friends with the girls, but really didn't get very romantic with either.

Vivian and Rose Marie were both very good in math and would take me to the library and help me with math if I got behind or didn't understand certain problems. This is where I first learned algebra. Not many of the seventh or eighth graders knew algebra very well. But Vivian and Rose Marie were the best in both grades and were always being asked for help.

"Johnny, it would be nice if you came over to our house to study. You could meet my father. He's a math professor at Melbourne High and for the local college."

"That sounds good. When would you want to do it?" I answered.

156

"How's Friday night after the football game?"

"Yea, like we are going to get a lot of studying done on Friday night after the game. No, I don't think so. I know you two, you'll want to play around and I'll be without my math tutors."

"Okay, when could you do it if we promise to restrain ourselves … cough, cough?"

"How's Wednesday afternoon?" I asked.

"It's a deal. You can ride home with us after school. Then your father can pick you up at our house that evening on his way from work at the Cape."

We did as planned, and I rode home from school with Mrs. Pearson. She was very nice and polite, also very pretty like her daughters. You could see where the beauty came from in that family. I didn't realize how short she was until we got to the house. After parking the car, she followed us into the house. Both daughters were taller by several inches. They looked like three sisters instead of a mother and two daughters.

Mrs. Pearson said, "Johnny, why don't you stay for dinner and I'll make a special homemade *sofrito* for you and the girls."

"What is that? I've never had that before."

"It a special meal I learned from my mother in Puerto Rico. Every American that I have made it for seems to really like it. I'm from Puerto Rico, but my girls were born here in Florida. I was born in our capitol city of San Juan. My family moved here to the States so I could go to work teaching English and Spanish after I graduated from the University in Puerto Rico."

"What is *sofrito*?" I asked.

"First, you must understand Puerto Rican food came from a mix of Spanish conquistador, African slave, and native Taíno foods. And while it's quite similar to other Hispanic cuisines, Puerto Rican food still has unique flavors, aromas and blends.

"*Sofrito* is a blend of vegetables and Latin herbs used in

157

seasoning. It's used in a lot of things—beans, stews, rice, and other dishes ... truthfully, no Puerto Rican dish is complete without the famous *sofrito*. A concoction of fresh roasted garlic, onions, sweet aji, onions, recao, cilantro, red bell pepper and spices. *Sofrito* is used as the base of any, or I should say every, Puerto Rican dish."

With that statement she knew she was getting too technical for me in the cooking end of things. So she changed the subject and asked me what I liked best about school?

Right away, I said, "Geography is my favorite subject, but football is my favorite pastime."

"You mean soccer?"

"No, ma'm, I mean American football. My father was a baseball player for the minor leagues and he just won't accept football as the sport for me. We have discussions that hinge on arguments all the time about the need to spend more time playing baseball."

About that time the girls came back into the kitchen where I was sitting at the counter talking to Mrs. Pearson. I told them I was ready for my math lesson. They told their mom we were going upstairs to study until dinnertime. Mrs. Pearson was in favor of the study session and said "See you later at 5 or 5:30. When Mr. Pearson comes home, we will eat."

The girls and I went upstairs to a study room that looked almost like a miniature library, with three of the four walls lined with books from ceiling to floor. I was very impressed.

"Wow, I've never seen a library in someone's home before. It must be really nice to have so many books at your disposal to read and study when you want."

"Yes, with both our parents being teachers I guess they have accumulated a lot of books over the years," Rose Marie said.

There were two desks in the room on opposite sides of the room, and a large conference table in the middle of the room.

The room was a light tan color and the windows were not covered with curtains or blinds. There were large fluorescent lights in the ceiling and a lamp on each desk.

"This is the type of room I would like to have when I get a home. You can study and read as much and as long as you want," I stated empathically.

We all sat at the conference table and each girl gave me math problems to solve.

"Johnny, each time you solve a problem I have given you, I get a kiss. Each time you solve a problem Vivian gives you, she gets a kiss. If we have to help you with the problem, you have to remove a piece of clothing."

"Hell, I'll be naked in no time," was my response to their laughter.

Both girls just giggled as they started the math lesson. *Kisses for math*, I thought, *does it get any better than this?* We studied until 5:30 when Mr. Pearson called upstairs for everyone to come down. By that time my lips were sore and I needed a break from those naughty little sisters.

Chapter 25

The pain you feel today,
will be the strength you feel tomorrow.
Author unknown

Hunting with Little Richard

Later that year, several of my friends and I planned a hunting trip in the undeveloped land about four miles southwest of Palm Bay. This land was rough, only used for cattle grazing, the other boys thought, and belonged to the state.

Harry Gardener, a school friend who was a year older, told me his dad worked for the state surveying for power lines in the area. Harry said, "My father comes home after work and talks about the good hunting spots and where we could hunt for small game."

Harry was a big guy, a good four inches taller than I. His family lived in a big white house about a half-mile from me to the west on what was called Palm Drive. Harry and I had fished together several times in the Indian River from the pier near our house.

Accompanying Harry and me that Saturday was little Richard. Richard and his family had just moved from Georgia. His father and mother worked for the school system there in St Lucie County. Richard and his older sister, Ellen, were always at the teen center and always dancing. Richard was small and short, but good looking, with dark, long, wavy hair. He combed it like Elvis, with a ducktail in the back. He always wore blue jeans and a white or blue short-sleeve shirt with the sleeves rolled up and the collar flipped up. Richard could really dance; thus the name "Little Richard" was bestowed on him because of the very popular rock-n-roll singer who had great dance moves.

He was a year or two older than I was, but smaller in size. I would watch Richard at the teen center awe the girls with his dance moves. It made me a little jealous when the girls would swoon over his beautiful, dark locks of hair falling into his eyes as he danced all over the floor. He looked just like Elvis or Ricky Nelson, only a smaller version.

We three were fishing one day down on the long wooden pier that flowed just a short distance from our house. I was sure it was a public pier because it was open all night. I had even gone there at three in the morning with my father to catch fish that were running at that time.

I had first met both Harry and Richard there at the pier. We fished several days without saying anything to each other, but one day Harry caught a hook in his sleeve trying to cast and I went over to see if I could help him get untangled. Richard saw us messing with the hook and line and came over.

We three began to talk and found we all went to Southwest Junior High together. Harry was in the ninth, Richard was in the eighth and I was in the seventh grade. That's why we really didn't know each other until summer.

That day we decided we would go rabbit and squirrel hunting on the following Saturday morning. We would all ride our bicycles to Harry's house and leave from there, since Harry lived the closest to the hunting spot.

I had a problem. All my father's guns had been lost in the flood in West Virginia. I was not comfortable admitting this to my friends ... that I didn't have a gun of my own.

Harry was going to take a .410 shotgun. Richard was going

161

to take his .22 with long-rifle ammo, which he said he used all the time for small game. I should have told them right then I had no gun, but I was too proud to admit my parents were too poor to afford to buy me one.

That evening I told Dad the plan I was thinking of and immediately Dad said, "What, are you going to be the bird boy? You have no gun." I wasn't sure what a bird boy was and asked Dad.

"A bird boy goes along on a hunt with a group of hunters, and when the hunter shoots the game bird, the bird boy goes with a dog to fetch it. He brings it back to the hunters to show them and then waits until the next kill. After he gets a few, he takes them to the cooler for the hunter."

That didn't sound too good to me. "No, I'd rather not be a bird boy on this hunt. What can I do?"

"Well, I saw a used gun store coming through Melbourne last week. Let's go take a look up there and see if we can find an old .22 or .410 that will fit you. You are nearly fourteen now; I got my first gun at thirteen. I think you're ready and you know that safety is the primary issue with guns, small or large," Dad said.

That gesture on Dad's part made me very happy and I told my mom and dad that I'd really work hard and pay them back for the gun. They both smiled and didn't say anything more about my request.

Friday night was usually family shopping night. My parents had made plans to go to Melbourne to do their grocery shopping. While Mom and Granny were doing the grocery shopping, Dad would take me and Doug to see if he could find what else was needed at our house.

By this time, I was fully aware I had a little brother, but didn't have much in common with him yet. We were more than five years apart in age and Mom was overly protective of Doug.

But Douglas was in the second grade now and was beginning to be someone I could talk with about guy things such as going hunting and fishing. On the way to the second-hand shop, I told Doug the hunting plans with Harry and Little Richard for Saturday.

In the shop there were all kinds of things—old bikes, furniture, pictures, paintings, and finally we came to a counter where a man by the name of "Ivan the Great" showed us guns. Ivan was huge—a head taller than dad and dad was six feet tall. Ivan looked to be a hundred or more pounds heavier than dad, with a long beard and thick, dark-red hair and tattoos up and down his big muscular arms. He looked to me like a real-life pirate.

Ivan said, "There are all types, pistols, rifles, shotguns, old ones, new ones, even hunting knives to look at."

Dad said, "Let's take a look at a few .22 rifles and a .410, first."

Ivan went to get three guns from the gun rack at the back of the counter. He laid them down and started telling the story of the guns. Then he went back and got two .410 shotguns from a separate rack. Dad and I talked and discussed what each was good for and what would be needed to take care of the gun. Finally, I chose the second Remington .410. It was five years old and owned by a local man who liked to bird hunt but gave that up when his eyes went bad.

The cost of the gun was $90. Dad haggled with Ivan, telling him it was my first gun and I was going to have to work and pay for it with my summer job. Finally, Ivan got tired and gave it to us for $75 if we would bring Doug back in a few years when it was time for him to have a gun. We all left the pawnshop happy that day.

We returned to pick up Mom, Granny, and the groceries before going home. When we got home that evening, dad laid down the law about guns and gun safety. He said, "The gun is not a toy; it's very dangerous and it has to be taken care of like anything of value." I was to keep it up on the wall where my fishing rod was so everyone knew when and where it was located. I was to keep it unloaded until I was in the field ready to hunt. He said this very sternly. He showed me how to load and unload the gun and made me do it ten times without any hesitation.

Dad then told me about hunting rules and courtesy in carrying and handling a gun. He explained why you should wear certain clothes, only hunting clothes, thick socks, boots, and heavy jeans or hunting pants and an orange or red hat or cap. Most of this I already had learned from either the Boy Scout meetings or playing with my cousin Smitty and the gang in the mountains. By the time we had finished, I was almost afraid to take the gun out for fear of doing something wrong without knowing.

A Long Way Back

Saturday morning rolled around and I was on my bike at 5:30 a.m., with my new .410 strapped to the frame like my dad had shown. I peddled toward Harry's on the gravel back road before the sun was up. It was hard to see, and I hit several chuckholes, usually avoidable during the day. Finally, there was the fork in the road where I was to meet Little Richard and I sat there on my bike in the dark, waiting.

The early morning was humid and warm. There were little beads of sweat across my forehead already. I could hear the noise of the night creatures very plainly sitting there on the bike. Looking around, I could see the many eyes watching me, or was I imagining the swamp-like jungle closing in as I sat still, waiting? How many snakes, gators and bobcats were there that I didn't see on this back road in the daylight? I could certainly hear the bullfrogs along the drainage canals, even if I couldn't see them.

After about ten or fifteen minutes, I listened closely and heard sounds of someone coming down the road. It sounded like a bicycle and in just a few minutes there was Richard's profile in view.

"Damn, it's dark on this road. I didn't think about it being dark this early when I left. My mother almost made me wait until it got a little lighter, but I wouldn't listen and told her we had to get an early start. I told her I would be late and ruin the entire hunting trip for everyone," Richard said, as we took off toward Harry's house.

"No shit, it's dark as pitch. Even though I've been to Harry's five or six times, it's a lot different in the dark," I told Richard.

Richard cried out, "Ouch, I hit a big hole and just about lost it when my seat hit my crotch. We are within arms-length of each other and still can't see shit … that's dark!"

I laughed. It was even harder as we continued to peddle to Harry's, about another mile in the dark.

Finally, I said in a half-whisper, "I think I see his front porch light."

"Harry said to just tap on the door and he would be ready when we got there." Richard went to the door and knocked three times, but no answer. He came back and asked, "What should we do?"

"I suggest trying to open the front door and see if there is a light downstairs in his room." Richard went back and when he turned the knob the door opened. Yes, there was Harry asleep by the front door. Richard shook him and told him, "Let's go or we'll be late getting in the woods." Harry was dragging, but he moved out of the door quietly with Richard, moving toward me waiting at the bikes.

Outside, we all got our heads together and decided to follow

Harry after he got his bike from the garage. Harry was waking up now and seemed almost normal. Because he knew he had cost us valuable time falling asleep, he tried to rush.

It was almost funny to see Harry trying to peddle fast; because he was so big and fat, it made the bicycle seat seem small. He could hardly shift from one side to the other when standing trying to peddle faster; his pants hung low and would catch on the cross bar each time his big body shifted. His pants hung, showing the "crack." But he was determined to make up the time and kept pushing his immense body to move faster and faster.

Richard was behind Harry on his bike and had no trouble keeping up. All of a sudden, Richard raised his head and said, "Damn, Harry, did you fart? There is an awful scent coming from up there."

"I'm not sure," Harry said, "I'm pumping so hard one might have slipped out."

"Aw hell, I think you shit yourself. Can you smell it back where you are, Johnny?"

"There's some god-awful smell around here if you didn't," I told both of them.

"You both are smelling swamp gas. It lays close to the low places until the sun comes up in the swamps and low areas where water stands," was Harry's explanation of the methane smell.

"We sure don't have that smell in Georgia," said Richard.

"We never had it in West Virginia either. I've caught it several times since moving down here but it sure is distinctive," I said.

Harry was laughing so hard now he just about fell off his bicycle. "You guys stop with the complaining; we're coming to our first stop," he said.

We all pulled our bicycles up to the open sage and palmetto field where the road ended, and we hid our bikes. The field seemed like it went on forever in the breaking dawn light. It was just before sunrise, but there was a faint dark-purple light in the eastern sky, enough to make out where to step as we carefully crossed the field. If we stepped in a hole, or one of the hundreds of swamp bogs, we could spend an hour getting out of the mud and swamp water. It could be like quick sand if you got stuck in a big one, Harry told us as we depended on his directions.

Harry was still leading the way cautiously, moving first left several yards, then right. Harry may have been big, but he knew the swamp and the way around these swampy woods. Harry had been with his father bull-frogging, small game hunting, and he even told us about an alligator hunt where they killed more rattlesnakes than anything else.

It was now getting light and we could see the fence line ahead, thick with palmettos and sage hummocks we had to cross to get to the hunting territory Harry's father recommended to us. Harry stopped abruptly, stooped down, and pointed; up ahead were three deer having their morning feed.

Harry said, "You know we don't have a hunting license, so if we see a State Game Warden, haul ass and make them try to catch us. Usually they are old, in their thirties and forties, and can't run or don't want to run in this heat and thickets."

"The deer are a little too far away to try to kill. I'm afraid we would only wound one, then we would half to spend hours tracking it down to field-clean. Let's wait and see what's on the other side of the fence," were Richard's last words about the deer.

"Ok, Harry, whatever you want to do. I just know that I'm anxious to use this .410, so lead me in the right direction for some action," was my opinion on shooting the deer.

Another ten minutes and we were at the fence line near a patch of brambles, palmettos, and sage that needed to be flattened if we were to cross it there. The fence was nasty, old, rusty, barbed wire, five feet high, with four strands instead of the regular three.

"Do you guys own a dog?" Harry asked.

"We have a Labrador Retriever, but he's back at our house. Why, what's that have to do with this damn old rusty fence we have to cross?" Richard said.

"No, I mean a real dog. Pit bull, mastiff, German shepherd—big head, powerful jaws, you know."

Richard looked at him, "What the hell for?"

"My father fights them. It's a big deal down here. Dad makes lots of money back in the swamp, but they keep them in big barbed wire pits for a week, throwing armadillos in there before they fight them, just to make them mad. But I would rather face them than to try to crawl this friggin' fence," Harry said.

"I don't think you can squeeze your big ass through these strands, Harry. I thought it was just the normal three strands we usually come across in the fields, but this is some serious fencing," Richard said.

"This is the first time I have been up this far. Usually I stay in the field we just crossed, go on down about another couple of hundred yards to some palmetto thickets. There's some good game in that area—rabbits, quail, dove and snakes. I don't know what's so interesting in this field across the fence that my dad wants us to see."

"Harry, I have an idea," said Richard. "Johnny and I will stand on this side of the fence, put our foot on the bottom strand, and pull up on the next strand. Then you might be able to squeeze through."

"Yes, you may be right. Let's try it."

"Let's set our guns down by the fence and get about six feet apart and both lift up at the same time. Hurry up, Harry, this is difficult," Richard said.

About that time, Harry took his gun, stuck it through the fence and started through himself. There was a violent shaking of the fence with Harry's weight, then an unexpected "Boom."

"What in the hell was that?" Harry said, as he was halfway through the fence.

"Oh hell, Richard's hit my gun! It went off and hit Richard. It looks like he's bleeding from the middle," Harry said. "I thought the safety was on when I put the gun through the fence. Anyway, help me get out of here so we can get him some help," yelled Harry.

I struggled trying to help Harry, while Richard was lying on the ground, moaning and groaning, "I've been hit, I've been shot, I've been shot, help me, help me." I broke into a sweat. Could I get Harry out in time and also get Richard to a doctor? I didn't even know where we were … it would have to be Harry to get us some help somewhere.

A rapid thought pierced my mind. *Richard could die if we don't get him somewhere soon.* I put Harry's hands on the fence and gave a big pull. Yelling, "Come on, Harry, move!" I grabbed the wire fence again and pulled with all my strength. With that, blood flew everywhere. I had pulled the barbed wire and hadn't noticed that I grabbed the barbed part. We could worry about my hand later. Harry was now free and bending over Richard. He opened Richard's jacket and you could see he'd been gut shot.

"Let's leave the guns here and carry Richard toward the nearest farm house. I know one about a mile across this field and toward the road," Harry said.

"Whatever you say, Harry, I'm a stranger to these parts so you lead the way and I'll carry Richard as long as I can."

I picked Richard up and put him over my right shoulder. We made our way across the open palmetto field toward the place Harry thought he remembered a farmhouse being. When we had gone about half a mile I asked, "How much further? Richard is

169

little but he's getting heavy."

"Just around this thicket of palms, I think," was Harry's reply.

"I hope so, Harry."

As we approached the thicket, Harry said. "Damn, I know there was a house here in this field and an old barn. But I don't see it anywhere now."

I squatted down with Richard across my shoulder and said, "Help me get him over to the other shoulder, I can't go much longer using this same shoulder."

Harry looked at me and said, "Damn, I don't know what to do. I thought sure that house was here at the end of this field. We've come it seems over a mile and down another mile toward the road."

"I trust you, Harry. Take a minute to go back in your mind and think about the old house and just where you saw it. Were you with your father or alone?"

Harry jumped up, "It's through the next thicket of larger palm trees. I remember the people there really liked palms and had them all over their property. Here, I'll carry him for a little bit while you rest your shoulder."

I helped Harry get Richard squared on his shoulders. When I did, Harry couldn't stand up. I got beside him and lifted Richard. Harry could walk with him once he had him up and balanced, but very slowly.

Harry was now crying because blood was all over me and it was now starting to cover Harry. We had carried Richard nearly an hour and were nowhere near the house yet. When we had gone another hundred yards or so across the field, Harry could no longer carry Richard and we had to switch again. Harry then lifted his head, looked ahead, and started yelling, "There, Johnny! There's the house, there's the house!" In another few minutes we were at the white picket fence and front gate of the farmhouse.

Harry ran to the front door and banged on it with his fist leaving blood prints across the floor of the porch and the door. "Sorry, this is no time to be polite and careful."

An older gray-haired lady came to the door with a dark green apron on, with her gray hair up in a bun like Granny wore. She asked what all the fuss was about. Harry told her the story briefly and asked her to call an ambulance; Richard was bleeding badly. She rushed back into the house and called the fire department because she wasn't sure the little clinic in Palm Bay had an ambulance.

Then she came out and asked me to lay Richard on the big blue metal glider on the front porch where they could get him. She went in the house and got two blankets and covered Richard. "To preserve his body heat," she said, "I'm not sure what it does but you always see it done at all the accidents."

I asked her if she had an outside hose that Harry and I could use to get some of the blood off our neck, face and hands before the ambulance got there. She was standing beside Richard and said, "God, he is young and so handsome, he looks a lot like one of my boys a few years ago. He looks so peaceful.

"Yes, yes, I'm sorry. The faucet is around the side of the house by the driveway. Get some of that blood off you before it dries. It's much harder if you don't," she stuttered.

We went around the side of the house and started rinsing off the blood. "Johnny, this is bad. There's a gallon of blood on us. How much does a person have in them and how much can you lose and still live?" Harry asked.

"Harry, I'm not sure of an answer to any of those questions. I only know you're right—it looks bad. Little Richard stopped talking shortly after I started to carry him across the field when we first started," I added.

About that time, sirens started blasting in town and it

171

sounded like they were coming toward the farmhouse. In less than five minutes a small red-and-gold truck that looked like a mini-version of a fire truck came screeching into the driveway.

"Where is he?" they asked us.

"He's on the porch with the lady that owns the farm. We are his friends and we carried him from the accident," Harry said.

The two men took a stretcher and ran up on the porch and spoke to the lady and then started lifting Richard onto the stretcher."

She said, "He hasn't moved or said anything since they brought him up here a few minutes ago. I put the blankets over him to help keep him warm."

"Let's go, boys. You ride with me in the front and Dave will stay in the back with … what's his name?"

"His name is Richard McDanielson," we said at about the same time, as we drove from the farmhouse with tires blazing and siren blasting.

Later that day, the Fire Chief took Harry and me to the home of the McDanielson family. He asked us to tell Mr. and Mrs. McDanielson the story of how the accident happened in detail. Our friend was dead. We couldn't believe it.

As Harry told the story, tears of remorse and guilt of our friend's death ran down his face like a waterfall. The big, gentle boy had gotten to really like Richard in the short time we were together. I looked at Harry and it made me cry also, as we told the story of how the trigger got caught on the barbed wire as we were pulling and shaking the fence trying to get Harry through. That must have caused the gun to go off by accident as we were tugging on the wire fence.

According to the coroner, Richard had died shortly after the gunshot wound because it had torn through the aorta. Richard bled out while we were carrying him. Richard's parents arranged for a viewing and service in Palm Bay, but they took his body back to Georgia for burial.

We never saw or heard anything more from the McDanielson family. They never returned from Georgia after the funeral.

Little Richard's Father's Dune Buggy and our Bicycles

Chapter 26

I never met a strong person with an easy past.
Author unknown

Friendship

That hunting accident in the summer brought Harry and I together as close friends. We fished, hunted and rode our bicycles all over the area. On a hot August night, Harry and I were fishing on the big pier on Indian River with four strangers when Harry hollered over to me, "Hey, you want a good cold Pepsi?" "Yea, that would be good, but everything's closed now," I told him.

"How about Mr. Sullivan's at the Jungle Park grocery? He sometimes stays open later when people are buying gas and groceries." Harry said, "Let's jump on our bikes and see ... we're not catching anything but trash fish tonight anyway."

By the time we got to the little grocery store it was dark and everyone, including Mr. Sullivan, was gone. The place had some big wooden benches in the front for people to sit and have refreshments. There was a single light pole with a big green shade over a bright glowing bulb with insects flying all around it. It made me think of the fireflies and my grandmother's tales about the Indian myths of the Great Smoky Mountains.

Harry said, "Damn, I guess it's a bit late for things to be open. It's about ten now. Why do you think grown-ups go to bed so early?"

"I'm not sure. I've wondered the same thing. I've lain in my bedroom at night with the radio under my pillow to muffle the sounds of the music playing from all over the country. I listened to rock-n-roll and all the big and latest sounds out there. Even Elvis is being given a run for his money with all the black singers on vinyl now," I told him.

"My father won't let me play rock when he's in the car or at the house. It's country western all the way with him. Now when I go to the teen club and at school I enjoy the rock songs of both black and white. What's the difference? It's the music," Harry added.

"Harry, why don't you dance at the teen club? You're always there with all of us."

"I'm fat, sloppy and have no rhythm like you and little Richard," with that statement he began to cry and hung his head. "I'm still sorry that happened with Little Richard!"

A few minutes later he said, "I have just followed my father's pattern, I guess. Eat, hunt and work, never cared much for girls until the last few years and by that time this fat you see won't come off. I just keep getting bigger."

"Well, Harry, I like you, so I don't see any reason why there's not a girl out there for you somewhere that will like you as much as I do and maybe a little more. You could get some lovin'. You've heard of Fats Domino, the singer in New Orleans; he has a few popular songs out now, haven't you? He's fat, and has been all his life, and they say he has women all over him." We looked at each other and smiled. "You could be the 'White Domino,'" I told him.

With that we both started laughing and decided it was getting late, so we got on our bikes and started our separate ways. As we rode off, I yelled to Harry, "I want to see you dressed nice tomorrow night at the teen club and we'll start our search for the White Domino!"

Chapter 27

A river cuts through a rock,
not because of its power
but because of its persistence.
Author unknown

A Devil in Blue Jeans

By the time I got to the teen club it was crowded. I began to search for Harry but couldn't find him anywhere. I asked several of our friends if they had seen Harry and none had. I thought Harry was probably in trouble for coming in late last night. After all, we had sat there in front of Mr. Sullivan's Jungle Park grocery for nearly two hours just talking.

After going around the club several times, I grabbed a pretty little thing and asked her to dance during a slow song. I didn't know this girl and had never seen her before. She was about my same height, but looked older. She had blue eyes, long blonde hair, and a great figure. After a minute or two, I asked her name.

"Jeanne Stiggletson," she answered.

"I've never seen you here before and as pretty as you are you'd be hard to miss. Just my misfortune, indeed."

She just rolled her big blue eyes and didn't say anything back to me until after the dance was over. "I know you from playing football at Southwest; that's where I go, but I'm in the eighth grade and have no classes near you so we haven't met before."

"Why, hello, my name is Johnny Stump and I think I'm in love with you. As a matter of fact, I know I am. Feel my heart beat faster and faster," and I took her hand and placed it on my chest.

"I don't hardly think so; that's from just dancing. You just met me, and when you meet my older brother you won't like me so much ... or you better not act like you're attracted to me. My dad will only let me come to the dances here if Joseph brings me, and he is certainly over-protective."

"Well then, we better keep dancing." We started grooving to the Big Bopper tune of *Chantilly Lace*. I couldn't keep my eyes off her.

After the Big Bopper tune there was *Only the Lonely* by Roy Orbison and I hugged her close and put her head on my shoulder. Just as she started to close her eyes and get into a mellow mood, she heard a familiar voice say, "What the hell are you doing? You know Dad said only fast songs and not to cuddle up with boys."

"Okay, after this one," Jeanne said, and she put her head back on my shoulder.

"Okay, Jennie, if there's anymore of this I'm going to tell Dad everything. I'm not taking the blame for everything."

As I looked at her brother, Joseph shook his fist at me and shook his head in the "no" motion several times. I smiled at him and went right back to wishing the song would never end.

Joseph came up to me after the dance was over, took me to the side and said, "If you want to live, then you want to leave my sister alone. My father and I know what punks like you are looking for in a girl as nice as Jeanne and I'm her brother and here to see you don't slow dance with her again."

He stood almost a head taller than me and was in Melbourne High School, I figured, because he was with all the other high school guys there at the dance. He was also blonde, like his sister, with a ruddy red complexion and a freckled face. I wasn't at all scared or worried about his threat. I knew I was going to see Jeanne again … real soon, and I told her as much.

"I want to see you again. I have a friend by the name of Harry. How about you and a girlfriend meet us at the movies in Melbourne Saturday at the matinee?"

"Okay, I'll try. My father's very strict, but he does let me go out with girlfriends to the afternoon matinee. I don't know who I'll get to go with me with such a short notice."

"It really doesn't matter. Harry has never been out with a girl before and I'm trying to help him solve that problem," I said.

"Great! Then we can go with my cousin—she'll go with anyone!" Then Jeanne laughed real hard.

"Then it's a date." I smiled and squeezed her hand and told her I'd see her later. I took another trip around the teen center and finally saw Harry standing with a group of guys just outside the front door, talking and smoking. I didn't know these guys, they were older and not in school with us. They were all wearing black motorcycle jackets with white T-shirts and jeans, standing in a semi-circle around Harry.

"Hi, Harry," I said as I walked up. "Are you coming into the dance? There's several girls that want to meet you."

"No man, not right now. I'm thinking about going for a ride with these guys. They are part of the *Night Riders* here in Palm Bay and looking for a few new members."

"Can I come too? I might want to join," I said.

"You two come with me—my name is Cowboy. We only go by slang names in the club. I'm driving this '52 Gold Caddy here," as he walked Harry and me over to the classy car. I didn't want Harry to go with them alone, so I played along with joining. I had liked motorcycles ever since my cousin Big Doug took me for a ride several years earlier in West Virginia.

"Well, how old are you guys?" Cowboy asked.

"I'm fifteen now," Harry said proudly.

"He's thirteen," Harry said, "but just ugly for his age." Harry smiled to break the tension in the car. "I know nothing about motorcycle gangs other than what I've heard about the *Hell's Angels* in L.A. I only know they all ride together whenever and wherever they are, and the police doesn't like them regardless. Where are we going?" asked Harry.

"I thought we would ride over to the 'Hut' where we have our headquarters and you can meet a few more of the gang, our members."

"That's a good idea. How many guys are in the gang?" I interjected.

"There're about twenty-five guys; we don't count the girls who come and go. We like for guys to have an old lady; that way they are not looking around at the other members' chicks all the time. That starts fusses and fights." Cowboy frowned and looked at Harry.

"I'm sure you know that in Florida you can get your motorcycle license at fifteen and learner's permit at fourteen. Most every guy worth his salt has a machine," Cowboy stated.

"I'll be fourteen at the end of this month … so I could get my learner's permit for a motorcycle?" I looked at Cowboy with the question.

"You sure could. You damn sure will score big with the babes when you get a bike," Cowboy told us.

About that time, we pulled up to a big steel-gray Quonset hut that looked like it was some type of military base outpost at some point in time. There were several old army trucks and jeeps that were wrecked, broken and scrapped in the yard.

There were a number of young people around the front of the place Cowboy had called the Hut. There was a bonfire going in a big open yard with a steel wire fence around it. The guys and girls around the fire had beer cans or bottles in their hands and were hanging on each other like lovers. They were all talking; some were singing along with the jukebox music that was playing from inside the Hut. Cowboy took us straight through the crowd and into the hut without saying a word to anyone.

Once inside, Cowboy showed us to a room in the back of the hut. In this room, with the door marked "Office" in black paint, was another older guy. We were introduced in a military fashion.

"Boss, Sir, this is Harry and Johnny. They are thinking about joining and wanted to see the place and meet some of the members," Cowboy told him.

Bruno, the boss, was older and had to be in his late twenties, as was Cowboy. They both had dark complexions and dark hair, almost like Indians or Mexicans, but they had no noticeable accent. Cowboy was shorter than "Boss" who was surely over six feet tall.

"Hi, my name is Bruno, but in the club everyone knows me as Boss. I am the chief of the club and everything flows downhill from me. This is not a democratic club, it's autocratic … what I say goes. Like in the military, I'm the captain and that's it. You see that Indian Motorcycle and the Harley-Davidson out there? Those are our bikes," Bruno, the boss, said as he looked at Cowboy.

"Sit down and let's talk. You've met Cowboy, my assistant or lieutenant, you might say. Then I have two sergeants, first and second; then you might say that everyone else is a private for right now. If you get too many chiefs and not enough Indians, you have a problem. There is a small service fee of twenty-five bucks each year for joining and staying in the club. It pays for the Hut and a few other benefits like shelter and a garage when it is needed. Do you guys have any questions?"

Harry spoke up first. "I've heard a lot of rumors over the last several years that you guys have a very difficult initiation that requires someone to go through some pretty rough stuff. What would you require us to do?"

"No, not at all, it's all in fun. The authorities may not see it that way with some of our requirements. But the guys and girls you see have been through the gauntlet and they are still here in one piece, so it can't be too bad," Bruno growled.

"I'm only thirteen, I won't be fourteen until August. Do you have any others in the club that young?" I asked.

"We have one young lady who'll be fourteen in a few weeks, who joined with her sister who was sixteen last month. We make exceptions for a few cute little things but not usually for guys," Cowboy said.

"Most boys younger than fourteen can't pass the test, to tell you the truth. They don't have the strength, speed or the balls to do the challenges," said Bruno.

"The challenges must be pretty rough, then. Would you mind telling me so I can see if I think I can do them?" I quickly responded.

"Basically, there's three things you must complete in a month," Cowboy stated.

"First, you will be taken into the swamp outside of town about a mile or two and tied naked to a tree. You must untie yourself and walk into town and get your clothes from a place of business where we'll let you know at that time.

"Second, you must throw a rock through a glass window with enough force to break the window and have the home or business owner try to catch you. You must outrun the home or business owner. If you're caught, of course, we will disavow any responsibility for your actions.

"Third, you must remove hubcaps or a wheel off a police car. Then call the police station and report a problem, like an attempted burglary, robbery, domestic argument, or a hit and run, so they have to scramble to change the tire to get to the reported scene. Of course, when they get there, nothing is going on.

"Remember, if you are caught in any of these pranks you're not a club member, and we will deny any connection with you."

Harry laughed, "I think we can handle that." Then he looked at me for an approval.

"I don't know, Harry, we better think about it. Your running speed is not what it should be, and with any of these there comes a possibility of getting caught. What would your parents say?"

"Can we let you know soon, like next week?" Harry said.

"Come on, let's go out and introduce you to the gang," Cowboy said, smiling at Bruno.

Outside, Boss and Cowboy started introducing us to the sergeants. Red was a big red-headed boy about Harry's size, way over six feet and 200 pounds. Tike was a shorter guy with blonde hair, built like a big block. It seemed like he worked with weights all the time, judging by his bulging muscles. After meeting these two guys, the others were introduced. They finally got to a girl and she stood up and said, "You know me, Johnny, we danced together at the teen club."

"Yes, you're Frances. I haven't seen you since that night," I quickly stated, in defense of my neglecting to follow up with her.

"Come on, Johnny, let me take you for a ride on my motorcycle. Harry will be fine here until we get back … is that okay, Boss?"

"Sure, Frances, go ahead," Frankie, her brother, told her.

I remembered Frankie, her brother, big, ruggedly handsome, with a persistent two- or three-day beard, with long black hair like the movie stars and male models. I found out Frankie was fourth in charge if you would put them in order from top to bottom.

I followed Frances, the buxom, black-haired beauty. She was much taller and probably heavier, but she was a knockout and I didn't care why she liked me. I climbed on the back of the little turquoise and white Triumph motorcycle she had.

She said, "Be sure you hang on tight; this little thing will move."

I put my hands on her hips near where her torn, short, blue jeans were cut off. She looked so good in the cut-offs, and the old light-blue dress shirt fell over my hands.

"No, no, honey, like this." And she took her hands and grabbed my arms and brought them all the way around just under her big breasts. "Now, doesn't that feel more secure?"

"By all means, just show me the way," I said, as we pulled out of the Hut parking lot with a roar, gravel flying as the powerful little bike grabbed the pavement.

I didn't have on a watch to time the action, but she had the speed up to seventy-five in less than two seconds, so it seemed, and we were still in town. Once she got out on the back road going up the beach highway, she gave it full throttle and we shot up to 100 m.p.h. I just hung on tight like she had told me and didn't say anything for a few miles. She began to throttle down as we approached the turnoff for the beach.

Frances said, "Now this may seem like a wild ride, but we'll be in the soft sand only a few minutes, then it will straighten up and everything will be fine."

She was right; the front wheel went right, then left, then right again and just like that we were on the hard sand and down next to the water. She pulled up on a hard spot in the sand and kicked at the kickstand with her boot. "Climb off and let's go for a stroll, Johnny."

"I thought you'd never ask. Damn, you can really drive that thing. When did you get started?"

"Oh, I was about fourteen when I got my first bike. My

183

father and brother are motorcycle mechanics and have a shop, so I've been around them all my life, riding with my father before I could walk. It was just natural for me to get a bike when I was ready. How old are you, Johnny? You talk and act much older than you are."

"I'm only thirteen, but I'll be fourteen at the end of August. I guess I'm just big for my age."

Frances said, "I know I'm bigger than you are, but I can't help it. My father is 6'7", my brother is 6'6'', and my oldest sister is 6', so they think I'm going to be like them. I couldn't be like my mother who is just 5'2", and my other sister who is only 5'3". Does the difference in height bother you, Johnny?"

"Hell no, I think it's wonderful if you're tall. I hope I get to be tall like my father's brothers, five of them, and they are all over 6'3". But the girls, his sisters, are all short like their mother's side of the family; you just never know what's going to happen with genetics."

"Come over here then, let's get a little closer. Give me a kiss; maybe we'll grow together," she said with a beautiful smile.

She pulled me close against her. She was so much bigger, I felt almost smothered when she hugged me tight. Reaching up, I pulled her head down to me. I felt a hot rush as we fell to the beach locked in an embrace that seemed to last forever. I wasn't sure because the night was beautiful with mild wind blowing the palm branches, and the moon reflecting in the surf and salt smell coming in from the Atlantic.

Was I dreaming again?

Chapter 28

Like Wildflowers; you must allow yourself to grow in all the
places people thought you never would.
Author unknown

Harry's Blind Date

The following Saturday afternoon Harry had his first date. I wanted to see that he was a hit with Jeanne's cousin. I didn't care what she looked like, as long as she was female and breathing.

Harry and I were standing in front of the movie, anticipating the girls would show up. We started talking about the "Biker Gang," my name for the bikers we had met. That night with Frances had changed my opinion of the gangs based on Frankie's explanation. I wanted to see what Harry's opinion was.

"Harry, are you planning on joining the Death Riders and going through the initiation that Bruno told us about?"

"That's a good question. I want to, but I don't have a bike, I can't run very fast and I'm really a chicken-shit at heart. I'm usually scared to do anything I'm not sure I can accomplish."

"Really!" I exclaimed, "You didn't seem afraid when at the Hut that evening with the gang."

"That's because they made me feel welcome and a part of the family. You see, I don't have much family. My father works all the time, and I don't see him until bedtime. Of course, I

185

understand why he works so much and is never home, my mother is such a nag ... always on my dad about something. Damn, I hope most women ain't like that."

About that time the girls walked up, and Jeanne made the introductions. Her cousin Penny was tall, slender, with dark brown hair pulled into a ponytail and had on glasses. She was friendly and talkative. I took the lead and went to the window to buy four matinee tickets and gave the lady a $2 bill. I decided to buy the tickets since Harry's dad brought us to the movies and would pick us up on his way back home that afternoon.

"Let's get a seat in the balcony," I whispered to Harry upon entering the theater. Harry had listened when I told him about the fun in the movies on other occasions with pretty girls.

"Wherever you're comfortable. Johnny and I will go to the concession stand and get us popcorn and Cokes," Harry said.

"Ok, Penny and I will get us a seat in the balcony so you won't have to walk up there twice with us," Jeanne whispered to me.

Harry and I turned to go to the concession area at the other end of the hallway, and Jeanne and Penny went to the steps to go to the balcony. Jeanne was very excited, and Penny was very charming, even if she wasn't as cute as Jeanne. Harry and I started talking as Penny and Jeanne got seats.

"Well, Harry, it looks like you scored okay," I said to him. "Just be a naturally nice guy like you usually are, and I think all will be fine. Somewhere in the middle of the movie reach over and take her hand and just hold it in yours and see what happens from there."

"Yea, so far, so good. She is pretty good-looking if she took those glasses off. But it doesn't really matter, if she needs them to see she needs them. We all need something, my mom says."

"Harry, let's buy them a box of popcorn and Coke and we'll share it. I've found that most girls don't really like to eat much on a date. Not that I'm a big expert or anything, but I have taken four girls to the movies and only one wanted anything but a few drinks of my Coke," I told him.

"Good with me. The less money the better. I may be saving mine to buy a motorcycle soon. You know I don't have a learner's permit or anything. My dad says I really don't need one until I'm sixteen, but if I join I'll want to have a motorcycle of some type." Harry sounded emphatic about that.

I didn't say anything, but I knew that I couldn't even think about getting a motorcycle at thirteen. My father would have a fit. Besides, I knew they couldn't afford to help me buy one even if I were old enough. But I could help Harry with his plan, just like today fixing him up with Penny, his first date. I felt good about that.

We went back to the balcony and enjoyed the afternoon mystery just released by Alfred Hitchcock, *Dial M for Murder*. We all enjoyed the thriller. Harry and I got a few kisses in with the girls between the screams, gasps and chills caused by the devious mind of the famous Hitchcock.

Harry and I waved goodbye before Jeanne's brother picked them up at the movie that afternoon, so our secret rendezvous wasn't discovered.

Not ten minutes later Harry's father was there to take us back to Palm Bay. Hardly a word about future plans was mentioned once we got in the car with Mr. Gardener. Harry did ask his father if he thought he should get his learner's permit; he felt he was going to be driving to pick up dates very soon. His father laughed and said, "We'll see if that pans out." He chuckled to himself, probably thinking about his escapades as a boy.

Chapter 29

Don't wait ... life goes quicker than you think!
Rosie Pendergrass (1960)

Harry's Commitment

When I got home that afternoon, none other than my grandmother, Rosie, greeted me. She was about my favorite person in the world outside of my mom and dad. I loved my little brother, but Mom would never let Doug out of her sight after he got home from school. I didn't know if it was because he was so timid, or if he was timid because she kept him tied to her apron strings. I loved Doug, but Mom would never let us do anything that would let us have a tight brotherly bond.

"Wow, Granny, am I glad to see you. Are you here for a visit or are you going to be staying with us for a while?" I asked.

"I'm just not sure yet. I don't know if your mother and father have enough money to pay me to watch you and your brother. Both your mom and dad say you are a handful, and Doug is a very needy child yet." She grinned at me.

"Aw, come on, Granny, I'm your best sidekick ever, you told me. We've hunted, trapped, chopped wood, fished, gardened, and you taught me the flowers and herbs for medical needs, what could be better than that? Oh, that reminds me, Grandma." With that statement I quit talking for a few minutes and looked at my mother and brother with a very solemn face.

"I was hunting a few weeks ago with two friends and we

were crossing an old barbed wire fence. While passing the gun through the fence, the trigger of one of the guns got caught on the barb and went off and shot my friend. We carried him fast as we could from the hunting spot, but he still died as we were carrying him."

With that I began to cry, and tried to finish telling the story, but became so emotional I went to my room, lay on the bed and cried myself to sleep. Mom finished telling Granny about the horrible accident, and about me and Harry carrying Richard nearly a mile trying to get help. That vision has been difficult for me to get over.

"That was one of the reasons why Flem wanted to come to work down here in Florida. Not only is it beautiful, warm and a lot more opportunity than in the mountains of West Virginia, but also the move would help get Johnny out of the area that reminded him of Curtis's death. Flem's got a good position helping to build the launching pads and foundations at Cape Canaveral for these rockets they're sending up now. We want to stay as long as the work is good," Mom told her mother.

"One other thing, Mom—I'm going to start working part-time for Mr. Sullivan up in his grocery store on his busy days to help ends meet for a while. I really could use your help in watching the kids during that time, at least until school starts in September," Mom told Granny.

"Well, it'll be like a summer vacation for me down here in the Sunshine State." Rosie grinned and said, "I remember not long ago I went to California, Canada, and Alaska with my second or third husband—can't remember which now—looking for gold. Damn, if that weren't an adventure. I saw my husband Henry Runyon shot in a brawl up there where we knew no one, and I had to carry him quite a-ways to get help. Fortunately, we had a horse and wagon outside the bar we were able to use. Hell, that was a bad, bad time for us but we survived."

"God, Mom, you never told me about that before.".

"There's a lot I have kept from you over the years. I didn't want to spoil your upbringin' when you were young. You had enough to deal with, all your brothers and sisters and tryin' to raise you younguns up the right way there in those mountains with very little income. We had to scrape for everything, but we made it," Granny said with a smile. "Koot, I'll tell you that story sometime when the kids are not around and we have the time."

Mom acknowledged the words her mother was saying and said, "I need to see where Doug is. He's not as independent as Johnny. We have some rough neighbors from Tennessee who have moved in a few houses down. I met the mother at the store last week. She has three boys and one girl. Her husband is an electrician with Indian River Power Company in Melbourne, and his oldest son works on a paint crew there. The other boys are about Johnny's age. The girl is a little older than Johnny, I think sixteen," she said.

Granny asked, "Why do you think they are such a rough family ... just because they're poor and from the mountains?"

"No, it's just the way they are letting the kids run wild, not much discipline and control, I guess."

I woke up and went back into the room to tell Mom and Granny I was sorry for getting soft and crying about the whole hunting incident. Doug had already come inside the house and gone to another room to play with his toys.

Granny said, "That's fine—no harm in showing your emotions." We began to talk again, and she asked if I could take her to see some of the beautiful sights—the flowers, trees, and water around the neighborhood. "I want to see where we are living; it's so lovely down here."

"Yes, we'll go over to the Indian River pier and see if there's any fish running tomorrow; you'll like that. You never know, though; sometimes they are plentiful, other times they are scarce. I'm not sure how you tell they are running," I said loud enough for Mom to hear in the kitchen.

"That sounds good, Johnny. Take Granny for a walk toward town."

"Let's take a short walk where you can show me around the neighborhood. It really looks like a jungle here with banana trees, palm trees, pretty little parrots, and monkeys in the trees. Our relatives back in West Virginia wouldn't believe this place—it's like a little paradise."

I went in the kitchen to get a drink of water and Granny went to her room, got something, and put it in her pocket. We went out the door talking like we hadn't missed a beat. It had been nearly six months since Granny had been with the family, and she was always with us before moving to Florida. Did Mom call her to come down or did she just come here on her own? No one really told me.

Chapter 30

"Yes, I'm old school. I have good manners. I show others
respect and will always help those in need.
It's not because I'm old fashioned.
It's because I was raised properly."
Rosie Pendergrass 1956

Rosie Comes to Town

As we were walking in Jungle Park, Granny took out a chunk of something that looked like a chocolate bar, unwrapped it, and with a small knife cut a piece off and put it in her mouth. "What's that, Granny?" I asked.

"It's chewing tobacco, a bad habit I picked up on the road with my second husband. Not as bad as smoking but pert' near. It keeps you from being hungry and you can sit in the woods while hunting and it makes you spit all the time, which occupies your mind as to what you're doin'."

"Let's see." I looked at the slab of Apple Chewing Tobacco, and then smelled it. "Granny, that smells awful. How do you stand to chew it?"

"Oh well, I'm a grandmother now and I don't have much else to stimulate me, so I use this for now. I'm not addicted like many people; I can quit for months at a time if I need to or want to. And I never have this tobacco around children. You are not what one would think of as a child anymore. You're a teenager. In some countries you would be out working, even supporting a family."

"Granny, I don't want to hear that."

As we walked along the sandy path going through Jungle Park, I thought of how nice it was to have Granny back with us. Then my mind shifted to the path we were on, and I began to think of what Mr. Sullivan had told me about the local snakes coming out at this time of the year and sunning for most of the day. "Granny, can you drive a car?" I asked her.

"Johnny, that's a good question. I have drove a mule, horse, oxen and wagon. When I was coming up, there was no need for a driver's license. Sometime after the war, each state enforced driving regulations, but you know West Virginia, Kentucky, and back in the hollers of Tennessee they never enforced it much except in the bigger cities like Nashville.

"Speaking of Nashville, you had a famous relative who had a hotel and bar there. I've never been to the place, but my husband stayed there when he was a railroad engineer. Big, nice place, George said. I think George said his name was Fredrick Stump. He was a mountaineer, pioneer Indian fighter back in the old days. Your father is a descendant of that clan of Stumps, I was told. The great-grandfather John George Stump was from the wine country of Germany. That must be why your dad likes a drink every once in a while. It's in his blood." With that she gave a loud chuckle.

"But to get back to your question about me driving. I turned sixty-five and never drove a car, except one time back in 1927, or '28, when Tom, my first husband, got bad sick in the winter and we couldn't get the animals out to hitch up because of the snow. I tried to drive him to the doctor in Tom's old Model T Ford and I just about run us over the side of the mountain getting us there. I didn't have any trouble steering but the gears! The car stayed in the same gear the whole time for twenty miles and wouldn't let us go more than ten miles per hour. No one had ever showed me the way to shift. After that, I never tried driving again."

I laughed, and Granny spit a stream of tobacco juice out of her mouth and laughed as well.

We were almost into the town of Palm Bay on the walking path when a car passed us on the gravel back road where we were walking. The old black Ford stopped and backed up. A passenger in the rear rolled his window down and asked, "Are you lost? You be out here all by yourselves?" His head trying to push out of the window, the young man's long, greasy, brown hair was matted and tangled. There was a scar across his nose like he had been in a bad accident.

I quickly said, "No, we just live over here in Jungle Park and we were taking a walk into town."

"This is not a safe place for an old woman and a young boy to be walking, if you know what I mean," the fellow said, as he got out of the car with another smaller boy following him. The car drove off, and the two came aggressively toward Granny and me.

"Whoa ... back up, kids," Granny said as they approached.

The boys looked to be about twenty years old, not much bigger than me, but definitely adults, with unkempt beards. The biggest had long, stringy brown hair, with pockmarks all over his face. The shorter dark-haired one was the talker and mouthier of the two.

"No, you better back up, old lady. We want some money, or we'll have that gold ring you're wearing," the bigger one said.

"Sorry, that's not gold but it is silver and made by my husband out of a silver coin for our wedding. I don't think I can allow you to have that now. I do have some good chewing tobacco here in my pocket you can have." Granny spit a mouthful of tobacco juice right in the face of the biggest guy. He cried out, "What tha' hell is this?!"

194

Then Granny hit the other boy square in the mouth and the blood flew. She turned back to the first and struck him in the head. He was trying to duck her fist while he got the tobacco juice out of his nose and mouth. I grabbed him and pulled him to the ground and we started wrestling, me trying not to allow him to swing, and keep a good grip around his neck at the same time. Granny went back over and kicked the big one in the side as he was trying to get up. He started yelping and yelling for help.

Granny said, "No help around here, buddy, it looks like your friends left you to do the dirty work and it's a little dirtier than figured. Need any help there, Johnny?" She kicked the boy straight in the face again. More blood spurted, and the boy wrestling with me started yelling for help and crawling away. Granny kicked him in his backside as he crawled down the gravel road on his hands and knees as fast as he could, with her right behind him for about ten steps.

"Come on, Johnny, let's go on into town; there's not even a good fight in either of these punks."

Granny and I left the two licking their wounds and going the other way to look for their friends. I didn't recognize any of them. I told Granny about the motorcycle gang and my encounter with them.

She simply said, "Johnny, let me tell you a story about when I was in Alaska during the Gold Rush days. This is when I went out west from Kentucky where I was living at the time with my husband, George."

Johnny with Granny Rosie

Chapter 31

*"Some old-fashioned things like Fresh Air, Sunshine
and Mountains are hard to beat!"*
Rosie Smith Runyon Pendergrass 1954

A Bit of Granny's Past

We walked along as she told the story of her adventure in Alaska.

"George and I had gotten word from a coal miner returning from California that there was a great deal of money to be made out there in the gold fields all the way from California to Alaska. The man had stumbled upon a job while he was in San Francisco. Another man learned that George's friend was a coal miner from the Appalachians, and he immediately offered him a great deal of money to stay there and join his west coast mining operation. All this was northeast of San Francisco in a settlement called Walnut Creek.

The miner went to the man's mining operation to see what sort of mine it was. He wanted to see what real gold looked like when it was mined. To his surprise, it seemed much easier than mining coal in the Appalachians. The man knew essentially nothing about mining; he simply had money to support the venture. He was looking for a mining supervisor he could trust.

"George's friend, the coal miner, picked up his bags and left the next day on a train to Houston, making a swing back toward home, calling on a few business associates along the way. But, he never got the man out of his mind and how desperate he was to find a mine supervisor.

"When George's friend saw George and told him of the incident, he thought that George would fit the job easily. George was a former coal-mining supervisor in the anthracite and bituminous coal industry. He had worked in Pittsburgh and in Coalwood's Olga Mining System in West Virginia, both having different types of coal that had to be mined differently.

"After hearing this, George came home and told me what the man had told him, and we decided to head for the gold fields of California and Alaska. We thought it would be better if he went ahead and got a place to live and the job secure before I went out," Granny said as we walked into Palm Bay.

"Johnny, it was almost two weeks later when George arrived by train in what is now Sacramento, to talk to the man about the job. George went to see the man and found his name was Sam Clay, the youngest brother of a Kentucky politician. Sam was sent out to San Francisco in 1890 by his brother to invest and to make his fortune in the Gold Rush.

"The gold had just about petered out in California by that time, but they were still making big strikes in Alaska. Each time they would make a strike, the mining company would send someone to see what the money-making potential was for the claim," Granny continued.

"'The big one, the big claim, is coming for sure. It just depends on where each claim is made. I think the next one will be a little further inland toward Klondike,' Sam told George the day they talked.

"Sam hired George on the spot the day he found they were both from back east in the coal fields. Everything seemed to be going good after George got a small house in the new community that was springing up around the mining operation in the Sacramento area. He sent for me and I was there in three days by train," Granny told me, as we walked down the street in Palm Bay.

"I told George when I got there, it seemed like half of the train was going to San Francisco to seek their fortune in gold. I met two women who had left their husbands, with plans to set up a brothel in Alaska and make a fortune from those men working in the gold fields. There were no laws there against prostitution, gambling and drinking, all the moneymaking activities a clever businesswoman could make.

"The women even asked if a young thing like me would be interested in going to Alaska to make a small fortune in only a few years while singing and dancing all the way to the bank. But I told her I wasn't interested. I had my man and he was a railroad engineer."

"Granny, I'm not sure what prostitution is. Can you tell me specifically? Things like that Mom and Dad won't discuss at home and the only education I get on it is from the boys' locker room at school and that's not very reliable," I said.

"Well, I've never been asked that question before, but I would say it is a woman who decides to sell her body for the pleasures of men. It is usually not legal, but is done in almost every society in the world that I know of, especially the male dominant places like Europe, Asia and Africa. A woman can work alone or for someone that has a house of women called a whorehouse where men may go and drink, gamble and hang out with those kinds of women."

"Oh, I think I understand. The women just learn to take the men's money through an affectionate relationship. Is that right, Granny?" I gave her a grateful smile.

"Let me finish my story I've started about the gold rush days. I've got a bad feeling about this entire venture already after talking to George. All these people are money hungry and willing to do most anything to get it, I told him. George had met me at the train station with a horse and wagon. The horse and wagon was borrowed from his boss, Sam Clay, to pick up supplies on the way home, about a fifteen-mile journey.

"George told me we needed a few barrels of flour, bacon, lard, cheese, potatoes, and whatever else you might need for cooking and the household needs. There really was not much to choose from there at the settlement. There was one new hotel and that's more of a flophouse. We found a shop and stocked up before we returned to the new place George had found for us. The horse and wagon was reliable but 'bout five miles from the settlement we could see some rough tents and campfires along the old dirt road.

"I asked George, 'Did you bring a gun or any type of protection?' You know I was afraid to carry one on the train, but there were several people carrying them; you could see them stuffed in their bags and belts.

"George said, 'Pull back that tarp and you'll see a nice new .30-.30 Winchester for you. I have my old Colt .45 pistol. I brought the pistol with me on the train when I made the trip.'

"When we were a few miles from the cabin George was living in, the cabin that was part of the deal he had made with Sam Clay for the supervisor's job, two men approached us on mules and acted like they wanted directions. George pulled back on the reins to slow the wagon and when he did the two pulled guns and asked for money. About the time they pulled the guns, I had the Winchester cocked and was firing at the one on the gray mule and hit him in the leg. He screamed and fell off. I said, 'Speed up, George, these are desperadoes.' The second man gasped, cursed and started taking aim at our moving wagon. Luckily, the mule he was riding was slow and there wasn't much chase. I got off a second shot, knocking the man's hat off his head and he pulled the mule to a stop and climbed off to help his friend.

"'Nice shootin' on your first day with your new gun, Rosie. You're going to fit in just right out here,' George told me. I told him, I hope it's not going to be like this from now on, I'm too young for this stuff. Is it like this all over?

"At this time, I was just a teenager of about eighteen, maybe nineteen, and already could, ride, rope, hunt, shoot and fight with the best of them from my Kentucky, Tennessee upbringing. This was the benefit of growing up in a big family of brothers and sisters. Back then Paw and Ma taught us to take care of ourselves from the time we could walk and if we couldn't, to ask a brother or sister to help with the task. Since I was in the middle somewhere, I helped manage the family problems." Granny's story continued.

"We went on to the cabin without further incident and unloaded the supplies. The one-room cabin had a fireplace with a pot bracket, two real windows of glass, and a coal stove with an oven for baking. There was a double bed in the far right corner with a small table beside the bed where George had a windup clock sitting. There was one picture in the cabin from a farmer's almanac calendar that read April 1894. In the front of the cabin there was a small porch and two window boxes for planting flowers or herbs.

"George told me the cabin had been lived in by the former mine supervisor who was now in Juneau, Alaska. Immediately, I liked the little cabin and went to work at putting the things away we had bought. As I walked across the floor, I noticed a trap door that wasn't covered with a rug. George told me it was a potato and wine cellar. Out here in the West, a lot of people drink wine like we drink moonshine and whiskey back East, was George's explanation of the wine and potato cellar.

"There were four cabins in the area that all looked the same. When I asked about the cabins, George only knew the other occupants worked for the mining company too.

"'Well, I've never had real store-bought wine, but I've heard good and bad about it. But if there's still some down there, let's give it a try. It's been a long day and a rough ride,' George said to me."

A California Company Edict

"The next day George left for work after breakfast at five a.m. His work and office was about a half-mile into town and he rode the horse the company gave him. I found the horses were kept at a community barn down between our place and the next neighbor. All four of the neighbors shared the barn but each person was responsible for the care and feeding of their own animals.

"Six months after being at the mining company head office in Sacramento, Sam came in and told George, 'There's been an incident at the Juneau site. I'm going to have to ask you to go investigate the whole incident and stay there until we can get a replacement.' George asked, 'What type of incident—was there an explosion at the site or something else?'

"Sam replied, 'No, I wish it were that simple and direct. It seems like we have some unruly and untrustworthy people in the mining community up there. Someone shot William Butler, our Alaska supervisor of mining operations, in an attempted robbery last week. We have three on-site armed guards there 24 hours a day, but some think we need more. It seems the cold makes the men meaner. The office personnel are getting scared and many want to close up and leave.'

"George came home that evening and told me the bad news, and the plan that Sam had given him to carry out with extra pay. I then said to George, 'I told you I had a bad feeling about this venture, now here we go again.'"

Chapter 32

Difficult roads often lead to wonderful destinations.
Mary Peffer

Alaska Bound

Granny asked me if I wanted to hear the rest of the story or was it boring? I said, "Sure I want to hear more Granny, this is like listening to a Western story on the radio except I know the star actor. I'm getting thirsty, though, and could drink a Coke after our long walk into Palm Bay."

"Oh, you call this a long walk. You've forgotten already our long walks in those West Virginia Mountains," she laughed.

We went into a drugstore to the soda fountain, climbed up on stools, and sat for a minute. When the waiter came over, Granny asked for two drinks—one Coke for me and an ice cream float for her. "Wait, wait, I think I'll have the same thing you're having; it sounds good. Granny, I really like your taste!" I told her.

Granny said, "Let's go out here and sit on this bench in front of the drugstore while I finish this story." After the man brought two ice cream floats, we went out to the bench on the beautiful warm day. There was a slight breeze blowing when we began devouring our treats. Somewhere in the middle of eating our treat, Granny started again with her story.

"The next week we set out for Alaska by horse and wagon. We had to take our things because we didn't know how long we

203

would be there in Juneau getting things straightened out for the company. We really didn't even know how long it would take us to get there, but since George was being paid by the day we figured we could chance it by taking the two-horse Conestoga wagon they had given him for the trip. I think they knew it would be a long time and we would need everything when we made the move. That way we would be ready for the cold weather with most of our supplies and clothes.

"We spent the next week slowly creeping toward our goal of twenty-five to thirty miles each day. We had to stop in the state of Washington because one of the horses became lame and George knew he would have to be put down. While there, we got the wagon wheels fixed by a blacksmith. The blacksmith asked if we had ever been to Alaska before and George told him no. The blacksmith suggested we trade the horses for two mules that would be stronger for pulling the wagon and more valuable in Alaska.

"We stayed in a hotel that evening and ordered a good hot bath and a real restaurant meal. The next day George took the blacksmith's suggestion and traded for the mules that were slower, but pulled longer without rest.

"In two weeks we were arriving in Juneau. There was hardly anything there but the mining operations and an outpost where traders and craftsmen brought their wares to sell.

"The town was full of saloons and brothels. I could see when we stopped for the evening and asked for a room at a local inn, George was told, 'Well, mister, I don't think you'll want to bring your wife in here for the evening unless you plan on sharing her with a half-dozen men that's in here every night. There's another inn that's better suited for you and the family life about a half-mile on the other side of town called the *Do Drop Inn.*'

"George and I drove the wagon on to the inn, and made a deposit on a room that included two baths each week and use of an inside bathroom for the next three days. It was a Friday, and common knowledge that most of the miners were out bathing, drinking, whoring and gambling—anything but working on Saturday and Sunday. The inn had twenty-five rooms on two floors. They put George and me on the second floor with three other couples.

"We went out the next day to look over the town and the site of the mining operation. It seemed like the entire town was built around the mine, much like George suspected.

"We counted twelve saloons and houses of ill repute before we found a church or a family eatery. There were over one hundred tent homes and fifty or more cabins much cruder than the one we lived in in California. They had no glass windows, or porches, but big fireplaces.

"George said, as we walked down the icy, mud-laden path the many wagons had carved into the earth, 'Rosie, I had no plans for you to have to deal with all of this. I wanted to keep you home in Kentucky on a nice safe little farm near your relatives, but look what I've gotten us into. It's a shame when a man has to chase the almighty dollar from one end of the country to the other to keep his family fed.'

"I told him then, 'George, it's fine. I'm with you and that's all that matters. We said we'd share our lives together, we didn't say how rough or smooth parts of it may be. I just want to see how long we'll have to be here. They say the winters can get pretty grizzly up here.'

"'Yes, I know. You can feel the chill in the air coming down that mountain now and it's only late September. What will it be like in December? We won't be able to leave except by train, and I'm not sure about that. I'm going to go see if we can talk to a railroad person today. But, part of the trouble is the fact that hardly any businesses have a name out front. Where's the railroad office do you think?' George stated.

"'Yea, but you can sure find the saloons and whorehouses easy enough, I told him gruffly.'

"George smiled and said, 'Yes, boys will be boys, won't they!' We entered what we thought was a hardware store, but it turned out to be a prospector's office where people would bring their digs to see what the certain or probable assay might be for that claim. George asked the proprietor where they could find a train schedule and was there someone in town who would deal with a real estate lease or sale. The store proprietor asked if he was a miner.

"'Well, in a way. I don't go into the mine anymore and actually dig, but I direct operations and personnel of the mining company.'

"'Sure hope you can fight and shoot if you have to direct these men to work in the mine. I'm from Sacramento and this bunch here in Juneau are just about the worst and roughest I've ever encountered,' the proprietor said.

"George said, 'That's why I brought Rosie. She'll help keep 'em in line.' All six feet three inches of George just quivered with laughter. We then left the Assay Office and went over to where we were told we could get information about the train schedule and possibly the real estate. The office was across the street and about a hundred feet south.

"The reason we knew this was the fact there was a huge post in the middle of the street with signs pointing North, South, East and West, with a few town names and how many miles away they were. The closest to us was further north another twenty-five miles, Skagway. South was Ketchikan, the town we came through with our wagon when first crossing the border into Alaska. According to the sign, it was nearly a hundred miles farther north to Anchorage. From what we gathered that day in town, there were about a thousand miners and merchants in the town established by the Tlingit Indians more than a hundred

206

years earlier, we were told.

"The location of the place was confusing to me because I couldn't understand the geography of the area. I only knew we were a long way from home and didn't know anyone in the area we could trust except each other. We went to bed that night thinking about our situation there in Juneau, but we could do nothing at that point except to deal with it."

Chapter 33

Always go with the choice that scares you the most, because that's the one that is going to help you grow.
Caroline Myss

Granny's Killer Winter

Granny continued, "After getting a telegraph and a letter from Sam telling us it would be six months before he could replace the mine supervisor, George and I leased a small cabin and barn from the mining company on the edge of town. I got busy getting prepared for what even the natives said would be a cold winter.

"What the natives said about a cold winter sure was correct because by September 30, there was six inches of snow on the ground already. George and I had gotten our wood sawed and chopped. The wood shed was only about five feet from the cabin, and it was piled ten feet high with wood. The coal came from the mining company coal yard.

"I had started my vegetable canning and salting of the meats like we did at home in the winter. A neighbor gave us a deer, a hindquarter of an elk, and a piece of bear meat—it was my first bear meat—for us to put away for the winter. Plus, we had bought some pork for cooking earlier when we first moved in.

"George took the hides and began the tanning process and our neighbor told us about a stream where the salmon, trout and other fish were always running, winter and summer. The neighbor who worked for George said he would even teach George to ice fish, something George had never done. George and I thought we were in good shape for the winter by mid-October.

"Days became routine as time moved into winter and the temperatures dropped below zero most days of the week, short days and long nights. On those days I sat and would knit and sew and made skin and leather clothes I had learned to make from my Cherokee mother. I enjoyed the quiet work time. There was only one problem—it seemed that George was getting home later and later each week.

"One nice cold starlit evening, George was still not home by eight p.m. This was the third evening of him having to work overtime at the mining office. I decided to hitch up our old mule, Miss Bessie, and ride into town to see what the problem was and if I could help. I had been holing up at the cabin for three days working and felt like getting out to stretch my legs a bit. I decided to strap the Colt .45 pearl handle pistol around my waist since there was a mile stretch of huge pine forest before town that could be dangerous, me being alone. I had no trouble going into town, passing only two other riders on horseback on the way.

"I approached the mining office first, since it was on the south end of town. It looked dark as I slowly rode by. Where was George and what had delayed him so much every night? There was a gang at the hotel and of course the saloon was always busy. I figured I would ride by the hotel to see if his horse was there, thinking he could be there in a meeting with some of the mining personnel. There was some reason he was late, and I wanted an answer.

"I tied old Bessie to the hitching rail and went inside. I looked around for something happening but after going in, I could see he was not there. There was only one other place left, so I climbed back on Bessie and rode across the street and down the block of wooden buildings about fifty yards to the saloon on the north end of town.

"I could hear the noise and music coming from the little saloon from many yards away. Everything was closed up tight to keep what little heat they had inside, but the sound found the cracks. I climbed off Bessie, and hitched her to the rail in front of the bar. I walked into the crowded saloon with more than fifty men scattered mostly along the long wooden bar. Sitting around two big round wooden tables, card games were being played.

"There was a small group in the far corner with a woman singing and playing the piano and another woman dancing on a little stage built on a stack of food crates above piano height. It looked like all were having a good time, as I looked around to find George.

"Then I saw him with his back to me at the card table farthest from the door. I slowly walked back to the game and before I got ten feet into the room, I had several offers to dance from miners.

"I stood behind the game for a few minutes to see what they were playing, and it was clear they were playing straight poker with deuces wild. George looked like he was doing well with nearly a hundred dollars in bills piled in front of him and another fifty in the pot. There were still four people in the game and the man to George's left had just raised, 'It'll cost you five bucks more, boys, to see this hand,' he said.

"George said, 'I'll see your five bucks and raise five more.'

"'That means it's going to cost ten more to see the winner,' a big guy with a black cowboy hat and long beard said as he threw his cards face down.

"'Okay, I'll call,' said another skinny man with a railroad hat at the table, and laid his two pair down.

"'Okay, George,' the man with the long beard said, 'What

do you have over there that you're so proud of?'

"'I hate to take more of your money, McCarthy,' George said, as he put down his hand with four sevens and a deuce. 'It will take four big ones, five of a kind, or a flush to take the pot. What do you have McCarthy?'

"McCarthy jumped up and yelled, 'You're a damn cheat! I have four Jacks, best hand of the night. You couldn't have had that hand without cheating. Did you have that deuce up your sleeve?'

"He pulled a gun and pointed it at George. I was standing behind the man, as he was about to put one in George's chest at point blank range. I hit him in the side of the head with the butt of my Colt. Blood flew everywhere. George fell backward on the floor. I was stunned, but pulled my gun back and took quick action, out of fear of the man. I swung hard for his beard and one hit in the head with the butt of the gun dropped him. I ran over to George and lifted his head into my arms. 'This is the shit you get into when you don't come home at night. I should have let him shoot you.'

"'Rosie, I know I shoulda' come home earlier all this week, but I was asked to play poker after work and I wanted to win some money to buy you a ticket home for the holidays. It looks like I won the money but lost the game in the end.' George closed his eyes as if to ask for forgiveness. I kissed him quickly on the forehead, grabbed his money from on the table and pushed him toward the door.

"We got home and I laid down the law to him. With a severe winter coming and this being our first time in Alaska, we didn't need any other problems like he was getting ready to bring home to me. A bullet hole in the chest would definitely put him in an unemployable situation and us in a bad position in Alaska. With that we made up and George brought me home to Kentucky that May after we endured a severe cold winter in Alaska."

Chapter 34

Chaos is a friend of mine
Bob Dylan

Old-Time Scrappin'

After getting back to Jungle Park and before dinner, I asked Granny something that had been on my mind since the boys jumped us earlier that day. "What was the most important part of being a good fighter?" We had been talking all the way back from the fight incident in Palm Bay and Granny's Alaskan adventure. I was convinced there was more to know about fighting than just being the biggest.

"Granny, teach me a little something that will even up the odds when a bigger guy jumps me," I asked in all seriousness because of the scrapes I had gotten into, and now with trying to watch over Harry.

"Well, Johnny, the most important thing is to try your very best to stay out of arguments and not get into situations that would mean it might lead to a fight," she said.

"Yes, I realize I shouldn't fight but there seem to be times when there is no other answer to a situation … like today when those guys jumped us."

"You're right, Johnny, there's times when you're put between a rock and a hard place, a situation that seems like only your fist can get you out of the hassle; but remember, if you get into a fight there's really no winner. Most of the time both people get into trouble."

"Yes, Granny, but I'm new here and have only a few friends and a lot of the older bigger boys want to pick on me just to show off or try me for some trivial reason like just because I'm new."

"I had a number of brothers and they made sure I could fight when I was very young. You have to realize you usually only get two or three punches off before the biggest person gets hold and pulls you to the ground. If that's the situation, you have to hit one of three places that bleed a lot. Remember, your opponent always hates to see his own blood."

"What are the two or three places?"

"The first place is the mouth and lips, but when you hit the mouth there's always the chance you will knock their teeth out and that spells trouble for them and you. Another place is the nose. It is a very good target and rather difficult to break but easy to make bleed by striking straight into the nose as hard as you can; the blood will fly and usually even the biggest person will stop, grab his nose or slow enough for you to get away or make another move away," Granny stressed.

"That's what I needed to know," I explained to her. "It was great today when you spit tobacco juice in that guy's face."

"Did you notice that was a detractor? It allowed me enough time to get a good punch in to his face. No one likes to be spit on and that was all I could think of then that may take his mind off us for a second.

"Just promise you'll do your best to try to stay out of fights. No one likes a bully or a troublemaker. Now let's go in and get ready for dinner and see what your father did at Cape Canaveral today. Your mom is home from picking up Douglas at school and they can fill us in on their day's activity."

"Granny, I'm sure glad you came down to live with us again. I feel like I can ask you anything and you'll tell me the truth, regardless if I want to hear it or not," I told her.

213

"You're right, Johnny, I will always tell you the truth because that was the way I was raised."

Chapter 35

When you have a bad day, a really bad day, try and treat the
world better than it treated you.
Patrick Stump

Gator Bait

I was getting familiar with the Melbourne area, having gone fishing with dad and the guys in several locations inland on the small lakes, ponds and seashore. We lived close to north Lake Okeechobee, the Big Swamp locals called it. It was full of gators, snakes, coons, wild boar, deer and other wildlife. I loved to go there with my dad, fishing and hunting.

Dad was a real outdoorsman and felt at home in any outside environment. I felt he enjoyed taking me along with him. Dad was the same as my grandmother, regarding the environment. She had taught him a great deal about how to survive in the outdoors, and now they were passing it along to me. I wanted to be appreciative of the time and effort.

One Friday, Harry called to tell me he had been accepted into the motorcycle gang there in Palm Bay and he was to have his initiation that Friday night. I asked him about my status.

"Johnny, you were not accepted into the gang because of your age. You're still only thirteen and won't be fourteen until the end of the summer. That's the minimum age to be a member," Harry told me.

"Harry, that's not a problem. I can join next year if you

survive," I said, and laughed.

"Oh, you think I'm going to have trouble, huh?"

"Naw, it's just you've had trouble getting out of a jam running and a few things like that because of your size. You'll be fine. What do you have to do?"

"Well, I'm not sure but I heard them talking about something on the old Okeechobee road out toward the swamp," Harry said with a slight tremble in his voice.

"I think I'll call Frances and see if she will let me ride along with her on the initiation get together. That way I can be there to laugh at your big ass when they put you through the wringer in the initiation ritual." I started laughing again.

"Stop, Johnny, it's not funny. A lot of guys have gotten hurt and had to be taken to the hospital doing these rituals."

"Is that right? Well, Harry, that should tell you something right there."

"Stop. I'm going to hang up now. Just wanted to let you know I had been accepted and you had not." Click, the phone was dead.

I thought, *What should I do? Let Harry fend for himself or try to run interference for him again?* I knew Harry was just doing this to fit in with the other tough kids in Palm Bay. He had a problem with his weight and couldn't seem to lose it or really didn't try. I felt fine not being accepted and would rather be an athlete, even though I did like the excitement of the motorcycles and the wild girls.

"Hi, Frances, this is Johnny. I was wondering if it would be all right with the gang if you let me ride along with you tonight on your bike? I know they rejected me from membership, but couldn't I go as your date?"

"Why do you want to ride with me tonight? You haven't before. I wasn't sure you really cared for me. Sometimes you seem interested, and other times there's no contact for days. I really like you, Johnny. I know I'm older and even bigger, but you are so nice and mature for your age. I want you as my boyfriend."

"Well, Frances, let's give it a try. I'm not saying that I'll be able to stick with a fifteen-year-old getting ready to turn sixteen who is as big and beautiful as you, but I'll give it my best shot," I said trying to ease her mind so I could ride along that night.

"That makes me happy Johnny. Meet me at my house at six. As you know, my brother Frankie is one of the leaders, Bruno his lieutenant. They both like you so I don't think there'll be a problem," Frances said.

I hung up the phone and looked at Granny. Everyone had been trying not to listen, but the house was small, and the phone was in the middle of the living room; it was impossible not to hear when someone was on the phone. I wasn't sure about tonight, but I was committed not only for the evening, but to Frances as well. I liked her but certainly didn't love her.

"Going somewhere tonight?" Granny asked.

She listened intently without saying a word as I began trying to explain my predicament.

"I'm caught in a hard place. My buddy Harry is heavy; actually really fat, and a lot of the kids make fun of him. But when you get to know him he is a nice, kind person. Ever since we carried Little Richard out of the hunting fields together on our back we have been real close. Now Harry is getting ready to join this teen club (*I didn't want to tell her a motorcycle gang*), and it involves an initiation doing some things that may be too difficult for him without embarrassment or some help.

"I'm trying to figure a way to help him without the others knowing. Harry is nearly sixteen now and feels he shouldn't have to be hanging around with a fourteen-year-old like me to help him with decisions and challenges. I think he is going to get himself into trouble."

217

"Why is it that you feel responsible for this boy's choices?" Granny asked.

"I'm not sure, I only know that I would feel better if he got past this initiation. He asked me to spend the night with him because he's not sure how long the ritual will last. It starts at six this evening." I was beginning to stretch the truth. I was not invited to spend the night with Harry, but in my mind, I wanted to be free to do whatever I needed that night to keep Harry safe.

"The other part of the problem is I've given my word to this girl that I would be her boyfriend, and I really don't want to get involved with an older girl right now. I don't have the money, the size or the influence to take care of her like a boyfriend should."

"How old is she?"

"I think either sixteen or turning sixteen very soon. The problem here is the fact that she stands nearly a head taller than me and probably weighs as much or more as me. She is tall, dark and pretty and I am short, blond and slender. What could she see in me?"

As we were walking back for dinner, Granny said, "I really don't think you have a problem with the girl. The problem is, if you stick your nose in where it's not supposed to be you may get yourself in trouble. You need to let your friend make his own decisions." Granny looked me right in the eyes.

The rest of the family was gathering around the table for dinner. I went to wash my hands. Mom asked Granny if she thought it was all right to spend the night with my friend.

"Yes, I think Johnny will be fine but I'm not sure about his friend Harry that's going to this initiation for this club. That sounds strange to me. In my day there wasn't much of that unless you were in the very wealthy class and were inducted into a society at a university or college, but that never was in my choices to make being humble and from the mountains." They all laughed at Granny's description and started the blessing when I sat down.

After dinner, I changed into a pair of jeans and a white T-shirt, with my comb sticking out of my back pocket. Granny asked me for a hug and slipped me a five-dollar bill and whispered, "Buy your girl a drink or a sweet treat tonight!" I smiled and thanked her.

I rode my bike to Frances' place, a beautiful large yellow bungalow with a red terra cotta tile roof with tall palms and red hibiscus and other tropical flowers all around the sprawling yard. This was one of the impressive properties that I passed when I rode the school bus during the year. I never knew it was Frances' parents' home.

Everyone was gathered at the garage where Frankie and his brothers had their motorcycles and cars parked. Frankie was the youngest boy in the family. He had two older brothers and their little sister Frances, who was a few years younger than Frank. There were three boys in the family with three cars and three motorcycles. They sure needed the garage because something always needed repair. The two older brothers didn't seem to be a part of Frank's organization.

I had been at the Hut several times, but most members didn't even acknowledge my presence. Tonight, though, Frankie did walk over and say to me, "I hear you would like to ride along tonight with Frances and be a spectator."

"Yes, I'm not sure what a spectator does but I'd like to ride with Frances. We are sorta' an item now," I said.

"That's another thing. I don't want you screwing around with my little sister even if you're only almost fourteen. I remember at twelve I was hard half the day." He laughed and slapped me up the side of my head with his huge hand.

I wasn't sure but figured Frankie was at least 6'3" because the oldest brother Nick was 6'6'' and there were just a few inches difference in their height. Frankie had played high school football as a defensive end but had been hurt his senior year with a bad knee injury that left him with a slight limp.

"Everybody grab your gear and let's move over to the Hut before the show starts," Bruno, the leader, said.

Frances came out of the house the moment he gave the command to mount up. She said, "Climb on behind me, babe … you're mine for the night."

The motorcycles fired up with a roar and the six rode over to the Hut where there were more than ten others waiting. I tried to size up the group. Some were male, some female, some young and some old.

The older guys looked to be the worst of the bunch—dirty, with half-grown beards, long hair and tattoos all over them. This seemed to be a theme with the older guys; most of the younger guys couldn't grow a beard, but long hair was a must. They all had on jeans with white (well, close to white) T-shirts and black boots. Some could not afford their own bike yet, so they rode with their friends until they could.

I was obviously the youngest and almost the smallest of the gang. There was one small, short, red-headed guy with a ponytail they all called "Shorty." He had big man-size arms and walked like a small gorilla and talked very little.

After a few minutes, a big Cadillac pulled up at the Hut. The back door opened and out stepped Harry. The guys ushered him into a room where Frankie and Bruno were waiting. I wasn't sure what they were doing to Harry or telling him, but he seemed okay when they brought him out blindfolded. They explained to the gang he was to be taken to a secret spot near the Okeechobee swamp, tied up, and left from seven o'clock until he could free himself, while blindfolded and naked. When free, he had to make his way back to Palm Bay and turn himself into the police to get his clothes that will have been left there by some unknown person.

I thought the only problem with this plan was who was going to tie him, how naked would he be, and could he withstand the varmints of the night, having no light and nothing to defend himself if there were a stray wild boar, alligator or some other predator?

We all piled on the bikes and roared out toward the western sunset and down alligator alley toward Lake Okeechobee, arguably one of the biologically richest places in Florida. The lake floodplain forest and swamp and the area immediately around it had more species of plants and animals than just about any comparable area anywhere in North America. It was a place not yet completely explored, much like the upper Amazon in South America, according to our science teacher.

The area surrounding the lake was a vast jungle wilderness where dozens of tributaries braided together and twisted apart, creating hundreds of small islands around the lake. Those islands, channels and tributaries were populated with numerous creatures capable of killing a person—especially an unarmed and unsuspecting person: bears, alligators, bobcats, cougars, feral hogs, foxes, and wild dogs, plus more than five species of venomous snakes and multiple poisonous spiders. There are more than 300 bird species and an untold variety of insects, amphibians and other reptiles.

But more than anything else, Lake Okeechobee was the home and hunting grounds for Indians more than a thousand years ago, and still is to a few surviving tribes like the Seminole.

The woods are spooky and dangerous, especially at night. Landmarks and trails vanish quickly in the swamp, leaving thick jungle and forest. The summer months come to life with the buzz of tens of thousands of insects and the chatter of an army of night birds, as well as the bellow of spawning alligators. A boat that would lose power in this jungle would quickly find itself in a dangerous situation, pinned against a cypress or gum tree by the dark murky water.

All this was going through my mind as I hugged Frances and rode quietly as her passenger.

When we arrived at the pre-selected designation some thirty minutes later, Frankie, Bruno, and Cowboy took Harry to see that he was tied up correctly. Everyone else was to gather some firewood and get a bonfire started. Nelson and Cheri were to bring the ice chest with the beer, hot dogs and hamburgers to eat.

Frances and I moved from her Triumph Sportster and got an old cypress log to sit on and rolled it up to where the fire was going. It seemed like Frances was going about this like she had done it before, so I just helped her get the area ready for the party.

It was getting dark by now in the dense swampy forest and the gang was scurrying around busily, so they didn't notice Frances pull me into the woods with her. There, between some palmettos and some mossy overgrowth, Frances made us a little nest. She said, "This is going to be our hideout for the evening after the party gets going and they all are pretty wasted. We can slip away and have our own party right here. How does that sound? You aren't afraid of the dark or me, are you, Johnny?"

I knew what she had in mind and that was about the only thing that would keep my mind off what was happening to Harry. We made our way back to the group. Someone lit the bonfire and a church key was being passed around to open the beer. Couples were getting their favorite spots around the fire. One of the guys brought a guitar and another pulled out a harmonica and they began to make what they called music.

Shortly after dark, the three leaders returned, and Bruno simply said, "Well, we have big Harry all greased up and ready for the roast. I don't think he'll be getting loose anytime soon unless he fools me."

I looked at Frances and leaned over and squeezed her hand. Frances soon saw the opportunity to sneak away to our little hideaway. We could see the fire from the tiny nest we had made. Big wild banana foliage, the scent of Poinciana, and fresh guava made this a perfect spot to lie and look at the moon. Frances and I covered the floor of our little nest area with banana leaves as we prepared for the evening.

"I really don't like the drinking and smoking, Johnny, so I hope you don't mind just cuddling up with me," Frances said.

"No, I really don't mind at all. I'm not much of a drinker and I don't smoke either," as I reached for her to come closer. She ran her fingers through my hair and down my chest.

"You know we're both the same size lying down, Johnny," Frances said as we cuddled.

Frances and I lay there looking up at the moon and stars on the steamy, humid, but beautiful starlit evening. We could still hear the gang noises as they were drinking, singing, and arguing about anything boys could argue about, especially sports.

I heard a strange sound from the swamp area where they had taken Harry.

"Stay here a minute, Frances. I think we have a visitor." I got up, slipped my boots on and crept into the darkness like a ninja. I was at home in the woods, ready for any animal, because I knew that most were more afraid of humans and would only attack if cornered or hungry.

However, this was a different sound. It was like a big animal tramping through the wild bananas, palmettos and underbrush of the area. The others couldn't hear it because of the noise of the party going on. Then I got a glimpse of the animal silhouette in the moonlight. It was big, like Harry, or some other big person roaming around the area. I had to get closer to really see before I gave my position away. I only moved when the shadow moved—the simultaneous movement would cancel out the noise created. I learned this from my father tracking and hunting animals in the mountains. After getting very close to the silhouette, I whispered, "Harry, is that you?"

The shadow jumped, and a voice came back, "Damn, Johnny, you just about scared the shit outta me. Here I am, naked as a jaybird and can't see much of anything except the bonfire. I've got cuts and scrapes all over me. I'm probably bleeding like a stuck pig. I'm trying to make my way around the fire to get to the road outta here."

"Harry, take my underwear and at least you'll have something on if you get out on the highway."

"Okay, that's a good idea if I can get them on; remember how much bigger I am than you."

"Do the best you can; at least they may cover the essentials." I took off my pants and gave Harry my blue boxer underwear.

After the change, Harry told me how easy it was getting out of the bindings and the blindfold. "They didn't know how to even tie a knot or anything, but getting through the swamp and back is going to be a bitch.

"You know I'm at home in the forest. It's just around people that I have trouble. I'm going to head toward Palm Bay. It may take me the remainder of the night to get there if no one gives me a ride—not that I blame them—but I'll make it to the police department sometime tonight."

"Okay, Harry, be careful. It was twenty minutes here going sixty miles an hour. You can calculate how far that is from the Hut," I told him.

I made my way back to Frances and our little love nest. I told Frances what had transpired, and that Harry was on his way back to Palm Bay through the swamp. She wasn't very concerned about Harry—she was more concerned about taking up where we left off with our lovin'.

Around midnight most everyone was ready to fire up the

bikes and make the trip to Palm Bay. We tore ourselves apart and followed in the designated riding positions we had been assigned by Bruno. On the way back, I kept looking in areas for Harry, but never caught a glimpse of him anywhere.

Upon arriving in Palm Bay, the gang first went to the Hut to either continue partying or to separate and get their vehicles. I was out for the night and wasn't sure where to go from here now that everyone was going their individual way.

I knew I couldn't stay at the Hut because I was not a member. I also knew that Frances was expected home shortly after midnight. I just asked Frances to let me off in the middle of the town of Palm Bay. From there I figured I could go either way toward the beach or toward town. She let me go reluctantly, asking me to call the next day to see what happened to Harry. We kissed, and I climbed off the bike.

I walked toward the center of town where there was a small diner open until two a.m. to serve the late-night crowd. I could wait there and drink a cup of coffee, even though I really didn't like the taste of the stuff. My father and mother would always sit up late on weekends there in Palm Bay, playing music and drinking coffee instead of beer and liquor like they did in West Virginia. I wasn't quite sure why the change, but they seemed the same either way.

Back in Palm Bay

As I sat in the Fish River Diner, I was amazed at the variety of people who came in late at night.

When I first went in a little after midnight, there was only one other person there. I sat in a booth at the far end and in the corner, so I could see everything. Something I also learned from my dad, "Always keep your back to the wall and everyone in front of you when possible."

First, a young black couple came in and sat two booths away

and ordered burgers and milkshakes. They sat there and acted like they were on a date, holding hands and flirting with each other.

Then, another young couple came in and they seemed argumentative. He was trying to convince her of something, but she was not changing her mind so far. They sat at the counter and ordered breakfast off the menu.

Next, an older couple came in, about the same age as Mom and Dad, with graying hair.

I told Miss Bessie, the owner, "I'm Johnny. I'll have a cup of coffee for now. I live over in the Jungle Park development and I'll stop in when I have the money to buy something. Right now, I'm waiting on a friend of mine to get to the police station. He has to pick up some clothes there. How far am I from the police station, anyway?"

"You are two blocks away, darling. Just walk out the door, go left two blocks, then right a block and you'll be there."

I had the five dollars Granny had given me and sat there until 1:45, ate two pieces of pie, and drank two cups of coffee. On my way out, Bessie wouldn't take my five-dollar bill and asked me to come back as soon as I could. I thanked her again and left, and followed her directions that brought me directly in front of the Palm Bay Police Station.

I wasn't sure what to do, but had to try something. I went in and asked the policeman behind a big glass window if a boy had been by there tonight to pick up his clothes that were left here. The big bulky policeman said, "Damn, son, you must have radar. We just took a boy back to lock-up for indecent exposure. Out running around in a skimpy little pair of blue underwear, all torn nearly half off, bloody and cut up like he had been in a fight. Luckily, one of our senior officers had a spare set of jeans and a T-shirt in his squad locker and let him get dressed here. He's in the back now, trying to get fixed up decent enough to go home."

"Can I see him?"

"I suppose so. What is your name?"

"Johnny, officer, Johnny is my name." As I followed the policeman back to the jail cells where several men were being held and yelling profanity from different cells, we passed into another room. The officer went to tell Harry someone came to see him, but they were working on Harry. He was all scratched and bruised up but still could smile. "Johnny, what are you doing here?"

"I just wanted to make sure you're all right and could get home. I'm supposed to be spending the night with you ... anyway, that's what I told my mother."

"This kind young Officer West said he would take me home when I got myself together enough to be sure my parents were not suspicious of anything. Now I can just tell them you and I were out night hunting or something like that, okay?"

"Okay, Harry."

Officer West came back and asked if he was ready. Harry asked if I could go home with him, and the officer said fine. Officer West was big and strong and just threw Harry and me in the back seat like a couple of criminals, turned the lights and siren on all the way out of town—we sure got a kick out of that. On the way, I asked Officer West if he had young kids like us. He responded by saying, "No, I'm not married but I have a beautiful young sister that you better not know." We didn't say another word.

Chapter 36

Either I will find a way or I will make one.
Courtney Stone

Prized Indian River Citrus

I was returning home one night from being at the teen club with our friends and Frances, who had become my "sweetheart," as she called me. It was a little before midnight. Dad and Mom always said, "Nothing good ever happens after midnight." I had danced nearly every dance with Frances and a few other girls. Harry and the gang were out riding with the bikers, so that left the younger boys like me at the teen club with the girls. I was fine with dancing every dance if the music was good, and it was especially good that night with a new disc jockey named Terry Madden.

I felt special that evening because my granny had bought me a new motorcycle jacket and I decided to wear it over my white T-shirt with jeans like the big motorcycle guys. The black leather with silver studs had cost Granny a lot of money, but she bought this as an early birthday present … and she was right, I was two weeks from being fourteen.

I was walking back home on the dark, lonely back road I used all the time to Palm Bay. This was the same shortcut road about a half-mile from my house that Granny and I had taken. It was more than a mile more to get into Palm Bay, but this was a short cut for cars and walkers. It had no lights, so most people only used the road during the day.

That night, few cars passed and no walkers as I strolled back from the dance thinking about the girls I had danced with. I went by the sign that read *Indian River Fruit ... prized citrus of Florida*. This sign I am sure I had read more than a hundred times, but never read the *No Trespassing* part of the sign. A big, high wooden and chain link fence assured there would be few who would disobey the sign.

I was hungry and thirsty from all the dancing, or maybe just a little curious like most teenagers, and went to the fence and peeked through a knothole. It was a huge expanse of orange trees with a house almost in the middle of the grove about a football field away. There were four big lights on poles in the trees in different corners of the grove behind the house.

I decided I wanted to have a big juicy orange if I could find the right tree. Getting over the fence was the first obstacle because the fence was topped with barbed wire. That was probably the idea behind the wire in the first place, but they didn't know the persistence I had when deciding to do something.

There was a large palm tree beside the fence. I went over to the tree and began to climb. When I got about even with the top of the fence I jumped, and landed well inside the fenced area. Now my mission was to find a plump, juicy prized Indian River orange, devour it, and be on my way. I looked and looked, and it seemed not all the trees had fruit and the ones that did were not ripe. Did I just break all those rules to be denied an orange? I continued to look for oranges throughout the grove. Finally, down near the house, there were about ten trees with big luscious oranges that were ripe.

When I got to the trees, I noticed there were no oranges on any of the lower limbs and that meant I would still have to climb with my hand bleeding and hurt from tangling with the barbed wire. I jumped up, grabbed a limb and pulled into the tree. As this was happening, some additional lights came on in the grove. A few minutes later, a loud siren sound started—three loud blasts, then they stopped for a few seconds, and then an additional three blasts. This went on for a few minutes, followed by a man's voice that came on the speaker, "You're trespassing—get out of my grove." This was repeated several times. Then the voice said, "If you don't get out, I'll shoot."

That's when I made my biggest mistake. I yelled, "Shoot, damn it, shoot if you are that good." Sure enough, there was a blast from the back of the house toward my voice and then another blast.

The next thing I remember, I woke up in the hospital with doctors and nurses all around, talking. I was on my side and felt a throbbing pain somewhere between my shoulders. One doctor said to another, "This is one lucky young man. Another few millimeters and the shell would have torn through the spinal column and he would never have walked again and possibly would have died. At least now he has a good chance at survival."

For some reason I could not talk and could only hear what was going on around me.

After they worked on me another hour or so, a doctor said, "Okay, I think that will do it. Go ahead, stitch him up and we'll just have to see if there are any problems from the lead. The good thing is that he's young, strong, and the lead was not in him long."

I drifted back off to sleep again. When I awoke the next time, there were familiar faces around the bed.

"Hi, Johnny," Mom said. "You really caused a scare at home. The police came to our door sometime after midnight and said you had been shot and you were on your way to the hospital. They didn't give us any details, just said to get to the hospital as fast as we could. What in the world happened?"

They really didn't know what had happened until after they got to the hospital and talked to Mr. Vincent, the owner of the orange grove.

He told them, "Johnny was up in my trees stealing oranges and used some profanity when I asked him to get out of the trees and leave my oranges alone. That made me mad and I grabbed my gun, but I grabbed the wrong one. I meant to shoot with birdshot but instead it was the gun I used deer hunting with pumpkin balls."

Mom related this with tears in her eyes.

"Johnny, you still have not said a word. Either you can't talk, or you are afraid to talk because of the trouble you're in with dad," my brother said.

"Well, let's not put blame anywhere yet, let's concentrate on him getting better and back home. Then we'll sort through the blame game. I feel better just seeing him able to open his eyes and hear what's going on. A few days ago, we thought we were going to lose him because he was unconscious and not responding," someone said. I drifted back off again.

A nurse came in and asked if everyone could leave because they wanted to do a brief exam of the wound. I was so weak that I couldn't even manage a goodbye to everyone. I just lifted my hand to wave, not enough to be noticed by most, I'm sure.

In the next five days, they were moving me up and about, walking the halls. Dr. Winston told Mom and Granny, "It's probably a good thing Johnny was wearing the thick, heavy leather jacket that night because it either stopped or greatly slowed the impact of the shell as it entered his back. That was one thing that helped save his life."

These words made me remember the new jacket that Granny had just bought me the day before the dance. No one had mentioned anything about that night, even when they came to see me for my fourteenth birthday spent in the hospital. Neither

Frances, Harry, nor any of the school gang seemed like they wanted to talk about the forbidden topic while at the hospital. *Where was the jacket and how bad was it torn up from the gunshot*, I wondered? I just couldn't believe I was here in the hospital on my birthday.

I would think about that later. I just wanted to get better and get back home. The summer was just about over, and I wanted to play football in the fall when school started back.

"Are you all right, Johnny?" a black lady asked me. I didn't recognize her at first, and then she said, "Did you forget Miss Bessie and her sweet potato pie?"

I smiled and said, "Of course not, who could forget that wonderful pie. You know I've been meaning to get back over to the diner to sample another sweet potato, pecan or maybe some apple pie." I laughed out loud and hard for the first time.

"I was here visiting my aunt and heard someone say that you had been in an accident and was laid up in here; thought I would stop by to say hello. You take care of yourself and I'll see you soon in Palm Bay." She winked and smiled.

Later that week, Mom and Granny came in and told me I was going to be released in an hour or two and would be able to go home. "We're here to take you back home."

When we came out of the hospital to get the car, there was a shiny new 1955 green Pontiac Chieftain.

"Wow, Mom, when did you get this?" I asked.

"Come on, get in, and I'll tell you all about what's happened in the past three weeks while you were in the hospital," Mom said.

"I had nothing to do with any of it," Granny said.

"I'm interested now—tell me more. I can't wait," I said with wonderment.

"Well, there was a lot of controversy when you were shot. At first everyone was on the farmer's side and said the thief deserved what he got. Then when everyone learned from a newspaper article that you were only thirteen and have had no strikes against you, the pendulum swung the other way. There was public outcry," Mom said.

"That did it. I went to the newspaper office and asked if anyone knew the person accused of this horrible crime was a thirteen-year-old boy with no record. A reporter took the information and turned it into a story about a farmer who was trigger-happy and money-hungry, protecting his prize fruit and quickly shot a young boy just wanting an orange to eat on his way home from a teen dance here in Palm Bay," Granny said.

"Then the following week an insurance company called me and wanted to set up a meeting to talk about the case. The farmer, Mr. Vincent, was going to press charges of trespassing and theft of property," said Mom. "There was this big hearing at the courthouse; Flem, your grandma, and I went. We had to get a babysitter for Douglas because they wouldn't let children attend the hearing," Mom said.

"Tell Johnny what the result was after the judge heard the case," Granny urged.

"Yes, Johnny, we were ready for a real fight to keep you from being charged with a crime and having it follow you the rest of your life. What happened surprised all of us.

"The judge looked up after hearing the case from both sides and said he was shocked that Mr. Vincent would even consider shooting someone for climbing his prize orange trees, let alone actually firing two shots at an unknown person. The excuse that he grabbed the wrong gun made it even worse, the judge said. The judge ordered the plaintiff to pay the hospital charges, and the insurance company paid ten thousand dollars, a part of which was to pay for school expenses while you were out of school doing therapy," Mom stated.

After hearing this story from Mom and Granny, I didn't

know what to think. I was ready to take the blame and punishment for doing the wrong thing and making the wrong choice. I knew I shouldn't have climbed up that tree and jumped over the fence, let alone attempt to steal the orange even if I was young and couldn't be charged as an adult. It was just not the right thing—those were not my oranges.

That night at the dinner table, when Dad gave thanks for the food, he also included a little sermon for me. *The fact that Johnny was wrong in the eyes of God, but was found innocent by his fellow man because of his age was a chance for Johnny to realize he needs to follow laws and directions as others are asked to do. Thank you, God, for delivering him back to us.*

To me this was a sign that I should be thankful from then on for the blessings bestowed on our family by the judge. It made me stop and think about the results of my actions and how they could have had an effect on everyone around me.

Chapter 37

"Embrace the glorious mess you are."
Elizabeth Gilbert

Fight or Flight

I was restricted from playing any sports the following year. If injury occurred, the wound could be breached by the trauma involved in sports. This broke my heart, but Granny thought this might be my universal punishment for the crime that I had committed and had to be paid for. She said it was something called Karma; I really didn't understand, even after she tried to explain it to me.

Not being able to play sports and be involved with physical activity was not a good thing for me because it led to a poor selection of friends, and that led to skipping school and going on little day trips. Dad had given me permission to begin practicing my driving. After all I was now fourteen and eligible for my driver's permit and my motorcycle license. I wondered why Florida was different from most other states and allowed an individual to drive at fourteen—regardless, I was now in that category.

I got to know the family that lived near us that had moved from Tennessee. Charlie was eighteen, the oldest, then the younger sister Betty, sixteen, and the little brother David, fourteen, the same age as me.

David started hanging around with me because of our

similar interest in music: Elvis, Buddy Holly, Chuck Berry, Nat King Cole, Etta James, Duke Ellington, and the new soul artist, a blind, black singer by the name of Ray Charles.

David's family had just moved down from the Memphis area and was big into country and western music. Dad and Mom were former country and western performers at the Grand Ole Opry and along the Appalachian and Atlantic seaboard. As a result, David and I got along well except that David didn't like school and I did. One day, David, Betty and I were walking to the bus stop, along with a few other kids. David said, "Damn, it's too nice a morning to go sit in class all day. Who wants to cut school with me on this nice October morning and go to the beach?"

"Friday should be an 'Off–Day' anyway. I'm game," said Betty.

Everyone had agreed except me and a cute thirteen-year-old girl by the name of Veronica, who lived three doors down.

"I'll miss seeing my girlfriend, plus I've got to start doing better in my classes. Missing a day won't help," I told them.

"Look at that surf and sunshine. We can get a radio, spend the day at the dunes just messin' around and having a good ole time," David coaxed.

I turned toward the group and said, "Veronica, be sure that you don't tell your parents about this. I know I'm going to regret this decision, but it is an awfully nice morning to have to go to school!"

Decision made, our group hid behind Mr. Sullivan's store until the bus came for the pickup. Veronica, who had decided not to skip with us, and Josh, a twelve-year-old, had gotten on the bus. We tried to decide where to go for the day and finally settled on a little beach about a mile south of town that few ever visited. It was called Jensen Beach and was more family oriented, but had a couple great coves for hiding and riding on

the beach. I remembered Frances taking me there the first time I
went for a motorcycle ride and I began to feel guilty until Betty
said, "Come on, Johnny. I can't wait to get your mind on
something other than that big Amazon you've been seeing for
the last few months. I think there are other girls who are a better
fit for you."

Betty grabbed my hand and pulled me toward her. She was
an attractive blonde, with blue eyes, freckles and a ponytail. She
had the perfect body, like the acrobats and gymnasts in school,
and not one blemish on her perfect skin. And best of all, we were
the same height.

"We look like we could be brother and sister, or at least
kissin' cousins," Betty said, smiling.

David said, "I don't know if Johnny wants to get involved
with us, Charlie, our oldest brother is quite different and not
someone to be taken lightly. Dad and Uncle Jimmy keep him
within arms-length ninety percent of the time and that's still not
enough to keep him out of trouble most of the time."

As we three walked along Indian River toward Jensen
Beach, we shared experiences and tales of each other's family
until I felt completely at home with the brother and sister from
Memphis. That day we walked the beach, talked about school
friends and ate at a little beachfront deli. There was nothing that
surprised me except how boring it was not to be in school.
School was always so much fun and social and interactive to me.

That evening I felt guilty and told my grandmother all about
skipping school, which I had never done before—who went with
me and what we did. She was not angry or upset while listening.
I told her, "I really didn't enjoy the day nearly as much as I
thought. I like being in school and probably won't do it again."

Granny laughed and said, "When I was young, I was a little
like that myself, glad to go to school to keep from having to work
so much on the farm; there was always chores, chores, chores

for us. School was like a short vacation each week."

However, several weeks after skipping school I was walking and talking with Betty, David and several more going toward the school bus stop. Charlie, their older brother, yelled at them, "Stop, I need to talk to you. Where you all going?" He was talking to David directly then.

"To school, Charlie," David answered.

"No, I need you to watch something first."

"What is it? We're going up here to Mr. Sullivan's store to our bus stop."

"Okay, that'll be fine, you all can watch the guy I want to make a point with. He's going to be stopping here for gas in a few minutes," Charlie said to everyone.

Charlie, a slender guy a few inches taller than me at 5'8" and about the same weight, ran on ahead of the group and stood at the red and blue Mobile Oil gas pumps. A large man wearing a red baseball cap, with dark hair, and about six feet tall, got out of his old Dodge pickup and started to pump his gas. Mr. Sullivan came out and began a conversation with the man.

About a minute or two later, Charlie ran three steps at the man and hit him square in the face without warning. His nose blew apart, blood flew everywhere and even his hair seemed to fly off with his cap. He staggered back a few steps and fell to one knee. Charlie hit him again on the other side of the face with all his might. The man fell over and lay there bleeding and moaning.

Mr. Sullivan was horrified and yelled at Charlie as Charlie just strolled away toward his father's house where the workers gathered each morning. Mr. Sullivan ran in and called the local Palm Bay police from his grocery store and gas station.

The other kids and I were all astounded at what had just occurred. No one had seen the man do anything to Charlie before the physical violence took place—all we knew was what Charlie had told us five minutes before it happened.

That day at school, I thought about the incident all morning. At lunch break, I asked David, "Is that what you mean by your father and uncle having to keep Charlie within arms-reach? Man, he really knocked the hell out of that guy for no apparent reason at all this morning."

"Yes, that is just what I mean. Charlie started doing that kind of thing, very physical, about two years ago. Just randomly picking someone and attacking with an all-out flurry of fist and fury then just walking away. My father has had to pay big fines in Tennessee and we think that was the reason Dad took this job in Florida. We have now been here three months and it's started again.

Johnny, what I am afraid of is my father, not Charlie. You see my father was a prizefighter in the ring for about fifteen years and retired when he just about killed another fighter during a match. Charlie went to see that fight the night it happened and has been like this ever since, but it seems to be getting worse."

"How could it get any worse? Charlie just sucker-punched the guy without him ever seeing him coming. He is really going to hurt someone without a reason," I said.

"No, he already has. He did the same thing to three sailors walking down the street in Memphis. He broke one guy's nose, the other had a broken jaw, and the third had a severe trauma to his eyes.

After that happened, my father had to pay several thousand dollars in fines and hospital bills and then in addition started looking for other places to live so Charlie wouldn't go to jail. We're not sure why we had to leave our home, but a judge said, 'Charlie's going to prison for a few years if this happens again, Mr. Shelton.'"

"Wow, I've never seen anyone do that to more than one person," I told David and Betty.

"Yes, it doesn't matter what the number is, if Charlie is in one of his moods they are all in trouble. He is so fast with his fist and has no restraint. Two guys he just about beat to death were bigger and older than Charlie but that didn't stop him."

That day after school when I got home there were two police cars sitting in front of Charlie's house waiting for Charlie and his uncle's work crew to arrive that evening. When the crew showed up, the two big cops put Charlie in handcuffs and guided him to the back of a police cruiser.

That was the last time I ever saw Charlie. The whole family moved within about two weeks of Charlie's arrest. He was eventually sent away to a prison in Georgia, his parents told Dad.

Sometime later, I overheard my mother and father talking and they said that Mr. Sullivan had the whole family kicked out of the Jungle Park subdivision. Mr. Sullivan felt the boy (Charlie) was dangerous and felt the whole family could have the same problem, so he just asked them all to leave. I never saw any of the family after that incident.

I thought maybe I would get a letter from David and Betty because David and I were close, but I never did. I think they were embarrassed about their brother.

Chapter 38

"Grow through what you go through."
Dwight Pailing

The Downhill Slide

After the Shelton family moved, it was another change for me. I had lost another buddy and I just couldn't throw myself into my schoolwork like before because of not being able to play sports that year. As a result, I found myself hanging with the "hoods" rather than the athletes where I usually was during and after school.

One night in late November after a Friday night football game, several of the guys asked me to go with them so they would have enough muscle to push a car. "Where's the car we are to push?" I asked the driver, Butch Castro. He was a big, burly Latino guy, about twenty, who had dropped out of school and was always fighting, drinking, stealing, or doing something that was on the wrong side of the law. I didn't like to judge, but I knew I shouldn't be there.

"We're going to pick up a vehicle that was left for us, but the car may have a dead battery and need a push. We need a couple of strong guys like you and Steve to help us."

Neither I nor Steve Ruddish, my classmate, knew Butch Castro before that night—we had only heard of him and his rough friends. Steve and I both were walking that night and didn't have a ride from the game back to Palm Bay. We decided we would take Butch's offer to help them out with the car this time.

After being in Butch's black '49 Mercury with fender skirts, glass pack mufflers and souped-up engine, Steve and I were relaxed and doing fine in ten minutes. Tom McClure was riding shotgun, another high school dropout also known for his unsavory ways. Steve and I were in the backseat just taking it in but not really knowing what was going on with the two of them.

"Drop me and the boys off up here at the corner. We'll walk from there and push the car out to the street and then I'll get in and you two push until it starts. Then jump in and we'll take the car to Butch's place. We can drop you in town when we return later," Tom whispered as if he didn't want anyone to hear us.

"Where's the car now and how far do we have to push?" Steve asked.

"Not far, fifteen or twenty feet if it's a straight stick," Tom said quietly as we started up the driveway of a large white house.

No lights were on at the house, like no one was home. There was a new white Caddy convertible sitting right in front of the two-car garage. Tom went up to the car and began to do something to the driver's side window. All of a sudden, the glass just fell straight down like someone rolled the window down. Tom reached in and pulled up the locks so the doors would open, stuck his head under the dashboard, and lit his cigarette lighter. In a minute his head came up and then he reached down and let off the emergency brake and the car began to roll ever so slowly.

Next, Tom pointed to the rear of the car for us to push. Steve and I began to push the big Caddy down the long drive with Tom steering. When we got to the road in about five minutes, he signaled to push harder. He touched something under the dash and the car started. He signaled to jump in and in just a minute we were gone … down the street with no lights on. When we got to the highway, Tom hit the light button and everything lit up in

ONE WILD AND PRECIOUS LIFE

the Caddy.

"How was that guys … just like it was meant to be? This is now my fifth heist and each one gets easier and smoother; with you guys, there was nothing to it," Tom said.

Steve and I looked at each other—we had just helped steal a car without knowing it. Now what were we going to do? We were now involved and would be hauled off to jail if this ever became public. Steve and I didn't say a word—just rode in the stolen Caddy to the hiding place.

"How did you get the car to start without the key?" I asked.

"Hell man, that's the easy part. Just pop the plate off over the ignition and pull the two wires down, cross the hot and the ground and *voila,* it fires right up."

"How did you learn how to do that?" was Steve's question.

"Well, I spent a year in a detention center, now called reform school, in Miami, and there were a lot of 'educated' boys in there who taught us a lot about surviving on the street and that was one of the useful things. We got to where we could hot-wire a car in two minutes."

We soon pulled into a garage parking lot. It had cars all around in different states of disrepair. Tom jumped out, tapped three times on the big metal door, and it slid open slowly and quietly. Tom jumped back in and drove the Caddy inside to a small enclosure within the garage.

"Come on, you guys, our job is done … it's all theirs from this point; let me stop and pick up my cut," Tom said.

Tom went over to two men. The men looked at him, but didn't say anything. One guy gave Tom three hundred-dollar bills and said, "Nice doing business with you again. I see you have a couple of new partners."

Tom didn't say anything, just took the money put it in his jeans and pushed Steve and me toward the door. "Let's go guys; we have to meet Butch in a few minutes."

That was how I got tangled up with a gang of thugs or punks without ever knowing, not really being discriminate. Guys who were youth on the edge of right and wrong and thinking the little wrong they were doing was not that bad. They did not see themselves as part of the escalation of crimes they would begin to commit over the next few years.

I knew better and was raised not to do things like that, but I found myself hanging around these types of kids when I was not allowed to participate in the athletics that I loved.

About two weeks after the car theft, I wanted to see if I could duplicate the hot-wiring technique that I had seen Tom do. One Saturday when mom and dad were at work and Granny had taken Douglas to the dentist, I saw a chance to try out the new skill I had observed.

Dad always left his car unlocked but took the keys with him to work. I got a screwdriver and some pliers and went under the dashboard like Tom had said. I saw the panel on the steering column covering the wires and unscrewed that; the wires were exposed and I pulled them down, took the pliers and snipped them, and then took the red wire and touched it to the steering column assembly, and the new Pontiac Chieftain fired up. I couldn't believe it ... I really did it!

Now what did I want to do? I decided to take the car for a spin. I knew I had no license or even a learner's permit, but I thought I sort of knew how to drive. I got behind the wheel like Dad and put my foot on the brake, shifted the Chieftain down into "DRIVE," and the car began to move. A big smile came across my face. I looked in the mirror and saw that I only could see the top of my head, so I applied the brakes, came to a stop, and adjusted the mirror to fit my view. Then I took off again with a little more push on the gas pedal. The Pontiac surged and spun the back tires, they hit the road with a slight squeal and a little faster than wanted or was safe, but I managed to straighten the wheels and get back on my side of the road. I figured I had command of the vehicle and now I would ride to Palm Bay, cruise around town, and then bring the car back without anyone knowing.

As I drove toward town I rolled down the window, put my arm on the window ledge, and began driving with one hand like I had seen dad do many times.

Driving through town, I saw two of my classmates and honked the horn at them and waved. I wanted to stop and show off a little but couldn't because I was unsure of backing up, so I continued toward the middle of town and stopped for a red light when a police car pulled up behind the Pontiac.

"God," I thought, *"this cop is going to take me in for sure."* I began to get ready to be stopped. The light turned green and I pushed easily on the gas pedal. The police car followed me a block and then, much to my relief, turned toward the downtown police station.

"Damn, that was close," I said to myself. I decided to drive back home and park the car as close to exactly where my father had left it as possible. I sure didn't want my father to think I had stolen the car and taken it for a spin because I was going to ask him for permission to get my learner's permit that Christmas.

When I got back home, I tried to pull into dad's parking position just like he would. I checked and made sure the ignition wires were tucked back under the dash and the little panel screwed back and there was no sign of anyone being in the car before I got out and went up to Mr. Sullivan's store where mom was working. I was relieved I hadn't been caught.

That evening at dinner, Granny said, "You know, Flem, Douggie and I saw a car just like yours today in Palm Bay. But we were a block away and couldn't see the man driving. I wanted to tell him how nice the car was but he pulled away before we got to the car."

I finished my dinner in a hurry, without a word that evening!

Chapter 38

Travel not to escape life,
but so life doesn't escape you.
Author unknown

Cuban Bananas

I came home one afternoon, and our next-door neighbor was visiting with Mom when I walked in. She said, "Hello, Johnny," and I replied, "How's my next-door neighbor with the beautiful garden? Are you in need of my help yet?" She had a beautiful yard, and I had been asking her for months to let me till and cultivate her flower garden,

"Well, I'm glad you brought that up. You know my husband runs a banana boat out of Ft. Pierce to Havana."

"I remember you said he ran a boat but I had forgotten where, when we talked earlier about the gardening," I said.

"My husband, Emanuel, has several men out sick due to a virus or something, and he was complaining he may not be able to make this week's pick-up and delivery. If that happens it means a lot of people don't get their weekly paycheck and we have a lot of unhappy sailors. Plus, we miss a payment on the boat that the bank will surely question.

He needs two men now for three days work. They get three hundred dollars and meals. They would have to load and unload the bananas when at port in Ft. Pierce and in Havana and usually stay overnight on the boat to ship out early the next morning for

247

the all-day trip. Do you have any friends that want to make some quick money? It's a little heavy work and only a few of the men speak English but they are all good young men on the crew."

"Let me ask some of my friends. When do you need the men?"

"Tomorrow morning," she said.

"That's not much time to find someone," Mom said.

"I know," Mrs. Alvarez, said, "That's why my husband is in such a panic."

"Mom, I have an idea. Let me call Harry and see if he can go. Harry and I could do the job and Harry is bigger than I am. Do you think Mr. Emanuel would let us go and do the work? Mom would let me go for two days with Mr. Alvarez as the captain. He could take care and tell us what to do. It would be an adventure for Harry and me, having never worked on a boat or doing anything like that. It would be fun at the same time. Come on, mom, please." And I begged her in front of Mrs. Alvarez.

"I think it will be all right. We just have to ask your dad tonight when he comes home from work. You talk to Harry and his parents and see if they are okay with the plan. I'm leaving it up to your dad. I'm not getting in the middle of this Huck Finn adventure you are hatching up," Mom said.

"Mrs. Alvarez, tell Mr. Alvarez I'm getting him some help and I'll be sure if we can do it by around six this evening," I told her.

"Oh, Johnny, my husband will be thrilled when I tell him this news. He's now very depressed and sulking all day because he thinks his boat is jinxed with disease and he is going to go broke trying to get the contract for Chautauqua Bananas filled. There's a lot riding on your young shoulders," Mrs. Alvarez said.

"I still think Harry and I can do it. I'll go call now and get back with you as soon as possible this evening," I told her with excitement in my voice.

I called Harry's, but there was no answer, no one home. I thought I would take my bike and ride out there. It wasn't that far, and Harry was probably in the garage tinkering with some project. I told mom I would be back soon and left the house on my bike.

When I got to Harry's place, there was no car or truck in the driveway and that meant no parents were home. *Well, I had come this far I might as well go on up to the house*, I thought. I knocked on the door, no answer. I hollered for Harry. "Harry, Harry, I need you. We can make a lot of money in a short time, but we have to leave tomorrow morning."

In about a minute, Harry came out of the garage wiping his hands on a greasy towel. "What the hell do you want, Stumpy? I heard you out here hollering and thought I better come and rescue you from something you've gotten into."

"Harry, I have come to tell you about a job my next-door neighbor has that needs to be done tomorrow. I think we can do it. We are supposed to be eighteen years old to work on the boat, but the man is in a pinch and will probably let us go this one time until his regular workers are over their illness."

"The boat? What friggin' boat you talkin' about?"

"Mr. Alvarez, my next-door neighbor, is the captain of a banana boat out of Havana bringing them here to Ft. Pierce and other places in Florida. But he has two men out sick and he is in a pinch to get the bananas loaded and unloaded. It takes several hours of hard, heavy lifting, his wife told me. I told them we would help them out this one time if you could go. My mom said it was all right since Mr. Alvarez will be responsible and he's our next-door neighbor. He will take us to the boat in Ft. Pierce and bring us home. We'll be in Havana overnight, but back the next night."

"Well, my dad told me I could join the motorcycle club if I wanted to, but I would have to work and make the money to buy a motorcycle. They cost over five hundred dollars for a second-hand one, so you hit me at the right time. I need the job, alright!" was Harry's answer.

Harry was unsure about his parents giving him permission to go out on a boat with a bunch of strangers, so Harry came up with a plan to go one way or the other. He would tell his mother he was spending the weekend with me at my house. Then he would call her and tell her we had decided to go camping and overnight fishing but not say exactly where. Then on Sunday he would call her when we got to Ft. Pierce and let her know we would be back Sunday evening sometime.

Harry had only one request. He wanted to ask Mr. Alvarez for more money. He thought four hundred dollars for three days would be better than two hundred each. Then he said he could borrow two hundred from me and put the four hundred together with the one hundred he had saved and that would be enough to think about a bike.

That caught me a little off-guard, but I didn't need the money right away for anything urgent like Harry, and as a result, I told him okay because I was more interested in going to Cuba. We would ask to see if Mr. Alvarez agreed.

I jumped on my bike and headed back home, but I decided to stop by the ice cream shop to get a treat. On the way, a motorcycle passed me by. It was Frances riding on the back of a big Harley Hog and she was all hugged up to some guy I had never seen before. I tried to speed up to follow them but there was no use; I was tired after just a half-mile of going all-out and decided to say the heck with her anyway.

That afternoon I called Vivian from the ice cream shop and asked her to go to the movies with me. I had to explain why it had taken so long to call, but I finally convinced her of my good intentions and the fact I had to work after school and any other excuse I could think of. She was so excited she asked where I was right then. I told her the ice cream parlor downtown. She wanted to jump on her bike and meet me there in fifteen minutes. She was home alone, and they lived right in Palm Bay. I agreed to wait, and in ten or fifteen minutes she was there.

I sat and ate ice cream and drank a soda with her for another hour. We kissed goodbye and I came home all giddy and happy about getting my girl back. I didn't know if I was more excited about my upcoming trip to Cuba or my date with Vivian. I had my eye on Vivian for more than three months. She was nice in class, quiet, dressed very smartly, and most of all she was pretty with big blue eyes and coal-black hair, a great combo for my taste.

I got home about four thirty and mom had packed a duffel bag for me. It had an extra pair of jeans, a T-shirt, and a hat for the sun, because I sun burned easily. She even put in a new toothbrush and underwear with a few comic books for Harry and me to read on the boat if we wanted. *What a considerate Mom*, I thought.

I waited until after five, then I called Harry. "Hello, Harry, what do you think? Have you asked your mother yet? I know your father doesn't come home until after five, but I told the Alvarez family I would let them know by six tonight."

"Well, my mother is not in favor of us going off with a bunch of strangers regardless if it's for work or not. She's heard of Cubans taking small boats to the Miami area then coming ashore illegally. She doesn't want me involved with that mess, she said. But I don't care. I'm planning on going with you. I need the money. What time are you leaving with Mr. Alvarez in the morning?"

"I think she said five, because we have to go to the boat docked at Ft. Pierce pier. I don't even know where that is but that's where we'll leave. I don't know how many of us there'll be from there. I don't know much more than you at this stage except I want to go but for a different reason than you. I want to see what it's like in another country like Cuba, Mexico or Canada. I have what my father calls wanderlust. I picked that up reading some adventure stories like Robinson Caruso, Huck Finn and others in class, I guess."

"Ah hell, you're crazy. It's all about the money for me. You have to have money in this country to travel or do much of anything. But let's do it … let's go … count me in regardless whether we have different reasons for going. I'll see you at five in the morning," Harry said.

That evening, when Mrs. Alvarez said her husband was home and would like to talk with me and my father, I thought something was wrong and became worried about the plans. After supper the Alvarez family came over. I didn't realize they had a beautiful daughter I had never seen who was in college in Melbourne.

They brought us a pineapple upside-down cake, mom made coffee, and everyone sat around the living room talking about West Virginia and how they wanted to know about Cuba where the Alvarezes were from.

It finally got down to business and I chimed in that Harry insisted on more money because he was saving for a motorcycle. Mr. Alvarez asked how much more? I told him Harry wanted $400; that way it was two hundred each, and he was going to borrow my two hundred to buy a motorcycle.

"You are not coming out so well in this deal," Mr. Alvarez said.

"Well, he's my friend and I want him to become more involved with the other kids. He's shy and insecure because he is big and fat now, but I told him he can work that fat off."

Tina Alvarez spoke up and said, "If it will help, I could go out with Harry a few times in public to a dance or the movies to boost his ego some and make him less shy," she said.

"That sounds perfect. He's more than a year older than me, taller and bigger. I'll introduce you guys after we return from our boat trip."

"Yes, getting back to business. Johnny, you think you two are up to this? It takes two strong men all day to load and all day to unload the fruit. You'll have to sleep on the boat with several other sailors and workers who don't speak English," Mr. Alvarez said in a gruff ship's-captain voice.

I saluted him, "Aye, aye, sir."

He smiled and said, "I think we have a deal, but if I were you I would build in an interest rate on the money you will be loaning to Harry. It's none of my business but just for safety and good business practice, that's what I would do. I'll see if I can squeeze out a few more dollars for you for getting me the help but it won't be much because my profit margin isn't much."

I could hardly sleep that night. I listened to the radio until after midnight and fell asleep sometime after that. I heard the clock go off the next morning, jumped up, showered, ate a good breakfast mom made, and was ready to go before five. At 5:15 there was a knock at the door. It was Harry, and he came in with a smile on his face. His father had given him permission this morning to go before leaving for work. He was so happy because he really didn't like going against his parents' wishes.

We said goodbye to mom. My dad had already gone to work at five that morning. We told her not to worry, we could handle the work and the strangers, and were anxious for the adventure. We piled in the Alvarez's Jeep and we were off on our voyage for Cuban bananas.

We arrived at the Ft. Pierce docks and Mr. Alvarez checked everything. There were already two big men on board. He introduced them as Chulio and Juan. They were from the

Dominican Republic and were staying at a Catholic mission for the disadvantaged there in town.

Chapter 39

Follow one course until successful.
Captain Alvarez

Cuban Adventure

The nautical terms we were taught on this adventure were sometimes overwhelming. We were out on the Atlantic, but only about five miles off shore, when Captain said, "I think we've caught it ... the Gulf Stream current is flowing almost due south and a leeward breeze to the south is good for us today." It was a beautiful morning and we were cruising about eight or nine knots on the big boat. I asked Chulio what kind of boat it was, but his English wasn't very good and all I got was, "Worka boat."

We spent the next eight hours cruising southward in the 85-degree sunshine with a nice cool breeze blowing from the north. Juan said, "Good sailing weather, making good time."

This was my first experience on a boat, but I didn't want all the others to know—not even Harry. Being from West Virginia and growing up inland, I was not exposed to open water like the intercostal Indian River where we lived, or Atlantic Ocean. I had been fishing on rivers, lakes and dams with my father, but he never had the extra money to buy a boat. Before coming to Florida, I never thought about boating or sailing.

Mr. Alvarez told us he had started sailing with his father at the age of fourteen and eventually moved to Miami and began his own boating business. Harry and I told Mr. Alvarez how we admired his ability to make that all happen during his youth, but he also told us that none of it came without a great sacrifice. He had to leave home at sixteen and begin working full time and that meant not finishing school and starting a family much later than usual.

"What I most missed was not being able to stay in school. I was pretty good at baseball and could hit the ball a country mile. In the summer of my ninth-grade year my father had a heart attack from drinking and smoking too much. The doctors told him to stop but he never listened, and the following year died. My family needed someone to earn a living and I was the only one, because my two sisters could not, and my youngest brother was only ten years old then. I told the principal, and he wished me luck and that was the last I was ever in a schoolhouse," Captain said.

That evening at dinner I talked with Harry about the story, and he too was amazed at the drive and determination of Mr. Alvarez. Harry asked, "Captain, at what age did you get married?"

"Harry, I was twenty-two years old. During those days you had to have something to offer the woman's family. You couldn't just jump into bed with a girl like you can today. You had to romance them and make their parents like you and know that you could provide for their daughter."

"I see, so even though you had a boat that wasn't enough."

"No, that was bought by my father and not completely paid for. I had to provide for my mother and family for the next five years until my sisters and brother were old enough to help. That's why it's important for you and Johnny to stay in school and get a good education so making money is not so hard.

"You see, the deal you made with me is like a contract. You will provide a service for so much money. When that service is accomplished, your work is finished. Then you are free to make another contract. If you become good enough, you can have many contracts with many people and be making big money just sitting on your own boat, office or at home. Working by the hour is labor-for-hire work, and you won't starve, but you will never become rich that way." The captain smiled at us.

Captain Alvarez told Harry and me it was time for bed and showed us the bunks where we slept with the other crewmembers in the belly of the noisy, big work boat that smelled like fish and gasoline. It took me an hour to fall asleep with the tossing and rolling of the boat, but it seemed like it was morning in no time. When I awoke, the men were already up and doing their jobs. Harry and I went up on deck and saw that we were in port.

"Where are we, Captain?"

"You are in Havana, at one time my home port. We will be here a few hours loading cargo. We are waiting for trucks to arrive from the fields in Guines, Matanzas and San Miguel where we get most of the bananas. I will be away to pick up some other merchandise here in Havana, but Juan and Chulio will take care of you guys. You go with them and start loading as soon as the trucks arrive."

"Yes, sir, Captain!" we both repeated.

The captain went to get Chulio and Juan to tell them to show us what to do and how to place the banana cargo in the boat to be able to get in the maximum amount.

As the captain left, he told the guys he would return before five that afternoon, and everything better be loaded. The captain looked at Harry and me and said, "I expect you two to work at your jobs, take the same breaks and lunch as Juan and Chulio and all will be fine. They will be supervising, but it's your job to load and unload the banana cargo."

"Aye, Aye, sir," came out of Harry's mouth first, and I

repeated it instantly.

In a few minutes, Juan came and asked if we wanted breakfast before the truck got there. "Sure, we haven't eaten anything yet." We finished the egg and cheese on home-style Cuban bread like a sandwich. About the time we finished eating, the truck pulled up. It was a big eighteen-wheeler. I was a little shocked at the size but didn't say anything, just followed Juan and Chulio.

They went with the driver to the back of the truck, opened the gates, and it was stacked to the top with green bananas. Juan acted as if he was in charge, and he got the driver to back the truck up close to the boat. They pulled a wide board from under the truck and placed it at the end of the truck and the other end on the boat.

"Walk this way with bananas," Juan said, as he crossed the board with a big stalk of the green bananas on his shoulder and took them below deck at the front of the boat, which he called the bow. He started putting them on one side and each one we brought in was placed beside it, not on top yet. When we got the first row finished, we put cardboard between the bananas so they didn't get mashed or damaged.

Juan and Chulio helped get the first row started and then said, "Now yours." That meant Harry and I were to finish the load that had taken almost an hour to get the first row done. Juan said, "I come back one hour. You finish."

I looked at Harry and thought, *No way would we be able to finish unloading the bananas in that time.* Harry just kept on walking and carrying stalk after stalk like a pack mule. After an hour, I said to Harry, "I need a break man and a drink of water. This is worse than helping my dad carrying cinder blocks; he at least let me take a break."

"Okay, let's take five minutes and I'll see if I can find us some water. There's got to be drinking water somewhere on the boat."

When Harry returned he said, "Look, right down the dock there's a pipe where fresh water is running out to wash and to drink; that's where the men said to use. I got mine and went to the toilet while I was there."

"I'll go now then, back in a few minutes; you say it's right on the pier?"

"Yea, yea, can't miss it. I'm going to start loading again so we can get this finished," Harry said.

Damn, I was impressed. Harry was like an old pack mule, slow and steady, and didn't say a word about all the lifting and hauling. I thought he would be crying by now and I'd have to do all the work but that certainly wasn't the case. Harry was doing more than his fair share of the work and I wouldn't forget it either. We worked two more hours and Juan showed up and said, "Eat time, some lunch. Wash hands and face and we go to favorite place."

Harry and I walked with Chulio and Juan about two blocks off the docks to an area where there were multicolor buildings of two and three stories. Some of the buildings were jammed with people shopping for groceries, flowers and different items. I even saw one man carrying a full-sized skinned pig and another with a big rack of what looked like ribs. I remembered my grandmother showing me what they did and looked like on the farm in West Virginia.

"Shopping and market district," Juan said to Harry, who was now walking beside him. Chulio and I were toward the back. Chulio was like me, younger and smaller; I guessed about 18 or 19 years old.

"You drink beer, Harry?"

"Sure," was Harry's reply.

"Here, best bar food with *chicas guapas*." We entered a crowded little eating and drinking establishment full of men and women. As I looked around, I had to be the youngest in the place, and the only one with blonde hair and a white face. Harry was darker with brown curly hair and not as noticeable and out of place as I was.

Here I was, not being able to speak their language and not looking like them. I felt sort of like our dog Popeye. He didn't look like any other dog. That was about what I felt like now that Juan and Chulio were my only connection to the outside world.

Chulio got us a small, round wooden table in the back of the room. Chulio and Juan began to speak quickly in the native tongue of Cuba, I assumed. They pointed to what I thought might be a menu and Juan held up four fingers. Chulio disappeared toward the front of the place.

I heard a rather loud guitar and what sounded like a band playing. When I turned toward the music, I saw three men and a woman on a small wooden platform like a stage. A sign in front of them read El Imperio De La Musica Cubana. The sounds coming from the guitar and drums were nothing like I had heard before and I asked Juan about it. He smiled and said, "Yes, *ked*, you like rumba music," and punched me in the shoulder playfully. "Listen, you will hear beautiful dance music … I come here, dance all night to the rumba and salsa; the drums and beautiful dancing woman makes your blood boil hot. Tonight we come and dance."

Chulio returned with four sandwiches and a big jar of something. He gave the others a beer and offered me a Coke … that I recognized. I didn't care; I didn't want to drink anyway. I found out later what Chulio was trying to say to us when he returned to the table, that our sandwiches were pulled pork which is very popular in Cuba.

I noticed Harry was moving even slower than he usually does on the way back and had a slur to his words when he would speak. *Oh, hell*, I thought, *he's half drunk*. Sure enough, when we returned Harry wanted to lie down and take a little nap, as he called it. Juan and Chulio were just laughing at him and maybe at me. I wasn't laughing because I had to start carrying bananas while Harry slept it off inside the truck. I figured I would do as much as I could and then when Harry woke up he could take over and I would rest.

An hour went by and Harry didn't wake up. Two went by and I was beginning to tire and decided to go over and see if I could get him up. Nothing I said even made him stir. Finally, after ten minutes of trying, I went to search for Juan and told him Harry was not up yet. He laughed, and told me to follow him.

He went to the water faucet where we had washed our hands and filled a big bucket and carried it back to where Harry was sleeping. He set it down and pointed to it, "You toss on him and automatic wake up his eyes!" I picked up the bucket and without hesitation I threw the whole bucket of water on his head. Juan was right, within a second Harry jumped up and started dancing like a madman, "What's up?! What the hell?! I'm soaked," he said.

I laughed and said, "Damn right. It's the only thing that's worked after trying to get you to wake up for fifteen minutes of talking, pushing and pulling on your big ass."

After a good laugh, we went back to work and at four that evening we were finished. The boat cargo hold was stacked full, just like Juan wanted. When we had finished, we were soaked with sweat from head to toe.

In thinking back on it, we probably lost five or ten pounds that day in the labor between walking and lifting the stalks of bananas.

We had been resting about fifteen minutes when Captain Alvarez appeared at the hold and was pleased to see that we had completed the first half of our mission.

Juan told him it was almost dinnertime and how hard we had

worked that day. He was happy and asked us to go to the quarters and clean up for dinner. That evening, the captain took all of us to a fancy nightclub for dinner, music and dancing. "Is this Latin music?" I asked the captain.

"Yes, this is the native sound here in Cuba and most all of the islands. It's a mixture of African, Spanish, and other influences along the way, but it's original. It's wonderful to dance and to watch these men and women move across the floor so gracious and flowing. Not like the jerking movement of the new American dance craze," he said.

The captain said, "Well, hope you guys have learned hard works pays. We work hard first, then in return we get a chance to play hard also. On the way back, you can see the beautiful coastline we'll follow to another port where we'll pick up a special cargo of tobacco. It's for something that is quickly growing in Miami and Atlanta—hand-rolled Cuban cigars. The most popular tobaccos right now are Bolivar, Cohiba and Cuaba, so we're going to stop in in the port of Santa Cruz and load up a few cases to take back to test the market. Our last trip I picked up a case of Bolivar and they sold just as soon as I let some men know in Miami. This time I'm bringing back a case for each port I call on for my bananas," Captain said.

We finished eating and the men had a few drinks. Harry looked at me and Juan when the drinks were brought to the table, and said, "I don't think I'll indulge; I'm going to pass." We all just smiled. Harry had learned his lesson.

On the way up the coast after dinner we were sailing toward Santa Cruz. That evening before sunset I saw a big stone lighthouse with all types of people and activity around it with green mountains in the background. Juan and Chulio said it was called the Northern Lighthouse of Cuba. I went in and lay down after sunset. It got dark and that was it for me. I was tired and essentially whipped. Harry said they stopped in Santa Cruz for a couple of hours, but I didn't move until the crew woke me in Ft. Pierce to unload.

Chapter 40

The ocean is everything I want to be, beautiful, mysterious, wild and free.
Ruthie Vysotskiy

Big Surprise

After being home for a few days after our successful banana voyage, everyone was talking before dinner. That evening at the dinner table it was a normal occurrence that Dad would ask everyone how their day went and what they had done. I already had a story ready for when it became my turn.

Doug began, "I'll start by telling how my first trip to the dentist getting my teeth cleaned and polished was, and how loud the probing instruments were. I thought they were going to stretch my mouth and make it even bigger than it is. It's true what the kids were saying that going to the dentist is about as bad as going to the principal. I can't believe I was that scared and the whole procedure wasn't bad or painful. After it was done, there was nothing to be afraid of other than a few unpleasant times getting his hand in my mouth." Then Doug started laughing at himself along with everyone else.

Granny then said, "And for being such a good boy we went to Mr. Gene's store and bought ice cream, didn't we, Doug?"

"Yes, and I had two scoops of chocolate and Granny had a scoop of coffee and butter pecan. Plus, we split a peanut butter cookie. We thought of you, Johnny, but not for very long—the cookie was too good."

"Johnny, how was your day and what did you do?" Dad asked.

I had talked and told about the trip to Cuba and how hard Harry and I had worked for the three days we were gone the night before. This time I made up this story of going down to the pier and going fishing with Harry and another boy and catching several big fish. I said, "I am disappointed my biggest fish flipped itself off the pier and I lost it." I was about to go into another fabricated fish story when Granny spoke up again.

"You know, walking is a wonderful way to get your exercise and to see this delightful little town. When Douglas and I were walking from Dr. Harold's office the other day, we saw so many people we had not seen in weeks. We stopped to talk to several on our way back home. We went to Mr. Gene's ice cream shop first because Doug had done so well with Dr. Harold that I wanted him to have a treat.

"As we were coming out of Mr. Gene's with our ice cream cones, there in front of our eyes was a car just like Flem's new green Pontiac at the red light. Doug and I tried to get up to where we could see the car better, but it was just a few steps out of our reach. I did see an arm sticking out of the driver's side and the driver had a shirt on—just the same color and type that Johnny has. But when we got back home the car was still here, just where it was when we left, so we knew someone in town has bought a new Pontiac like yours, Flem."

She looked at me as if she were asking me a question, but I didn't say a word other than, "Pass me the green beans, Doug, please."

Doug said, "I really thought it was Johnny driving. The guy had hair as blond as his and it blew in the wind like Johnny's does when the car took off from the red light. But we could only see the driver from the back and didn't want to yell at him, so we just kept walking and wondering."

Everyone stopped eating and waited for me to say something, but I just kept eating. I knew if I stopped and tried to deny anything I would stick my foot in my mouth.

After a few minutes, Dad said, "Well, someone other than me has good taste in automobiles. I feel like some of this car is Johnny's, because of the orange grove shooting incident and the insurance settlement. But Johnny will have to wait a few more months before he can get his daytime driving permit.

That's one difference I've noticed between here and West Virginia. They let kids begin driving at fourteen down here with a parent or another licensed driver during the day in the vehicle. That allows them to gain a year of experience before night driving, when most accidents occur. Of course, you have lots of kids that drive tractors and farm trucks and work their parents' farms as well."

"I agree, Dad, most of the kids that are driving at fourteen are driving with their parents or on the farm or just to school and home. Short-distance driving allows them to get experience with the mechanics of the vehicle. That's where most of the problem is with driving a car. Here in Florida they give a permit to ride a motorcycle at fourteen ... that travels seventy-five miles per hour. Yet, there are fewer accidents with the motorcycles and scooters than the cars.

"That's why I like starting the drivers at fourteen. Helps them a year or two before the age of sixteen like other states. You can't devote the attention to driving details when there's two or three in the vehicle with you ... especially teenagers," I said.

"It sounds like you're an experienced driver already, Johnny. Have you had a chance to drive any down here with any of your friends?" Mom asked.

"Well, I've driven Frances's motorcycle a few times with

her. Harry's father has an old beat-up Ford farm truck that he lets us drive around the farm and down the dirt roads around their place and that's given me a little experience. But I've come to realize there's more to driving than just getting behind the wheel and steering the car. I want to be a safe driver, when I can drive, that is," I said.

That said, Dad, Doug, Grandmother and Mother dropped the subject of driving. They weren't sure I had taken the car. Though Granny did see enough of me to be almost certain, there was a slight margin for error, so no one forced my admission. Instead, my parents thought it would be a good chance to teach me the importance of safe driving now that I had turned fourteen. My father was in favor of letting me get my driving permit and using the car that I had a role in getting.

That Sunday, dad and I left and went out on the back roads of Brevard County to give me some experience behind the wheel. From that point, I realized how much my parents cared about me and how much I cared for them. I decided at that moment I was going to stop getting into trouble, skipping school, and running around with the wrong crowd. Now, I could understand what my grandmother said about "being judged by the company you keep."

I knew I was very lucky we didn't get caught lifting the Caddy the other night. I knew I would be in a world of hurt if that little misjudgment of character by Steve and I had gone wrong. *There were many small things I had reason to be thankful for now that I had turned fourteen and was a real teenager, almost a grownup*, I thought.

Later that year, just before Christmas break, Dad came home from work and at the dinner table announced he had gotten a promotion, but it meant the whole family had to be in on the decision for him to take the new position. Dad explained he was being sent to Delaware to supervise the building of a new building at the DuPont headquarters in Newark, Delaware. The new construction was scheduled to begin later that year, but they wanted him there to look over the blueprints with the engineers and the architects. It was a huge job of over 200,000 square feet of office building, a two-story steel and masonry construction.

"I'm not an engineer but they are treating me and paying me as if I were. I guess all the years of building the two-story stone buildings and brick churches have paid off. You know, now that I think of it, I have supervised and built nearly seven churches and two office buildings in three states over the past ten years. Not counting this Cape job. That's pretty good for an old hillbilly like me," Dad laughed.

"When do you think we would move? If we could get up there over the Christmas break before winter sets in, I would be in favor of the move," Mom said.

"What do you think, Rosie?" Dad asked, for he respected Granny's opinion a great deal even if she had little formal education. He used to say she had the best common sense of anyone he knew.

"You know I have a sister living in New York I have only visited one time in twelve years. When we get settled up there, I'd like to take Johnny and go to New York to visit Sarah, little Jake, and their family. If that's okay with you all," Granny said.

This was Granny's way of voicing her approval for the move. She never liked to come out and say yes or no when asked an opinion about something that wasn't her decision.

"It would allow Johnny to separate away from the unfavorable crowd he has started running with and expand his chance at another beginning at a new school and get more education and travel in his life.

"Johnny, what's your opinion?" Dad asked.

"I'm torn. I have made some good friends here in Palm Bay. I really care for them and would hate to leave and never see them again. On the other hand, I realize this is a chance to have a new beginning in school and with my athletics, as well as new friends—I say let's do it, Dad!"

"Doug, we realize you are the youngest, but your opinion matters as well. What do you think about moving north to Delaware?" Mom asked Doug.

"I just started school and I like my teacher, Mrs. Workman, but the kids say that next year we will get Mr. O'Conner and he is real mean and tough, so if we leave it would be a good thing for my future that way."

"Then it's settled. Everyone is in favor of the move for different reasons but still approve. I'll let my boss know tomorrow and your mother will let the school principals know so we can get the proper paperwork done for the schools in Delaware. I hear the schools in Delaware are ahead of the Florida public school system. That means you two will have to study more to catch up." Dad looked at us.

We had everything in order and planned to leave within the next month, destined for Dover, Delaware. But before we left, Dad took me to get my Florida driver's permit and let me drive the car for the next two weeks.

As usual, Dad never liked to live too close to the job he was working. He had contacted his brother-in-law, Clifford Thomas, the husband of his sister Sally, saying that he would enjoy a long drive to and from work. A long drive, he felt, would give him a chance to think about the plans for the day, and the drive home allowed him to reflect on the day and think about what a wonderful family he had and to be able to provide for them in such an interesting way. As a result, he asked them to find him a place at least twenty-five miles away from the job site.

Dad asked Clifford to send him a map of Delaware and he would start looking for a new location for the family to live around Dover—that's where my Uncle Clifford recommended a nice place to live and raise a family.

Chapter 41

Be somebody nobody thought you could be.
Michele C. Cook

Our Move North

We made the move from Melbourne, Florida, to Dover, Delaware. We ended up staying with my Uncle Clifford Thomas, and his wife Sally, one of my dad's older sisters. Cliff was a tough construction worker who had been a coal miner like my dad. They had worked together in West Virginia twenty years prior. They had gone their separate ways after marriage and family came along.

We were there for what seemed like months during that summer. Amish people settled much of the area where we were. Uncle Clifford and Sally had a daughter, age 24, by the name of Gloria Jean, with two daughters, Mona and Debbie, about three and five, both very good and always wanting to play when we would see them. Gloria Jean's husband, Richard, was a sergeant in the Air Force stationed at Dover Air Force Base.

I was somewhat aggravated that I had just gotten my driver's license in Florida, yet could not drive at all in Delaware. As a result, I took to hitchhiking everywhere, because we had left my bicycle in Florida along with a house full of things. Mom never liked that I hitchhiked, but Dad didn't mind. It was eight miles into Dover from their farm and would normally take me half an hour or more to get a ride into Dover. After a few weeks, I decided to push the envelope and hitch all the way to Rehoboth Beach, another fifteen miles south of Dover.

Oh, did I discover a new playground then! Here were the homes of the rich and famous. I met and got rides with politicians, attorneys, professors, and other top professional people. As we would ride along, these people would either spill their inner secrets about why they thought the beach was so relaxing, or they would be interested in me and what a young man such as myself was doing hitching to the beach. If I told them the truth, that I was new from Florida and I wanted to explore the area, they would often take me to a new area and drop me. I even had several men and women take me to a restaurant they liked and buy me a meal.

Amish Country

This went on for weeks unless my parents wanted me to do something special that day. Sometimes I would help a neighboring farmer with chores to make a little money as long as my parents knew where I was.

Living down the road a half-mile was Mr. Jakob Bern who had a big farm, was building a huge barn, and needed help. Uncle Clifford told dad and dad enlisted me to go down and offer my help in what they called a barn raising, where all the neighbors would get together and share labor and materials for different projects that were needed.

One Saturday, my Uncle Clifford got me up at six in the morning and said he wanted to take me down and introduce me to the neighbor having the barn raising.

On the way down to their place, Uncle Clifford told me not to use profanity around anyone, don't look or stare at any of the women if they were around and to keep my shirt on even if it got hot. "The Amish Mennonites have a lot of strange beliefs and customs, but it's their religion and they are still nice people," he said as we got out of the truck.

"Mr. Bern, I want you to meet my nephew, Johnny. They are staying with me until my brother-in-law gets on his feet and finds a home in the area. I told Johnny you are building a barn and could use his help for a day or two," Uncle Clifford told Mr. Bern.

"Well, we are getting ready to start over there with Mr. Mantz. He is the leader of the framers. We have a man in charge of three other men on that job. You will be the fourth framer, Johnny. Have you ever used a hammer?"

"Yes, sir," I said to him. "I have worked with my father on several of his construction sites. You just show me what you want done and I'll do it," I replied.

I was sent over with Mr. Mantz and I introduced myself to the others. I noted there was one other young guy in our group who seemed to be around my age by the name of Conrad. We were all sent to a huge stack of lumber and Mr. Mantz told us what to carry over to get started. I counted about twenty-five guys there to work. The foundation had been poured and was set. I heard several say moving the wood was called the bull work, as we began to carry the massive 8"x12' beams over to the point Mr. Mantz showed us.

I saw uncle Clifford get back in his pickup truck and go down the long gravel drive between the manicured fields to the paved road. We continued to carry the oak and pine lumber for the next several hours without a word being spoken. It was almost eerie the way the men worked together in silence. A few of them whistled, and that was the only sound on this beautiful Saturday as the sun was coming up in the eastern sky. The men didn't start to talk until the sun was well above the skyline and the sweat began popping out on them. At first it was low, almost like whispers, and then it got louder. In an hour it was like I had heard on most construction crews, talking, shouting, laughing, and swearing.

At ten that morning, everything seemed to come to a halt and all the men just sat down. Four young women brought wooden buckets of water out and passed the pail around to each man and they drink as much as they wanted from a long-handled metal dipper that was in the bucket, but the girls carried them from one man to the next.

When it was my turn I remembered what Uncle Clifford said about looking at the women. When the girl handed me the big wooden handled dipper, I looked directly into her big blue eyes and smiled, then I realized what I had done ... just what they told me not to do. I couldn't help it. It occurred without me realizing what I had done. I always tried to look someone directly in the eyes and smile especially if they were giving me something. The girl's face brightened and a smile beamed from her face. Then, just as suddenly, she turned to the next man to give him water.

I thought about the pretty Amish girl for the next hour. She was probably fifteen or sixteen, wearing a long, blue cotton dress with a white bonnet and heavy brown ankle-high boots that looked handmade, like her dress. I thought about the fact all the men had on similar type shirts, blue or drab-gray pants with a green or white cotton work shirt.

At exactly noon, a man yelled "LUNCH, let's eat!" Again, everyone stopped, and all the men went to an existing barn to wash their face and hands at a trough with a hand pump and a big bar of what looked like homemade soap. The guy, Conrad, who had been working with me all morning, came over and said, "Johnny, come and I'll show you our eating procedure."

"There's an eating procedure?" I said to him.

"Yes, there's a number of unwritten rules we are to follow as a young Mennonite. I'm fifteen and shall turn sixteen at the end of the summer, then I will qualify as a man. Let's sit down on this bale of hay over here and talk while we wait. We are expected to wait until the older men get their food, then we can get in line and the women will serve us," Conrad said.

We walked toward the barn, where the hay was under a shed roof out of the hot sun. Two other guys were walking the same way.

Conrad introduced me, and I realized we were the only four that were under sixteen, so we could not be with the men.

"We are all in the same class at our Mennonite school up the road about two miles. It goes to the eighth grade according to Delaware law, but in standard test we are at a high school level. After that we can choose to continue in the public school system, or we can quit school, go to work and start our families," Conrad stated.

"I am going to the University of Delaware to pursue a teaching degree. I want to study more history of the Mennonite and Amish movement," said Zurich, a small-framed guy with black horn-rimmed glasses. He spoke with a strange accent I hadn't heard before.

"The Amish Mennonite movement descends from a 16th century fellowship known as the Swiss Brethren who were known to be a radical reformation group of English people. It spilled over into other parts of Europe like Germany, Switzerland and other areas. That's why I want to know more of why this became such a strong belief system that it is still a movement today, even here in America," Zurich said.

"Well, hell, I'm done with all that religious crap. When I turn sixteen in November, I'm out of here. I'm going to work at International Latex, DuPont, or the Chrysler plant and make lots of money. I'll get a beautiful woman, smoke cigarettes, and drink whiskey like the movie stars," Gabe said. Gabe was the biggest of the group, blonde hair, blue eyes, well over six feet tall with big hands, and seemed as strong as an ox.

They all laughed at Gabe and Conrad said, "Pay no attention to Gabe—he is our resident optimist of the school." They all laughed again, and I joined in.

A few minutes after our laugh, there was an older man of about 70, with gray hair and a white beard, who came over and said, "Now, come on over, boys, and get yourselves some food the ladies and God have prepared for you to keep you strong as the oak wood we are using today." He walked away hastily, with a slight limp on the right side.

As we got up, I asked Conrad why was it most of the men had beards and long hair and wore hats even when they were working? He responded, "That's another of the distinctions between being a man and a boy in our culture. I'll explain if we get a chance to talk again."

We were guided to a long wooden table, one of about ten in the big two-story barn with a tin roof. The barn was fixed up to be an eating area with a kitchen. It had huge doors opened at each end of the barn, so a slight breeze would tunnel through the barn. As the men finished eating, we were the only ones left in the barn.

I asked Conrad about the place where we were eating, and he told me it was a community meeting hall. The Mennonite Community was about fifty or sixty families strong in and around Dover, and they all met in the barn about once each month to discuss community wants and needs.

Just as we sat down, two of the water girls came out to bring us our first bowls of a bean soup. I noticed the cute blonde with the water bucket and nice smile was one of them. She didn't say anything but seemed to linger by me longer than necessary. I didn't look at her this time like I did the first time. I just kept talking with Conrad, Gabe and Zurich as if she was not there. Next, they came in with a course of fresh tomatoes and corn. This time she gave me the tomatoes and stood and waited for me to look up and tell her how many ears of corn on the cob I was going to have. I asked her if it was yellow or white corn, and she said yellow. Then I said, "That's good. I can eat more yellow corn than white, can't you?" She didn't know what to say. She really didn't get the joke I was trying to make.

"Are you for real?" she said and started to turn around to leave.

"Yes, I'm real and I would like to know your name, please," I said to her.

"Why? Why would you want to know my name?" she said.

"In order to call you to talk with you. I want you to know you're the first Amish girl I have ever met or tried to meet. If they're as pretty as you, that's why the parents keep you hidden."

"You are full of cow dung, you are doing nothing but flirting with me. My mother said most American guys are like you, just talk and no action."

I said, "What do you mean no action? I'd sure like a chance to see you off and away from this farm. I don't even know your name."

"It's Veronica, and that can be arranged tonight. Talk to Conrad."

"We younger Mennonites have a little hiding place that no one outside knows about, where we go for entertainment at night. It's down in the woods where we hunt," Conrad said.

Gabe laughed and said, "Yea, if our parents only knew what we get into they would be shocked. But they said they want us to know what's happening in the world."

Zurich said, "I'm about the only one left that's still unconfirmed of our group. Soon as I work up the nerve, I'll cross over the line too."

"Zurich, what do you mean 'unconfirmed'?"

"Never mind him, I'll tell you this evening." Then Veronica

turned quickly and left.

"Johnny, come to the end of Mr. Bern's lane after dinner, about 7:30, and I'll meet you there," Conrad said, in a low whisper.

An older man walked in then and asked for a cup of coffee and some water and the girls were off to the kitchen. By the time they returned, we were on our way back to the construction site.

It looked to me like the framework was just about complete. I figured the roof would go on soon. These men attacked the work like it was on a deadline. They each knew the next step— there was no guesswork to getting it done. It looked to me like they had all done the work many times before and they were certainly good at it.

I was on the ground as were the other boys, carrying the sheets of tin to the hoist area they had rigged to pull up the material for the roof. It took the next three hours to get the tin up on the roof, but it was just about done when Conrad said, "You can leave these last four sheets of tin where they are. We need a water break for sure," as we walked toward the kitchen area. I tried not to look at Veronica when we got in the kitchen area.

"If the elders see someone looking at the girls, they will put them on restriction for a week," Gabe said.

"No problem. I'll close my eyes if I need to until tonight."

Two other women came out to bring us water and asked if we wanted a snack, and of course we agreed. The fresh blueberry cobbler she brought within minutes was still warm out of the oven, not just one slice each, but we were given the whole pie. I kept looking up and around to see if I could see Veronica, but evidently she was working somewhere else in the afternoon.

That evening we all stopped around six when the sun was beginning to set in the western sky. The men waved and thanked me for helping them. Mr. Bern said, "The barn is now dry and usable; we can finish in the weeks to come before winter arrives. I appreciate your help and it was good to meet you."

"It was my pleasure to meet you and all the fine men today. Please let my uncle know if there is anything else I can do up here on your farm to help you. I need the money to buy clothes to go to school this fall," I said to him. I wanted him to know I would work, but not for free next time. I waved goodbye, walking out the lane toward my uncle's place.

Getting an Amish Education

That evening after dinner, I sat on Uncle Clifford's front porch with dad and him while my mom and Aunt Sally washed dishes. I told them I had been invited back this evening for a game with the other kids. I didn't say male or female because I really didn't know. Uncle Clifford said, "Johnny, I've heard from some good sources that you can get a mighty fine education over there in the evening if you're a young man." And he looked at my dad and laughed. "Now go in there and take a shower put on some clean jeans and you'll be ready. I wish I knew at your age what I know now. I'd have that '58 Plymouth Fury over there (he points to his car) out every night trying to score with all these little girls around here on these farms."

That was all the direction and incentive I needed. I got cleaned up and put on my black loafers, blue jeans with peg legs, and a white shirt with the collar turned up. I stuck my trusty comb in my back pocket and told everyone not to wait up. I would tell them all about the party tomorrow. Mom said, "You better not go out of here without a kiss for your momma." I laughed and gave her a kiss.

There were no lights on the road at all, much like the old back road I traveled when in Palm Bay. I walked the half-mile in total darkness down the lonely road. I got to the place I thought was theirs when I read the mailbox at the end of the lane.

I only had to wait a minute or two before Conrad showed up on a tractor. "Jump on," he said. I climbed up to the seat and stood behind him like I had seen guys do going into the field.

"Just sit back and enjoy yourself tonight. If you like, join in and above all don't tell anyone what we do tonight," Conrad said. "We have had this little club ever since we started the sixth grade, so we could compare notes on what the boys are told as compared to the girls, and we both want to find out what outsiders like you think about the Amish."

About that time we hit a big hole coming across the field in the dark and I just about fell off the tractor. Conrad slowed a bit until I could get another hold on the seat and he shifted it to a higher gear, "Sorry about that. I'm not used to carrying anyone with me."

We were on the tractor another couple minutes and then the plowed field turned into a forest. Conrad said, "Stoop down or the tree limbs will take your head off. We try to keep it thick as we can here so our parents won't venture back here." A few minutes more and he shut off the engine and said, "Get hold of my arm and follow quietly. The cabin is about a hundred yards on the other side of this berm and water moat we made."

"Damn, you guys really did a good job of hiding this place," I told him.

"You haven't seen anything yet. Just be ready to see the coolest hideout in your life. It is almost totally invisible, even during the day." Conrad stopped and asked me to look ahead. I looked and could see nothing. He laughed and said, "See, I told you. We're three feet from the front door."

Conrad told me to stay where I was; he would be back shortly. I did as he asked. In less than five minutes he was back, tugging at my sleeve. "Ready, Johnny. Come on in." When I walked in, I could hardly see in the dim light but there were four lanterns burning, one on each wall. There was a large table in the middle of the room and there was an old cot in the corner with a blanket or sheet in behind it when I looked. They had a little stove, wash pan and a fire pit dug into the floor near an open window. It was six paces by six paces, he said, when trying to explain the cabin in the faint light.

"Looks like you and I are the first here. We never know who will be here because some of us are put on detention for the littlest things and end up not being able to come. We try to meet every Wednesday and Saturday night when our parents are in having services. We all must go to church on Sunday, so we know there is not much chance at other times.

"There are ten of us in the club—six guys and four girls. Two of the guys are brothers and two of the girls are sisters and there's one with no brother or sister. You met him—Zurich."

In just a few minutes we heard a rustle in the bushes and Gabe walked in with a big smile, carrying a six-pack of beer. In another five minutes Zurich, Zeb, Lila and Veronica were there, all carrying something to drink or eat they had brought for the party tonight.

Conrad introduced me to Lila and again to Veronica and Zeb. Zeb was a tall, skinny, dark-haired guy unlike the others. Lila was another light-haired beauty like Veronica. As we were being introduced, Suzanne, who was the girl serving water today with Veronica, walked in with another girl I hadn't seen today at the barn raising. She was short but well-built one could see even in the dimly lit room. Her name was Celia, with dark hair and skin as well.

Celia got the party started by taking a church key from the bag hanging in the corner. You could hear the "pssst" as the can of beer was broached. Suzanne turned on the radio and tuned it to a rock station. In five minutes everyone was dancing, except Zurich. He and I just sat there and watched and sipped on a beer Gabe had handed to us. In twenty or thirty minutes smoke filled the room as someone had brought smoking material.

That's when Veronica grabbed me and pushed me out the door. "Come with me. I can't go home smelling like smoke and alcohol. Next door is another part to our cabin. It's a private talking, praying and contemplating room that is open to us in times of need. I think this qualifies as one of those times of need," Veronica said.

"I can't see a thing," I told her. She reached out and grabbed my hand and pulled me toward her. "Stay close, just a few more steps and we'll be there," she whispered.

We both took a few more steps. She took out a cigarette lighter and flicked it a few times until there was light. There, just ahead, was a crude door and an opening into a tiny room made somewhat as I imagined an Alaskan igloo or a small Tepee would be.

"Come over here and sit on this, it's a pad like the Japanese use on their floors. You know the Japanese sleep on the floor and then roll up their bed in the morning and put it away," she said.

"No, I didn't know that. How did you learn so much about Japanese customs, Veronica?" I asked.

"My father was stationed there for three years when I was in the first and second grade. Then he was transferred to Dover Air Base after Japan and that's how we got here. I was born in Pennsylvania and my parents wanted to get as close to that as possible because that's where my grandparents live. A member of the family isn't very healthy and we go see them often."

"I see your family moves around like mine. We just moved here from Florida. My dad was working at Cape Canaveral building the launch pads," I told her.

I felt a soft hand across my face as I was talking. The hand was very gentle and moved from my neck and face to my shoulders then to my chest. I felt myself being pushed downward to the grass mat. Then there was one hand on each side of my face guiding me to her lips. I could feel her hot breath and a smell of bath oil. She started kissing me and I was intoxicated by her charms.

A few minutes later, we heard Zurich call out, "Veronica, John, where are you? I've decided to take the plunge with Celia. Do you mind if we share the pad?"

I felt Veronica move and asked her, "Is it time to leave?"

Doug and John Practice Guitar

She responded, "Yes … Zurich is losing his virginity tonight. We need to find another nest."

The party went on until around 11:45; then just like clockwork everything was stopped. They picked up all the debris and everyone disbanded into the night just as they came. Conrad and I got back on the tractor and he let me off at the end of the lane and said goodbye. "I'll call you as soon as the coast is clear again, Johnny. Hope you had a good time partying with the Mennonites." Then he was off, and I drifted toward Uncle Clifford's place thinking how right Uncle Clifford had been in his assessment of his neighbors.

I was excited that I might have found a sweet little girlfriend right up here in North Dover, and we had been here less than a month. However, before we could even do more than call each other, dad came home and one night at dinner said, "Well, Cliff, it looks like we've found the perfect house just across the state line over in Henderson, Maryland. It is a small farm house that needs a little work, but it's the right price and it has enough bedrooms for all of us, Granny included."

"Hate to see you go but I know how you feel. Until you're

settled where you want to be, you stay restless and uneasy—at least I do," Aunt Sally said.

"We are going over there tomorrow and talk to some of the people about the house. We'll take Johnny and if we can make a deal, we'll begin to move this weekend. We don't have much to move so we should be able to get it all in a day or two if the house is livable," Mom said.

That was the end of my relationship with pretty little Veronica. I left word at her house with her mother that I had moved with my parents to Maryland, but I never heard from her again or any of the Amish people.

Chapter 42

*Don't allow someone to make you feel like
you're not good enough.*
Linsey Flavo

Mind, Muscle and Merriment!

These three words may sum up my school days and years quite accurately. As far as the *mind* part goes, many thought I had lost my mind at times, and not sure about having a mind at other times. I had more muscle than brains at that juncture of my youth. All I was interested in was having fun with a capital *"F"*.

I remember back in my junior high school days in Florida and how I got involved with the "wild bunch," being able to drive and ride motorcycles at the age of fourteen. I didn't think with my mind at that point—it was how I could use my muscle to be recognized among my peers. I had gotten used to fighting for everything I ever attained. With almost no family and very few friends in the new places and areas where we moved all around the country, my early youth was rough, to say the least.

Mom really liked the rural feel of the Dover area because it was not big and metropolitan like other cities we had lived near. She could drive without horns blasting and dealing with traffic jams for hours like other cities north of the Dover area. Dover had open spaces and farms with Amish people still driving horse-drawn buggies, and horse and farm wagons piled full of hay up and down the two-lane roads. Mom said it reminded her of her girlhood back in West Virginia.

Dad was a good mason and would have had no trouble going to work a week after we landed in Delaware if he had wanted the work at that time.

Mom was the one who was unsettled, and I'm uncertain to this day as to why. The only thing I know for sure is that she didn't want to stay with Uncle Clifford and Aunt Sally any longer than necessary. She often would take Doug and me with her to look for a house.

One day, coming home, I wasn't paying attention, and neither was she. Doug had fallen asleep in the back seat. We were talking, and somehow ended up in Maryland. We turned onto a county road and followed a sign to Goldsboro. There we found a gas station with a helpful lady clerk happy to sell us drinks and snacks, and tell Mom where she was in relation to where Uncle Clifford lived.

We turned north toward Henderson, Maryland, a small town north about eight miles away, right on the state line, the lady had said. After getting to Henderson, we stopped at another gas station. A man came out to see if we needed help, and Mom asked him if she was on the right road to Mud Mill Pond. He gave her specific directions back to the Hartley-Dover road.

Mom felt we needed to drive through the town of Henderson south to north and then east to west until she had seen the entire town. There were only a few houses in each direction. We learned later that the entire town was only six square miles since it had been settled in the early 1920s.

During that excursion my mother fell in love with the little town of Henderson, of less than 300 people, two gas stations, two grocery stores, one general store, one post office, three churches and a constable by the name of Grover Thorpe who acted as sheriff and judge.

Sheriff Thorpe took us to the state line to help mom get back to the road to Dover. I didn't realize at the time, but my five-foot six-inch mother was a young good-looking woman with long, brunette, natural curly hair and blue eyes. Every man usually tried to act like a gentleman, but stay in her company as long as possible in those days.

I had always measured my growth against my mother's. We were now the same height, but I didn't give her beauty a second thought. That day with Sheriff Thorpe my mother saw a *For Sale* sign in a yard in Henderson and asked him about the house.

That afternoon we went back to Uncle Clifford and Aunt Sally's place and told everyone over dinner what happened that day: That she had seen a nice little place, and that the Lord must have guided her there, because she was essentially lost when she discovered it. But she wanted dad to see it as soon as possible.

That Saturday my father and mother went to Henderson and made an offer on that house and the offer was accepted. We moved our meager belongings to Maryland the week after dad and Uncle Clifford painted and did some carpentry, sprucing up the old farm house. It was great when we finally moved in later that month.

The master bedroom was on the first floor and there were three bedrooms on the second floor with a huge closet, one bedroom each for Doug and me. Dad, Uncle Clifford and my cousin everyone called big Doug, my grandmother's grandson on my mother's side, helped us move. Doug was a giant of a man of over 6'6" and 250 pounds. He came over from Dover with a helper, and in one weekend built us a new bathroom and remodeled the kitchen to suit my mother.

I didn't know we had all these relatives here in Delaware from West Virginia. But at the time my father took the job in Florida with DuPont, his sister Sally moved with her family from West Virginia to Delaware to go to work for International Latex Corporation, making space suits right there in Dover.

The rest of Aunt Sally's family moved to Delaware a little later because the coal mines were shutting down and jobs were being lost. The relatives had moved to Little River, just east of Dover, where the crabs and fish were plentiful on the Delaware Bay, and the price for houses and rents was modest. Uncle Clifford found his place between Hartley and Dover by talking to an Amish family in Dover.

Here we were now living in Henderson, Maryland, and it was the end of July 1959—hot but not nearly as hot as Florida had been. I was just about to turn fifteen and felt like I needed to explore the area as I had done in Dover and see where I was living.

One morning after Dad had gone to work, I told Mom my plan for exploring the area where we lived. She knew I was stir-crazy and wanted to get out and explore. I promised to return home by the afternoon to go with her and Doug to Greensboro where we would start school in the fall. I agreed and took off to explore.

In those days we never thought twice about walking or hitchhiking to locations that were a short distance of eight to ten miles away. I was always hitching in Florida and figured it would be fine here as well.

I had Denton as my target that day, because Denton was the county seat and the largest town in Caroline County where we were now living. It was almost eight a.m. by the time I had eaten and done my chores.

When I walked out, Henderson was abuzz with activity. Trucks, tractors, and big railway cars were all parked across the highway beside the railroad like they were in line for something. I wanted to see what was happening and ran to the corner.

There was a factory of some type down the road about a quarter-mile because smoke was billowing from the huge smoke stack. For some reason it had gone unnoticed by me when we moved there. It seemed every truck, tractor and wagon around was in line to go to the factory. The rail cars were boxcars not coal cars. They were sitting open and ready for hauling like I had seen in West Virginia hundreds of times.

I walked down the road toward the factory. I could see stacks and stacks of what looked like tomatoes on the back of trucks and farm wagons being pulled to the factory. As I approached the factory, I could hear the clamor and chatter of the work crews around a big concrete pad where all the baskets of tomatoes were being stacked. I crossed the road and walked down the dirt side-road where all the trucks going to the factory had lined to unload. This is where I stood with several truck drivers watching what was going on for the next half hour.

I asked a truck driver what kind of factory this was, and he said, "This is a processing cannery for canning tomatoes. The far end of the factory is a storage building where the boxes of huge #10 cans are being stored. Then the boxes are taken by tow motor to a train with boxcars to be loaded and shipped to larger companies like Campbell's or Green Giant. We drivers come from the many different farms around here that grow tomatoes."

"Hey, boy," a man called and looked toward me. "You want to make a few bucks?"

"What do I need to do?" I asked the man.

"Fifty cents an hour for unloading those baskets of tomatoes when they come onto the slab. This is the slab. You would be responsible to be sure there're tomatoes here when the tow motor driver comes back for another load," he said.

"These have a little more than half a bushel in each one. Make sure they are full. Sometimes you have to take from one to give to another, so keep a broken basket of tomatoes near you to fill the others up each time," he said.

"How much do the baskets weigh?" I asked.

"Oh, about 35-40 pounds when they are full of good ripe

tomatoes. Why, are you hurt or something and can't lift?"

"No, I'm trying to build muscle for football season; this way I don't have to worry about lifting weights. The work of lifting these baskets will help substitute for weights. Sure, I'll do it. My name is Johnny and I'll work each day if you need me to," I told the older man that morning.

"We'll be running at least for the next three or four weeks, ten to twelve hours each day, to get this fruit out of the field. We're hauling from Chris Lee's farm right now. When we finish that one we'll see how much you have left in your tank," he said with a laugh. He told me the boys that pick the tomatoes get ten cents per basket, and the loaders of the wagons and tractors get fifty cents per hour.

"Oh, by the way, my name's Mr. Baynard and I'm the outside loading dock foreman. I work for Mr. Logan and Mr. Ford who own the cannery. We'll pay you on Friday, just like the rest of the men, if that's alright with you?"

"It sure is." I grabbed a basket and started unloading right away.

"Here, let me show you how to get started." He grabbed a basket from the truck and carried it, and set it about twenty feet back on the slab on a big crate-like wooden thing he called a pallet. Then he carried another and put it right beside that one on the pallet, and then a third. On the fourth, he started another row toward the front of the pallet.

"This way the pallet will be loaded for the tow motor and he gets them stacked for the boiler inside the cannery. You will put twelve of the baskets on one pallet and then start on another as soon as you finish with one. That way you always stay one pallet ahead of the tow motor driver and he doesn't have to be waiting around for product," Mr. Baynard said.

"I think I have it," I told him. He watched me for about ten minutes, enough time to unload twelve baskets and set them on the pallet correctly and start on another, then he said, "By God, you're a fast learner and I like that. I think you'll do just fine for this summer job."

There was nothing to the job as long as the drivers didn't fall asleep in their trucks or leave them too far away from the loading dock. At noon a whistle in the factory blew. Mr. Baynard came out and told me to go to lunch but be back ready to go at one o'clock.

I said, "Thank you for hiring me to do the unloading. I'm very dependable and only live a few hundred yards up the railroad. I'll see you at one."

When I got home, I must have been covered with tomato waste and smell because my mother said, "Stop, don't come in the house like that. You're filthy, where have you been?"

I was very excited and took my T-shirt off and left it outside and put a clean T-shirt on in place of that one and went into the house to wash up and get some lunch.

"What have you been doing all morning? It looks like you got into a tomato fight or something equally interesting."

"Yes, Mom." And I told her all about my new job and where I would be working for the summer. "I'm not sure, but I know the next four weeks are filled with tomatoes that are still in the fields, according to Mr. Baynard. I'll bring you some fresh tomatoes for dinner when I come home tonight. We work until six or seven loading the tomatoes, Mr. Baynard told me."

I told Mom the baskets weren't very heavy, and the tow motor drivers are rather slow, so I don't feel pushed or pressured. "Mr. Baynard said he would give me a tour of the plant when I get back before the conveyor belt starts again; for some reason they don't like for the belt to stop."

The next week when my mother went to Dover shopping, she brought me back a book to read for the summer by John Steinbeck called *Cannery Row.* She said it was very popular a few years ago. I had to laugh because here I was working just like Steinbeck described in his book. I went on to read three more Steinbeck books that summer and put him at the top of my favorite author list for many years.

Red Bridges

Delmarva Peninsula was the name of the place we lived. Geographically, it was a Peninsula formed by three states— Maryland, Delaware and Virginia. This was taught our first week at the new school in Greensboro, Maryland, twelve miles south of Henderson, and a few miles from the First State— Delaware.

Greensboro was a nice little red-brick school with only grades seven and eight, with about one hundred boys in the entire school. Being an eighth grader had its advantages and disadvantages, but mostly it was good. I couldn't wait until they called for all those interested in playing football, something they hadn't done by the second day. I went to the principal's office and asked why. I remembered what an ordeal I had getting on the team when I transferred schools before.

"Well, Johnny, you are two weeks behind since football practice started before school started. All the boys have been hard at practice this whole time and you are just deciding you want to play."

"Well, no, sir," I told him, "I just found out about football from a student in my classes today. I live in Henderson and had no transportation this summer to come to practice early."

"Those that want to play find a way, their parents bring them or a friend drives. Somehow they get here when they're interested enough," Mr. Conner said with a stern face and no smile.

"Well, I'm very interested and I will do my best to comply with the rules now that I know the schedule that's expected.

Where and when is practice?"

"It is 3:45 until 6:00 p.m. every school day. They are getting ready to go out on the field now. Come on, I'll take you down and introduce you to Coach."

"Great," I said and followed him down the steps and out to the field house where the coach was explaining a "pull" from the line by a lineman, in this case a right guard.

"Excuse me, Coach," the principal interrupted. "There is someone I want you all to meet," and he extended his arm toward me as if to introduce me, but he didn't say a word. I realized after a minute he expected me to introduce myself to everyone.

"Hello, my name is Johnny Stump, and I would like to join your football team. I played football last year in Melbourne, Florida."

"Hi, I'm Coach Maggs, football coach and math teacher here at Greensboro. We're pleased to have you join our team. Just sit in on this instruction about pulling linemen and the primary job of blocking, then we'll get your workout gear after practice today," the coach said in a matter-of-fact sort of way that I liked.

After practice I went with the rest of the team into the locker room and while the others took showers and got dressed, Coach took me and fitted me with my practice equipment.

This was the start of my eighth-grade year. As it turned out, I lived the farthest north of the boys in the school who played football. As a result, after school each night I would be hitching a ride home. Usually there was someone going at least halfway, but the other six miles was never easy and sometimes took hours. I even had to walk more than five miles several times

Eventually, I played first-string quarterback after Coach let me play, and scored or threw twenty TDs that year. I became instantly accepted during football season and a leader in school

293

activities. I was doing well, the best I ever had in school, and then everything changed when I decided not to play basketball.

After football season my family took a trip back to West Virginia to visit one of our relatives who was very ill. I think it was my grandmother's brother, Hillard Smith, who lived in Welch, the county seat of McDowell County. Welch was only a few miles from the Virginia state line, so mom and dad visited Bluefield, Virginia, to see another relative while they were there. As a result, we were gone over a week and I had missed the basketball tryouts and the official beginning of the season.

Johnny with his 1954 Chevy

The Monday we returned home, I was in homeroom class and one of my friends mentioned we had a new basketball coach who was also our physical education teacher that semester. He was new and had just moved to town from West Virginia.

I was excited that the new coach was from West Virginia and thought we had a bond before we ever met. Our PE class was the last hour of the day, that way if any athlete had to miss a class when traveling to a game it wasn't an academic class. That afternoon in PE when the bell rang, everyone assembled as usual in the gym and lined up for roll call. We always lined up alphabetically and with my name being Stump I was near the end of the line.

A man came out of the locker room dressed in the school colors with gym shorts and a T-shirt with GREENSBORO on the front of the shirt. He had a flattop haircut that was popular at the time, but his light hair didn't cover the balding spot at the top of his head. He was young, I guessed about twenty-two or three because he had a shiny new wedding ring on his left hand.

He was coming down the line checking roll, asking names and making comments. He got to the boy beside me by the name of Palmer Smith who was very tall at 6'1", but didn't play sports. He asked Palmer why he wasn't on his basketball team. Palmer then told him, "I have to work on my father's farm after school and can't play any sports because sports don't put food on the table, my father says."

"We'll see about that. That shouldn't be a reason not to play basketball while I'm here. A guy your size would be a good asset to our team."

"Yes sir, but my father says the farm comes first and so we three boys all must work after school."

"Things are going to be different around here. I'm going to see that everyone plays if they have the potential," Coach said.

Then he moved to me. He looked me straight in the eye and said, "So you're the football hot-shot."

I didn't say anything. We were the same height and his steel-blue eyes looked deep into my eyes with what was supposed to be a stare-down tactic. I wasn't intimidated and just kept a straight-ahead gaze without looking directly into his eyes, much like I heard my cousin say that Drill Sergeants do to recruits in the Army.

That day was the beginning of an awful year of school. Coach Dorsey Scott tried every way in the world to get me anxious, annoyed or infuriated that year. One day in PE class he threw a basketball at me, meant to be a normal basketball pass, so hard it went right through my hands and smashed my nose and mouth. Blood was just gushing and he was laughing and said, "Not such a star now, are you? 'All-thumbs Stump' is what I would call you. You wouldn't be my star. You're not that good."

Tears came to my eyes, but I didn't lose my temper like I would've the year before. In another incident, he made me run laps all class long because someone was talking when he was talking and no one in class admitted to it so he blamed me just to have someone to punish.

On St. Patrick's Day I had painted an old pair of loafers bright green and wore them to school, since we were to have a class play and I had a part in the skit about St. Patrick's Day. He got me suspended from class for the day for being a "disruption to the class because of the green shoes."

I tried talking to him one day after talking to my dad about the situation. I waited after class and asked Mr. Scott what I had done and what I could do to remedy the situation. He laughed and said, "You should have thought of that when you decided not to play basketball this year. You could have been a good point guard. You are fast, with good hands and quick reflexes. But no, you wouldn't play because you wanted to mess around with those degenerates and hippies that are all over the place now."

"No, Coach, I didn't play because I didn't have a ride home after school and practice. We live in the last town north in the county and the four guys in Henderson who drive are all at North Caroline High School. I had to hitch home every night from football but it's warm then. In basketball season the weather is cold with rain and snow on the ground, so my parents questioned my desire to play," I said.

"Oh hell, that's a poor excuse to use not to play for your school," Coach Scott said. "Nevertheless, I would think that you knew why I have it out for you. I'm going to give you a hard time all year and you can just take it as payback for not playing."

With that, he pointed to the door and said, "See you next time, loser."

Hurt and dejected, I didn't know what to do. It was the first time an adult had come right out and said why they were going to give me a hard time and there was nothing that I could do about it. If I went to the principal with a complaint, Coach Scott would deny the story and that would make things worse. The best thing, my dad said, was to try to stay away from him and do what he asked.

One day toward the end of school May Day activities and prom season, a small group of my classmates hatched up a plan to disrupt the entire week of the prom. They wanted us all to get out of school for a few days during the first of May when the weather was beautiful and everyone wanted to go to the beach, swimming, or do something besides our routine school activities.

That Friday night, those boys told me they had stolen Mr. Webber's cow. Mr. Webber lived nearby on a small farm that bordered the town of Greensboro. I wanted to have a good excuse and not be around when this happened, so I went partying with several couples to a little beer drinking and necking spot called Red Bridges between Greensboro and Goldsboro all of us guys knew about … it was the place to park with your lady!

Mr. Webber had two daughters in school with us, one in the seventh and one in eighth grade. That Friday evening the four boys took his Jersey cow and led her to the school. Then the four guys, and I was not one of them, went to the school and found an open window, climbed through and went to the gym and opened the big double steel doors and lead the cow into the gym. They milked the cow and left some hay for her to eat before they left the school. Then they went back to the school Saturday night to milk the cow again.

When they looked around the gym they burst out laughing, because it sure had caused a stench that was awful, and that was their intent … to have the place knee-deep in cow manure on Monday morning. They laughed so hard they forgot and rolled on the floor in the crap the cow was providing for over ten minutes before they could milk the cow and give it more hay.

They planned on taking the cow back to Mr. Webber's farm the next evening but didn't know Coach Betsy Hunter and Coach Scott planned a community pick-up game Sunday afternoon to get the local folks involved with the school's end-of-the-year activities. Coach Hunter was surprised when she opened the gym. "Damn, Dorsey, you'd better get down to the school as soon as you can, right away, and look to see what happened," Miss Hunter said.

She went back out and told the twenty or twenty-five people waiting to watch and to play basketball there was a problem and she would have to see if there was something that could be done after Coach Scott got there to make an assessment of the situation. Everyone could smell the farm odor coming from the gym when she opened the door. As more people gathered, it was apparent they wanted to know the extent of the problem.

"This is the problem." As she opened the double gym doors, the smell was awful, and everyone started gagging and spitting as they ran back out of the gym doors.

Dorsey got there a few minutes later when everyone was gagging from the stench of the gym and wondering what to do. Then he said, "Those damn boys. I know who did this. I'll get their ass. It had to be several of them to get this milk cow in the gym. I'll get them all kicked out of school for good! Call Mr. Conner, and see if he doesn't agree with me."

The boys responsible had told me something was going to happen because Coach Scott was not only holding a grudge against me, but also hostile and abusive to several other boys who didn't play basketball. I didn't have a network of conspirators and friends other than the football team because I was a new boy in school, but they had grown up in Greensboro and gone there from Greensboro Elementary School. They would take care of Dorsey they assured me, that Friday we left school.

That was the last time I had any trouble with Coach Scott. As it turned out, the coaching staff had to clean up the mess because Mr. Conner had said, "Coaches Scott, Hunter, and Griffiths, and their assistants were responsible for the basketball games." Good or bad, he couldn't place the blame without concrete proof, even if Mr. Conner knew the boys who had been behind the smelly prank.

I couldn't help but laugh when I told dad of the prank that was played that week. I was glad I wasn't a part of the plan this time and only knew of the hoax by the upper-classmen.

Chapter 43

If someone sticks by your side in your worst times, they're the ones who deserve to be with you during the best times.
Margaret Wolf

Duck and His Souped-Up Old Ford

The next year was my freshman year and I was to go to North Caroline High School, located another ten miles south from Greensboro. I had worked in the tomato, corn, and cucumber fields and canneries for two summers.

Before school started my first year at North Caroline, Mr. Thompson, who owned the store where my parents bought groceries and gas each week, asked if I wanted a job at the store stocking shelves, cutting meat, and waiting on customers who needed gas. Of course I told him yes, never realizing that meant getting up at four a.m. to get the Sunday papers, *Baltimore Sun*, *Philadelphia Inquirer*, and the *New York Times* ready for the customers coming to the store to get their papers and gas before and after church every Sunday.

This is when I met Duck Thompson. He was Roland Thompson's son and one year older than me. He had a '53 Ford that I thought was super cool. Duck's name was really Donald, but everyone called him Duck for a nickname because of Donald Duck's popularity and his fun nature.

Duck had the best personality of anyone I had ever known up to that point in my life, always smiling, laughing, or telling a joke. Later, I realized he was a small guy, only 5'8" and weighed 120 pounds soaking wet, and I was then about 5'10" and weighed 170 pounds. Duck had more heart and guts than any of the 200-pounders on our football team. He had blonde hair and blue eyes just like me, so we called each other "brother" and started hanging around together from morning to night after I started working for his dad.

Duck's mother, Matilda, whom I came to love, would get up at four a.m. and fix Donald and me pancakes and eggs on Sunday morning before we started our paper sorting. The sorting took about two hours before they were ready for the customer.

Duck also had an older sister named Lorraine who had the beginning stages of muscular dystrophy and could not walk very well without assistance. She was very pretty and popular, about two years older than Duck. Lorraine was the person responsible for teaching me to eat salted peanuts out of a Pepsi bottle. Lorraine stayed at the store during the day but couldn't get up and down to assist the customer or use the gas pumps. This was one of the reasons Mr. Thompson hired me to do the physical work Lorraine was no longer able to do.

When I started hanging with Duck, it seemed my whole game stepped up a bit. He introduced me to several of the older guys who lived in or around Henderson. Most of the people would come to Thompson's Market or The Ragged Robin on the north end of town for gas and odds and ends.

There was a group of guys and girls about our age and all at North Caroline high school. There was Billy, Frank, Stanley, Bunky, Donald, Wayne, Richard, Duck, and Eddie to name a few. There were a few girls I got to know after Duck introduced me to them—Christine, Kay, Patty, Norma, and a few others, and all drove to school. I was now part of the Henderson gang, but was low man on the totem pole.

At that point, I was 75 percent interested in sports and 25

percent interested in girls, and I was the youngest of the gang. All the guys had their own cars or their parents' car and would drive to school, but I usually walked up to the store and rode with Duck or caught the bus.

There was one scrape that summer I won't soon forget. The whole gang was invited up to Duck's Uncle Smudge's farm to enjoy the summer activities. He owned a big trucking operation with dozens of eighteen-wheelers going in and out of the farm each day, carrying milk mostly.

This Saturday was hot and sticky, one of those dog day afternoons when you just wanted to lie around in the cool water. There were several new girls in town for the summer. I wasn't aware of it then, but the Eastern Shore of Maryland was a favorite summer destination for the wealthy from Baltimore, Washington, and Philadelphia. They had summer homes down on the Shore. Well, that summer was an exceptional season for love, or I just woke up and noticed the sweet scent of the flowers in the air.

We were at the big acre site where there was a large pond on the farm and a smaller area for gardens. There were about fifteen teenagers there and one or two adults from the farm, mostly young mothers whose husbands were drivers on milk runs. The young mothers would enjoy sitting in the sun and swimming with their children.

Someone long before me had monkey-rigged a high dive of about ten or twelve feet out of some old construction material. All the guys and girls were climbing up to take their turn at jumping from the high perch.

Duck, Billy and I had three lovely girls from Michigan over on a blanket, smooching and trying to take it further, when this girl by the name of Sarah told Billy or Duck (I couldn't tell exactly who she was talking to), "If you can dive headfirst through that inner tube floating over there, I'll take my clothes

ONE WILD AND PRECIOUS LIFE

off for you. If you can't, you'll have to take yours off and be my slave for the day."

Neither of us guys were big divers at the time, so as a result Billy said right away, "You would have to do a lot more than take off your clothes if I dive through that inner tube. I want action."

"Well, that could be arranged also. I think all us girls will take that bet and promise you boys the treat of your life if one of you can dive through that tube."

"Hell man, here the sweet spot is being offer to us right on a silver platter and you guys aren't willing to dive through that tube?" Duck said.

I couldn't let Duck down and knew already that Billy didn't have the guts to take the chance. I said, "Hell, yes, I'll take that bet from you girls if I can choose the time and place."

She said, "Hell no, big boy, it's all today or no way." She grinned a big "I dare you" smile and licked her lips.

The girl was near sixteen, had auburn hair and a beautiful smile. Duck's father was a friend of her family that came down during the summers. The father owned a big farm outside of Henderson, Duck had told us. Two of the girls were sisters, and the challenger was a friend of the sisters, Michele and Dawn. She had called my bluff and was going to hold us to the challenge.

I pulled off my shirt and walked toward the diving board. I guess the word got around very quickly, because a crowd gathered below the diving board and everyone cheered as I climbed the ladder. I wasn't thinking about the danger of what could happen, but of how nice it would be all hugged up to this sweet young thing from up north. I had worked hard all summer and now getting ready for school in a few weeks made this challenge like the cherry topping on a dessert.

I looked down at the tube—it looked smaller than ever. The

303

tube hole I had to fit my entire body through looked only inches now. One of the guys had brought it under the diving board. I motioned for him to move it a foot or so out more because it was too straight down under the board. I really didn't know how to approach the dive—I had never tried it.

Duck hollered out, "You can do it, Stumpy, there's room, just be careful and tuck your head so the valve doesn't scrape you as your head goes through."

Someone else yelled, "I'll bet he chickens out and doesn't do it."

Another returned, "I'll take that five-dollar bet."

Then another chimed in with, "I'll take some of that action," as the crowd got more into the scene.

I couldn't back out now after all this ruckus and betting was going on that beautiful, hot, humid Saturday afternoon. The bet with the girls was a dream come true. Before I knew it, I was diving for the tube.

I awoke on the side of the pond where someone had dragged me. Seems as though I made it through the tube, but my body wasn't quite straight up long enough to get my entire body through the tube and it caused me to sustain a whiplash effect as my body was pushed into the tube. The valve had cut the back of my head and that was bleeding.

As I sat there, things began to come into focus and I felt like I had been hit with a freight train. I was in the arms of a man hovering over me asking me questions and making sure I was breathing, and the blood was being stopped from my head wound.

After ten or fifteen minutes, the group helped me to my feet and a big cheer broke out from the crowd huddled around. I still felt like hell and couldn't move very fast as I was helped to the blanket. The girls made me a spot with pillows and a blanket spread out, looking very inviting.

"Lie down there, big boy, you need some tender lovin' care," one of the girls said. I wasn't sure which one because I still wasn't thinking right. I lay down on the blanket and someone started rubbing my neck and back and I fell off to sleep and didn't wake up until after sundown.

I awoke and a female was right beside me. "Are you all right, can you move, do you hurt?" she said.

"Hi, you're not Sarah the girl I had the bet with. Which one are you?"

"I'm Michele, the young shy one, I've been told."

"Well, it's just about dark out here. I can hardly see anything, aren't you scared of the dark?"

"Not as long as you are here with me. You are the brave one to dive through that inner tube from that high dive," she said.

"Where are the others?" I asked.

"They've gone for a joy ride in Duck's souped-up Ford and I drew the short straw to stay here with you and be the first to kiss you awake."

I still felt like hell and my head was just pounding but once she mentioned what our purpose was for the evening, I remembered and began to feel better. I lay back down on the blanket and pulled her down next to me and gave her a warm gentle kiss to express thanks for the company. What a wonderful way to end the summer, I thought!

Johnny's TR3

Chapter 44

Train your mind to see the good in everything.
Positivity is a choice. The happiness of your life
depends on the quality of your thoughts.
Ronel Wilken

High School Days

On my very first day at North Caroline High School, I couldn't believe who I saw ... yes, you guessed it ... Dorsey Scott. He was the new basketball coach and physical education teacher. Again, I tried to steer clear of him and his staff of basketball people that he had assembled over the summer. Someone had told me when going back to school there were some changes in the physical education department, but I had no idea this was what they were talking about.

I did well during football season, making the first string, not as a quarterback, but as a defensive middle guard. Our quarterback, Freddy Lawton, was a strong, fast guy from Ridgley, one of the towns along with Denton and Greensboro that formed the boundaries for the new high school.

As freshmen there were only a few of us that played with the varsity squad. One was the son of the superintendent of schools for Caroline County, Roger Hoopengardner. Jackie Goode, Steve Reddish and I were the others. We had three additional guys with fathers who were tied into the school system who became good players that year as well. I tried to

307

forget Dorsey was at the school because I avoided him whenever possible.

About midway through the season, we had only lost one game. Coaches Payne and Johnson, both from North Carolina out of Lenoir Rhine University, were the kind of coaches I was used to in West Virginia. They were tough on you, but fair, and would let those that worked hardest play, regardless of who their parents were.

I had made a good showing for myself that season on the defensive squad when a first stringer got hurt and I went in as a backup. I made six individual tackles as a freshman. From then on, I became a first stringer on the defensive squad at middle guard. We had some big, tough, old farm boys who loved to hit and play defense. Our only problem as a team was our lack of depth on offense. It was somewhat limited with some guys able to block for runs, but limited at passing defense, and we had a better running team.

Coach Ed Payne and Bob Johnson, our varsity coaches, decided to run a single wing that year. Bob Bickling was the signal caller and Freddy Lawton and my friend Duck played tailback on certain plays. Duck was fast, shifty, and could catch, but was very light. As a result, Coach didn't use him much for blocking. I was not a good passer if the play went more than twenty-five yards, but I was fast and could block and tackle pretty well. Coach Payne had me play a pulling guard position on offense behind Gordon Walls, another big 200-pounder but who was slow. About the third game I outran a play, and the fullback dug out the first down without much help. That's when I got wrath from not only the coaching staff, but my teammates as well.

After the season was over I saw my friend Gordon Walls, the right guard, sitting in front of the assistant principal's office. I was in the hallway walking to my next class. I waved and yelled, "Walls, you should have behaved yourself." He smiled and waved.

About that time, I felt a hand on my shoulder and then I heard a ripping sound and felt my shirt being pulled and tugged. I had just bought the shirt with my hard-earned money from Thompson's Market. It was being ripped off my back. Before I got turned around to where I could see who my attacker was, my fist was flying toward them. My fist connected ... to Mr. Scott's big mouth, and he went sprawling back into the trophy case in the hallway where all the school trophies and honors were displayed.

"I'm sorry, Coach Scott. I didn't know who was behind me grabbing my collar and ripping my new shirt," I said quickly.

As he was getting up from the floor he had his fist clasped and he looked angry and ready to fight. "Why, you punk, I should kick your ass right here in front of everyone."

"Go ahead, Coach, give him your best shot," said Steve Reddish who was walking with me. About that time, I hit him a second time in the middle of his chest because I knew I was going to get into bad trouble for the first hit anyway. Down he went again.

By that time there was a group of students standing around yelling for me to give him another. Then I heard, "John, what are you doing? You know better than to lay your hands on a teacher." It was Mr. Holsinger, our principal, and Mr. Smith, our assistant principal, taking me by the arm and escorting me to the office just a few feet away from the scene.

I knew I was in trouble and there was no way out. I did hit him twice and I meant to with the second punch. I wanted him to remember it.

"I'm sorry, Mr. Holsinger. Coach Scott came up behind me and grabbed my collar and ripped my shirt without any cause. I just spun around with my fist because I thought it was another student who grabbed me. The strike was a reflex; I couldn't take it back after I threw it."

"Well, John, you have really gotten yourself into a mess this time. There's nothing I can do. We have a rule that you can't touch a teacher regardless of the circumstances. I'm going to have to expel you for an undetermined length of time, depending on what the school board decides," Mr. Holsinger said. He sounded almost sorry.

"I understand. I know I was wrong, but I worked one whole week just to get the money to buy that shirt. My family doesn't have much and can't buy me fancy clothes and things, so I was instantly mad when I felt the fabric rip," I said.

"What were you doing that made him grab you?" said Mr. Smith.

"I suppose it was waving to Walls who was sitting at your door waiting to see you. I waved and told him he should have behaved or something like that. It was an innocent gesture to say hello," I said.

"I see. Well, that doesn't give you permission to turn and hit someone whether they were in the wrong or not."

"I understand," I repeated.

I was told to go get my books and Mr. Smith would drive me home and tell my parents what happened.

When we got to our house there was no one home. My mother had gone to my Uncle Rink's place about five miles away and my dad was still at work. He let me off and told me to be sure to tell them the truth, and that Mr. Holsinger would be calling them after school to discuss the problem.

That evening at dinner, I told mom and dad, "Well, I got into big trouble at school today. I punched that teacher, Dorsey Scott from West Virginia I got into it with last year. To make a long story short and to the point, he came up behind me, grabbed my new shirt by the collar and ripped it, trying to turn me around. I automatically spun around with my fist already in action to jack some student's jaw. I worked all week to make enough to buy that shirt and now, mom, you'll have to sew it up or throw it away."

My father didn't say a word until I had finished with my side of the story. "Why are you so volatile that you would just turn around and start punching without seeing who it was in the first place? Don't you have any self-control? I thought your coaches were teaching you how to channel that aggressive behavior you've developed over the past few years.

"Now you won't be able to participate in your favorite thing—football, or any sport for that matter. You just may be kicked out of school all together for good. It would serve you right, then you would have to get out and work off some of that hostile attitude and temper. Remember a few years ago what you said about Charlie down in Florida?"

Dad had no sympathy and neither did mom. They only told me to go up to my room and do homework until they heard from the school. A little after five p.m. they got a call from Mr. Holsinger. Doug brought me the news. They talked for over an hour before dad hung up the phone, shaking his head.

My dad was a patient, polite gentleman, and didn't show anger much, but when he did, you knew it. This time I had set off a dynamite stick under my father. He raced up to my room, slammed the door and said, "Do you know what I've got to do now? I've got to take you to a special meeting of the school

311

board on Thursday night to plead your case to see if we can get you back in school. This is Tuesday and that only gives me a day to determine what to say or do. Boy, you have put us in a jam this time. I think I'll just let you get kicked out and have to work for a living now."

"There is nothing I could say I haven't said before that will change anything, I guess," I said honestly.

Dad said, "I'm going to call Roland Thompson to see if he can help somehow. Boy, you are going to owe me big time for this screw up."

Dad left the house after he called Roland and was gone about two hours before he returned around 7:30 p.m. that evening. "Johnny, Roland says he's not sure what he can do, but he's going to try to see if he can't get us some help before we have to go before the board.

"You know your boss at the cannery told everyone that you were one of the best workers he had ever had. One of the men he told was Judge Logan, one of the owners of the cannery, and father to Brooke Logan in your class at school. Now, you'll probably be facing him if you have to go to court on charges stemming from hitting the coach."

"What does all that mean?" I asked.

"Roland thinks he can put in a good word with Judge Logan before this comes up as a case against you. You know sometimes they charge the parents instead of the child in many states and I'm not sure about Maryland. Anyway, we'll see tomorrow when we meet the board," Dad said.

I thought about Charlie down in Florida being almost uncontrollable and finally taken to jail. Was that going to happen to me now? I was sorry but it was too late, the damage was done.

I really didn't know what to do other than admit the truth. I knew Coach Scott had it out for me and told me so, but I had no witnesses. Coach Scott had tried when we were at Greensboro school to get me kicked out. Now here at North Caroline he was still trying to take me down, and this time he may have succeeded.

I stayed home the next day and just read my textbooks and did lessons that were outlined on Monday for the week in some of my classes. My father got home early and put me in the car. He drove to the school without saying much of anything.

"I'm going to wait and see what they have to say about the circumstances and then we can see what the choices are. You are set on going to college to play football, but I know I can't afford to pay for your college. Maybe there are other ideas they have that can help. I'm not worried about this incident. I understand you lost your temper, but Mr. Scott should never have grabbed you if he didn't expect a response. Yours was just a lot more direct and violent than most would have been."

"Yes, dad, I am really sorry for the lack of control on my part. I do intend on trying to go to college if I can get over this hump I've created for myself. Dad, you decided not to go to college. What would be my future if I didn't go to college either, because of this incident?"

"Pretty bleak. I see all of these guys coming out of college with engineering degrees. They can't even do what I do, but they make twice the money just starting. You need to try to go back to school and finish. I would like to see you with an engineering degree or something beneficial you will use. Remember, even if you play football, that's only four years. Then you will graduate and go to work.

"Well, here we are, let me see if we can find a parking spot and we'll talk more on the way home," dad said, as we pulled into the parking lot.

We walked into the administration building, then to the main office where dad said we were to meet. When we arrived, there were five others there. Judge Logan introduced everyone, and they asked me to sit off to the side of the main table like I was on trial. For that matter, I guess I was, but hadn't thought about it in those terms.

The first thing they did was call the meeting to order and check the roll. Everyone was present except one member they said was sick. Judge Logan was the Chairman of the Board and Roland Thompson was the Vice President and member from north Caroline County. There were four other members from east, south, and west Caroline County, and what was called a member at large.

Once the meeting was underway, it was a short agenda. One of the members read: "John Stump has been accused of striking a teacher, one Dorsey Scott, coach of the boy's basketball team, and physical education teacher at North Caroline High School." None of the members said a word.

Judge Logan stood and gave a little background on my family being from a humble background. Me being adopted in West Virginia, my father being injured as a coal miner and us having to move to South Carolina, Georgia, Florida and Delaware for employment. Then he told of my dad being transferred to Delaware to work at DuPont in Newark and then International Latex Corporation in Dover, causing me extreme duress in school and trouble getting along with others because of an unsettled childhood background.

I didn't know how Judge Logan had gained that information about my background. After Judge Logan's talk, I was asked to stand and give my side of the story.

I stood and said, "It started last year in Greensboro School where I was an eighth grader. I had just moved to Caroline County a few months before school, and didn't know about the school rules and schedule. I was introduced to the football coach and the team two weeks after school started. All went well that year during football season. After football, I was to take physical education and my teacher was Coach Dorsey Scott. I heard from the other students he was from West Virginia, my home state. I thought that would be a somewhat good subject and beginning conversation to talk with him about. It was not. He only wanted to know why I hadn't signed up to play basketball. I explained that my parents only had one car and my father drove to work in Newark. If I played I would have to hitchhike back and forth from school after practice in the winter when it got pretty cold standing waiting for a ride, which I did," I told them.

"Did he understand your situation?" asked one of the board members.

"No, he said he really didn't care—that I should want to sacrifice to play for my school, was his answer."

"Did he offer to see if he could get you a ride after school home in Henderson where you live?" another board member asked.

"It's more than ten miles from school to home each day. I couldn't ask anyone to come and get me because we were new to the area," I responded.

"So you think that is what started a vendetta against you, Johnny?" said a board member.

"Yes, I think it is, if I know the meaning of the word 'vendetta' like I think I understand. Is it a grudge?" I said.

"Yes, I think you understand the meaning quite well," another member said.

"You then had several other incidents at Greensboro School during the year?"

"Yes, but evidently they meant a lot more to him than to me. I realize that I am what they term a 'free thinker,' but I've been told by several of my friends' parents that's what Harvard, MIT, and Yale are full of—that I should keep that attitude. Because in the long run it allows you to explore more territory with your mind and body," I stated.

"Right now, Johnny, you're a long way from Harvard and MIT. We just want to try to get you out of high school. You aren't making it easy for yourself or us with the path you've chosen," another board member stated.

"I know, I'm sorry. It's not that I don't like Coach Scott. He just doesn't like me, because I wouldn't play basketball for him and he's made it difficult for me ever since. This is what he told me, and I can see now that he has carried out his word," I explained.

"You have absolutely done the wrong thing by hitting him in school. What do you think would be the best recourse for you and for us as board members to now advise?" Mr. Thompson interjected to me from his position.

"I really like school and I don't have trouble with any of my teachers or the material, except him. How would it be if you said I am suspended to only school activities, and I could not participate in any extracurricular activities the remainder of the school year? Would that work?"

With that there were no more questions from the board members.

Judge Logan stood again and said, "I think we can all agree that there was a misunderstanding. There was no malicious intent on Johnny's part when he spun around and hit Mr. Scott in the face with his fist. It was a reflex act and not premeditated.

"Although Johnny broke the rules as they are written in this case, the three days he has been off will be sufficient punishment for the accidental incident. He is not to participate in any further extracurricular activities the remainder of the year. If there are any dissenting opinions or votes let them be heard now or forever hold your peace."

The room was quite for a minute and then Judge Logan said, "So noted. Meeting dismissed."

With that evening in my background, I went on to play three

316

more years of varsity football as a middle linebacker, became the captain of the football team, ran track as a 100- and 200-yard sprinter, and threw discus and shot-put. I was nominated as president of the junior class and was an honor roll student every semester until graduation. You might say I turned my life and path around. I saw just how close to the edge I came at allowing my "free spirit" to go too far.

After my incident with Coach Scott, we did not communicate the remainder of my time at North Caroline High School. He did not speak to me and I avoided him.

There were several harrowing times, like when Duck got his neck broken in a football game at Southern Lothian on the Western Shore of Maryland. My best friend was carried off the

field to an ambulance, never to play football again, and we had to try to come back from that devastation.

There were several incidents that sounded inviting to me at the time, like when Jester, Adams and Reddish took off to New Orleans for Mardi Gras in a vehicle stolen from a family member. There were stories galore about the wild fun and good times of the trip, but in the end, it cost them dearly for the good times they had.

Johnny gets ready for Maryland

I remember one of the best times in February 1964. Duck asked me to go to Baltimore with him to see the heavyweight champion, Sonny Liston, fight a new hot-fisted Cassius Clay at the Baltimore Civic Center. I couldn't believe the fight results.

Most of the people there were betting on Liston, but Cassius Clay, then 22, who would eventually change his name to Mohammad Ali, totally dominated the fight and was declared the winner. He went on to win the World Heavyweight boxing crown. Ali went on to become the first fighter to capture the heavyweight title three times.

JUNIOR OFFICERS
Mrs. Butler, Advisor; J. Hall, Treasurer; S. Chaffinch, V.-President; J. Stump, President; J. Aden, Secretary.

North Caroline High School

318

Chapter 45

Young love is two hearts with only one thing in mind
Author unknown

A Secret Love Affair

In my junior and senior year of high school, I had saved my money and bought several motorcycles and an old junker of a car, a blue and white '54 Chevy six-cylinder. Having much more mobility now, I became involved in several love triangles, none so secretive as the time I was invited to a regatta at the St. Michael's Yacht Club on the St. Michaels River on the Chesapeake Bay.

I was a senior, pretty much on my own, and getting ready for college. I had been working, as usual, but this Saturday I had a special secret invitation from a faculty member of our high school to be a guest of the event. This intimate thing we had gotten into was innocent in the beginning, but at that time my hormones were raging, and the least little indication of interest was fair game.

One of my teachers was very attractive, with a stunning figure. She was always very coquettish with me and that sent my radar up. I volunteered to help her put supplies away one day, and she came on to me. We continued to find times and ways to grab a kiss or two in-between classes. She invited me to the regatta at the yacht club, giving me the name of the boat where we would meet.

I had never been to the yacht club before and arrived on my motorcycle. When I got there, the party was in full swing and it was about six in the evening. I went to the docks to search for the name of the boat she had given me. There seemed to be hundreds of boats—sail, power, fishing, and pleasure craft, and they were all over the place. People were drinking, smoking and partying on nearly every boat.

I finally found the boat. She was anchored down at the end of a long line of sailboats. I guessed it was too big for the average slip. I didn't want to go aboard without permission. I stood there and milled around for ten or so minutes, then decided to go next door where there was a big party going on. I knew no one and they certainly didn't know me. I got on board the beautiful 45-foot Morgan.

I seemed to be dressed appropriately in jeans, T-shirt and deck shoes with no socks. Most everyone else was only in swimwear or cut-offs. The average age was early twenties and thirties, I figured, with about twenty highly intoxicated people dancing to *Great Balls of Fire.*

In the dim light of the unlit boat, a woman put her arms around my neck and began a wildly passionate dance and seductive slithering movement on me. I returned the motion, enjoying the fun she was having. After about ten minutes she said, "Are you alone?"

Since I hadn't seen my teacher friend, I said, "Why, yes, I am."

"Well, follow me for more fun than you'll be able to contain. I know the owner of the boat real well and you might say this is for him!"

She guided me below and forward to a small berth in the bow with a single bed and a small wall lamp. As she turned on the light I could see this was no girl, but a fully developed woman. She was striking, with big blue eyes, black hair, and a deep tan.

"I'm Connie. They call me Conita. Let me show you the fun spot," as she seductively undressed and came on to me like no one had before. Then and there, I got my first education of what a woman wants more than raw sex. I soon learned what to do.

After about a half hour, I heard a man's voice say, "Conita, are you down here? You BITCH—what are you doing with that guy?! Let me get my gun and I'll shoot both of you."

She said, "Oh hell, it's my husband. You need to get outta here 'cause he will shoot you like he has two other guys trying to seduce me. Sorry, babe. It was nice." She ran and I ran.

I grabbed my pants and ran by him while he was looking for his gun in a drawer. I don't remember even touching but one step. I knocked down one guy and a woman at the top of the hatch that was in the way. Then I heard shots ring out. I had hit the water. I must have stayed under for fifty yards before I dared come up.

Johnny's 1963 VW in Maryland

When I did, I was about thirty or forty feet from the boat. It was as dark as pitch out, so no one could see my naked body swimming in toward the pier. With my pants in my teeth, I had to come up to put my jeans on. I swam back down toward my teacher friend's boat and away from Conita as far out as possible. Then I climbed onto the pier and lay there, saying a silent prayer. I crept to my bike and got out of there as quietly as is possible on a motorcycle.

I decided then no more messing around in school or with married women for me. I settled down to a nice, sweet, young brunette in my class for the remainder of the year. I learned that grown people are serious about their women. That night was an "education" in more ways than one!

Chapter 46

*"Too often we underestimate the power of a loving touch, a
smile, a kind word, and a listening ear, an honest
compliment, and the smallest act of caring, all have the
potential to turn a life around."*
Written in my high school Yearbook in 1965.

Peanut

I graduated and was off to college, much to the surprise of
many of my teachers who had known me through middle school
and high school. My grades since my freshman year were a B
average and my last year was exceptional with a 94 GPA—it
was my discipline that was always in question.

My senior year was extremely good because of the influence
of a sweet girl called Peanut. In our senior class there were
several who tried to keep me on the straight and narrow that year
of 1965, but none more loveable than Peanut. I really thought
our relationship would go somewhere because I settled down
and saw the benefits of her suggestions, and we even made
future plans together.

But I left for college and, as things will happen, she ended
up marrying my good friend Jackie. I held no animosity or hard
feeling toward either Jackie or Jean, I just wanted them to be
happy together once they fell in love.

There were others that helped with the endeavor of keeping
me on track that year. My friends Sammy, Fred, and Rusty

323

became my closest friends during my last couple of years. Rusty was never in trouble and was too small to be a viable athlete in school. He was only 4'10" but funny as hell, great sense of humor and friendly; he never met a stranger.

After Duck graduated, I missed his bubbly personality and found a replacement in Rusty. He went on to become a very successful professional jockey after we graduated and then we saw the real athlete come out in him.

Another guy who was one of my best friends for quite some time in high school was Sammy. Sammy was a tall, slender guy with dark, curly hair and brown eyes, good looking as described by the girls in school. I found him to be very reserved, quiet and shy, but we seemed to hit it off and started hanging around. He played football our senior year and that seemed to bring him out of his shell a little more. Sammy had a posh Hillman convertible during our senior year, and I had a lavender Triumph TR-3 convertible. Between us, we established the first British car club in Denton, or at least in North Caroline High School, that we knew.

There were several other good influences on me that year. There was Freddy, a tough, fast guard on our football team, quiet and rarely into any trouble.

Other good friends, Steve and Billy, were very mischievous most of the time and were always trying to go down the wrong path just for the hell of it. Their fathers both were staunch Bulldog supporters, and were always at athletic events, regardless if Steve and Bill were there or not. Steve's father had played college ball and wanted his kids to follow suit. Steve was our tackle, big, strong and tough, but never wanted to apply himself in the classroom. Steve was in one of the groups that stole his brother's car and got Jester, Adams and QR to go with him to Mardi Gras in New Orleans. It didn't matter if the cops in three states were looking for them or not.

That's the kind of fun and outrageous things we liked to do, but Peanut talked me out of those opportunities.

Bill, on the other hand, was as mischievous as one could be in school, but rarely got caught at anything. He was an end on our football team and was a great high hurdler on our track team and dated my good friend Donna Smith who lived near me.

There were many other good influences—friends, teachers and adults, who made suggestions that year that helped me stay on course and I am grateful to them. Here is a partial list:

Dr. Gordon Wheat, the Denton chiropractor who helped me so much while in high school. Mr. Webster, Coach Scuarto, Coach King, Miss Brown, Mrs. Stivers, Mr. Stone, Miss Fogelsong, Coach Harrison and Coach John Nussear with his great Geography class. He was one of my coaches and I had class with him as well. Mr. Nussear will go down as one of my favorite teachers and counselors of my high school days.

I had several scholarship offers while at North Caroline that Coach Payne was instrumental in getting, but I decided to accept one at the University of Maryland.

I worked that summer at Choptank Electric as an assistant to the field engineer that plots new electric lines. My boss and supervisor was Billy Torbert, a cigar-smoking 40-year-old graduate of the University of Delaware. Billy liked to work hard and play hard. He would come into work many a morning too hung over to drive and I would drive us to the designated location. Then we would set up the transient to shoot the line for the electric poles to be located.

Just about the time I began to understand the math and setting up the tangents and angles or targets, as Billy called them, for the electric lines it was time for me to go to Maryland.

I had to leave and go to College Park, Maryland, outside of Baltimore the beginning of August that year because I was a designated freshman slated to play football, my passion and goal since the sixth grade.

I spent the last few days packing and getting my '63 Volkswagen ready for the trip over the Chesapeake Bay to my new home for the next few years. Of course my family, mom, dad, Granny and Doug, threw me a little family party the night before I was to leave home.

In those days, most guys took the opportunity at that stage of life to spread their wings and go out on their own. As I look back now, that is exactly what I did after I was safely in Maryland.

This is the story of my life up to the age of 18. It is true and factual according to my memory. I have had some help on the names and places from my friends, relatives and acquaintances whom I thank immensely. I could not have accomplished this book without their help. I have not used last names in many cases since I could not seek permission to use them.

Epilogue

After sixty years and nearing my retirement, I found the time to investigate my past. I tried to locate some of my West Virginia friends and relatives to see if they could help me fill in the blanks of my childhood.

I found that I have four siblings. We all were children of Pansy but by different fathers. I got to talk on the telephone with Catherine Stevenson, my half-sister in Princeton, West Virginia. In addition, I have a second sister Judy and a younger brother Mike, both adopted by different parents. I have never seen or talked to them.

According to a conversation with Catherine, Pansy had four husbands and passed away around the age of 85 somewhere in Ohio where her last two children were born. To this day they can't say what really killed Curt but it is thought now that it may have been an endocrine tumor like you will read about in my next book, that almost took me out.

About the Author

John L. Stump was born in 1946 in Welch, West Virginia, and was educated at the University of Maryland. He completed his doctoral training at Palmer College of Chiropractic in Davenport, Iowa, and Post-doctoral (PhD) at Shannix College in China, and a third doctoral degree (EdD) in Sports Medicine at the United States Sports Academy. After returning from the 1988 Olympics, where he was a team doctor, he settled down on the Gulf Coast in Fairhope, Alabama.

Dr. Stump spent forty-five years as a Chiropractic Physician specializing in acupuncture and nutrition and wrote several professional books, including *Somatovisceral Aspects of Chiropractic; Energy Medicine: East and West; Applied Kinesiology Essentials: The Missing Link;* and *A Stroke of Midnight. The Beacon* referred to him as "the poet laureate of natural medicine," and over the years he received many recognitions and awards in the United States, as well as from Japan, India, China and Korea, where he taught and studied. One of his favorite authors was Oliver Sacks.

Dr. Stump's early life memoir, *One Wild and Precious Life,* was published in 2019. He retired from active full-time practice and devotes his extra time to his family, grandchildren, writing, lectures and travel.

John is now trying to become a creative fiction writer after forty years in the non-fiction genre.